Trauma-Informed Practice in Education

ALSO AVAILABLE FROM BLOOMSBURY

Why Do Teachers Need to Know About Child Development?
edited by Daryl Maisey and Verity Campbell-Barr

Why Do Teachers Need to Know About Diverse Learning Needs?
edited by Sue Soan

Why Do Teachers Need to Know About Psychology?
edited by Jeremy Monsen, Lisa Marks Woolfson and James Boyle

Trauma-Informed Practice in Education

Making Safe Spaces for Learning

Edited by
Mike Carroll and Christine McKee

BLOOMSBURY ACADEMIC
LONDON • NEW YORK • OXFORD • NEW DELHI • SYDNEY

BLOOMSBURY ACADEMIC
Bloomsbury Publishing Plc, 50 Bedford Square, London, WC1B 3DP, UK
Bloomsbury Publishing Inc, 1359 Broadway, New York, NY 10018, USA
Bloomsbury Publishing Ireland, 29 Earlsfort Terrace, Dublin 2, D02 AY28, Ireland

BLOOMSBURY, BLOOMSBURY ACADEMIC and the Diana logo are
trademarks of Bloomsbury Publishing Plc

First published in Great Britain 2026

Cover design: Ben Anslow
Cover image © Christine McKee

A catalogue record for this book is available from the British Library.

A catalog record for this book is available from the Library of Congress.

ISBN: HB: 978-1-350-49825-9
PB: 978-1-350-49824-2
ePDF: 978-1-350-49826-6
eBook: 978-1-350-49828-0

Typeset by Integra Software Services Pvt. Ltd.
Printed and bound in Great Britain

For product safety related questions contact productsafety@bloomsbury.com.

To find out more about our authors and books visit www.bloomsbury.com
and sign up for our newsletters.

Contents

Section III Responding to Trauma

Section IV Building Systemic Responses

List of Figures

List of Tables

About the Editors

Mike Carroll is Associate Tutor at the University of Glasgow, UK, and was formerly the Director of the MEd Professional Learning and Enquiry.

Christine McKee is Lecturer in Teacher Education at the University of Glasgow, UK, a former teacher and support for learning assistant, and an adoptive parent. She is also the Vice Chair of the charity Scottish Attachment in Action.

Acknowledgements

We would like to thank the many contributors to this book, those within the School of Education at the University of Glasgow and from other organizations. The conversations that have ensued have been thought-provoking and inspiring. We hope to continue collaborating with this like-minded community of dedicated practitioners.

Our thanks go to those from other organizations who shared their experience and wisdom, not to mention their precious time, in conversations with Christine. We feel that these voices from practice are an invaluable part of this publication.

Our immense gratitude goes to Andrea Cardow, who transcribed these conversations with incredible efficiency.

Mike: I'd like to thank the many children and students that I've had the good fortune to meet throughout my career in education. They have taught me that 'The past is never dead. It's not even past' (William Faulkner).

Christine: I'd like to thank my three children, who've taught me more than they'll ever know and to whom this work is whole-heartedly dedicated.

1

Introduction

Mike Carroll

Exposure to early adversity in childhood can have profound and lasting negative effects (Felitti et al., 1998). Crucially, poor outcomes are not inevitable if we view and respond to distressed behaviour in trauma-informed ways. Prioritizing relationships within environments which focus on safety, trust and wellbeing are key to trauma-informed practice as is an acceptance that it is a shared endeavour with all members of a school, community or organization.

This book will appeal to several different practitioner audiences by introducing those with little knowledge of trauma to fundamental ideas, as well as those with some experience by drawing together up-to-date research informing the conceptualization of trauma and trauma-informed interventions. In addition, professional dialogue with practitioners provides a strong focus on trauma-aware practice (see Chapters 5, 9, 14 and 18). Chapter 2 introduces the reader to key ideas linked to understanding trauma, while Chapter 3 examines thinking related to Adverse Childhood Experiences (ACEs).

Exposure to traumatic experiences places children at increased risk for a number of problematic developmental outcomes, including problems with learning and socialization (Sonu et al., 2021), as well as an increased likelihood of poor mental and physical health outcomes in adulthood (Steptoe et al., 2019). Research suggests that preventing traumatic experiences could have broad positive health, social and economic impacts; consequently, trauma awareness is advocated by UK policymakers to help inform the training and practice of a wide range of professional groups including health, social work and those working in justice services (White et al., 2019). Investment in interventions that seek to reduce the impact of trauma is likely to improve outcomes with respect to physical and mental health as well as educational attainment (Shonkoff and Garner, 2012). Awareness that our actions and policies can both re-traumatize but also heal is an important aspect to consider. This would not only benefit those who have experienced trauma but also help enhance outcomes for overall population health and prosperity. NHS policymakers (2018: 7) describe such investments as a 'preventative-spend' approach.

The notion of trauma-aware education (Howard, 2022) has developed out of this growing understanding of the potential long-term negative impacts of trauma and the need for schools to take an active role in addressing the various manifestations of trauma in and out of classrooms (Sharkey et al., 2024). A core belief of trauma-aware practice is that building safe and secure relationships is more likely to mitigate the impact of adversity as well as facilitate healing from trauma. Exposure to traumatic experiences does not necessarily predict negative outcomes; however, the likelihood will increase in the absence of protective relationships that help facilitate healthy adaptations to stress (AAP, 2012: 225). Wu, M-H (2024: 2) argues that it is 'essential to recognize that adverse and positive events regularly coexist in daily life, contributing to an individual's resilience and ability to adapt to life's processes and challenges'. A trauma-aware teacher is more likely to create a positive classroom climate in which healthy relationships can thrive. Chapter 4 examines this relational context in terms of attachment theory.

Among the more visible symptoms of exposure to trauma exhibited in the classroom are acting out behaviours and aggressive defiance. Siegel (2020) refers to this loss of control as 'flipping their lid'. Children who have experienced trauma struggle to regulate emotions and trust others. These 'extreme' behaviours are the result of toxic stress which is defined as dysregulation of the biological and psychological stress response due to altered brain architecture (Ximenes et al., 2019; Harris, 2020). Chapter 6 examines the link between the structure of the brain and exposure to trauma as well as introducing polyvagal theory. Viewed through a trauma lens, these dysregulated reactions are 'not an attitude or a "choice", but rather a physiological and psychological reaction to stress' (Rossen and Cowan, 2013: 2). However, the impact of trauma on an individual can depend on many factors so the perceived harm to one's physical, psychological or emotional well-being can vary substantially (Rossen and Cowan, 2013). In other words, two individuals may go through the same difficult experience but, based on their relational history as well as their current social context, may demonstrate quite different behaviour in response. Some will move on quickly, while others will display fight, flight or freeze responses. Consequently, differentiated solutions are essential (Giboney Wall, 2021). Schools that do not develop a trauma lens will tend to quash such behaviours by creating an authoritarian learning environment, not realizing that this only exacerbates the situation as it replicates, in the mind of the child, the behaviours of those responsible for inflicting trauma in their lives (Giboney Wall, 2021). Chapter 8 examines teacher responses to 'problematic behaviour' and the perceived increase in behavioural issues. Schools that apply a trauma-aware lens to the everyday life of the school are better equipped to provide educational and social-emotional supports needed to help children learn (Phifer and Hull, 2016). Chapter 11 examines a number of different theories of behaviour and what these mean for the trauma-experienced child. By building trauma-aware 'Cultures of Care' children may feel that they belong, and that there are people who care about them (Lipscomb et al., 2024) and support their disparate needs. These Cultures of Care provide a layered system of support, with each layer building upon the previous layer (Golding, 2020) (see Figure 1.1). Children move through the layers, depending upon their needs, with

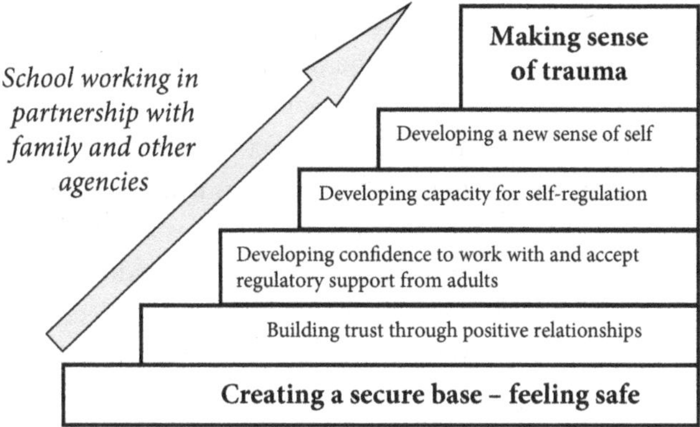

Figure 1.1 Layered support.

the ultimate goal of making sense of their experience of trauma and the impact that this has had on their life trajectory with a view to remove – or at least minimize – the likelihood of future harm. Practitioners who are trauma aware will be better placed to support the social, emotional and academic development of *all* children, particularly those who would otherwise be marginalized as a result of their behaviour. Taking a social justice approach to resilience and enacting 'resilient moves' may help create an environment which can help children face the trials of life (Hart et al., 2007) and ultimately, with the right help provided by the right people, recover from trauma. 'Safe nurturing relationships, particularly in the early years and into adolescence[,] are the key to developing resilience at an individual level' (NHS, 2018: 37). Chapter 12 explores developing understandings of resilience from social ecological and social justice perspectives.

Trauma-informed practice (TIP) is increasingly coming to the attention of educators as they grow in awareness of the impact that trauma can have on children (Sharkey et al., 2024). Different terminology has been used in different jurisdictions, but in this text we use the terms 'trauma aware' and 'trauma informed' interchangeably. Although educators are growing in their awareness of the need to develop a whole-school, trauma-informed approach, they are also aware that implementing and creating a trauma-informed climate can be challenging (Wassink et al., 2022: 471). To be efficient and effective, such an approach requires the rhetoric of policy to permeate all aspects of the life of a school. Being a trauma-informed school must become a way of being for all involved, with the school requiring change in practitioner attitudes and behaviours. The NHS (2018: 7) in Scotland has described the shift in thinking required as moving from asking, '"What's wrong with you?" to "What happened to you?"' and to follow through with '"How has this affected your life?" and "Who is there for you?"' Focusing on staff well-being is also necessary to facilitate such a cultural shift. Chapter 17 looks at an initiative designed by Scottish Attachment in Action (SAIA) to address this via reflective supervision for staff.

Not all children experience trauma in the same way, and as such this requires a responsive tiered approach to meeting the disparate needs of children (Phifer and Hull, 2016). The baseline tier requires all teachers and educational support staff to receive training to enable them to become trauma aware so that children encounter safe learning environments. Within these classrooms teachers and support staff will utilize trauma-informed teaching and learning practices as part of their classroom routines. Moving up this tiered approach will involve providing progressively more intensive interventions to meet the needs of, hopefully, a decreasing number of children whose social, emotional and academic learning is compromised by their exposure to traumatic experiences (Howard, 2022). Moving up the tiers requires schools to work in partnership with mental health care, social work and youth justice services (Phifer and Hull, 2016). Chapter 10 outlines some key aspects of a multi-tiered system of support drawing on thinking from Australia.

Throughout the book we will suggest that policies and procedures designed to support the development of trauma-informed practice should seek to:

- Provide a safe environment within which children have a sense of belonging.
- Cultivate supportive relationships centred on the children as it is these relationships that can help facilitate the process of healing.
- Establish routines and structures as these will provide children with a sense of stability, which is often missing in their lives.
- Create opportunities to actively listen and respond to the voice of children so that there is a genuine sense of shared agency.
- Provide opportunities for children to regain a sense of control over their lives through developing strategies that promote self- and co-regulation.
- Provide opportunities for social-emotional learning in order to help children realize and grow in terms of their self-esteem and self-efficacy (Giboney Wall, 2021). Chapters 7 and 13 will outline ways of supporting social-emotional learning with respect to bereavement and through Story Drama.
- Provide opportunities to care for and think about the well-being of education professionals.
- Include all staff in a school/learning environment as each has a role to play in fostering a Culture of Care.

Most of the contributors to this text work within Scotland, where policy and practice strive to highlight that trauma is everyone's business (NES, 2023a). Chapter 15 examines developments taking place in Scotland to implement a multi-disciplinary and multi-agency approach to addressing the impact of trauma. The launch of Getting it right for every child (GIRFEC) in 2008 set in motion a national approach to improve the well-being and outcomes of children by offering the right help at the right time from the right people (NHS, 2018: 63). *Getting it right for every child (GIRFEC)* (Scottish Government, 2022a) has facilitated a positive change to the philosophy underpinning policy and practice initiatives that are focused on children in Scotland, placing them and the family at the centre of decision-making (Davidson and Carlin, 2019). The most recent initiative is the *National Trauma Transformation Programme (NTTP)*, which builds on this ethos and seeks to develop the whole workforce (NES, 2023a). Despite the beneficial changes in attitudes, thinking and behaviour that Getting it right for every child (GIRFEC) has engendered amongst practitioners, it remains centred on an 'individual pathology' of adversity as it fails to fully address the role of socio-economic status, particularly the relationship between poverty and the increased risk of child maltreatment (Walsh et al., 2019). It is essential that practitioners realize that children and young people who have or are experiencing trauma is not as the result of some individual deficiency but rather as a result of betrayal by the persons or the environment in which they live (NHS, 2018: 52). Providing support for children, and their families, to develop resilience in the face of adversity can only be one part of the process. In addition, it is also necessary to address the 'structural determinants of health, education and well-being inequalities' (Davidson and Carlin, 2019: 480). Chapter 16 will offer a critique of trauma-informed practice in terms of neoliberal ideology.

We argue in the text that a school's adoption of trauma-informed practice will help support children who have experienced trauma to understand, cope and develop strategies that facilitate healing and growth, thus opening Siegel's (2020) window of tolerance, as discussed in Chapter 11 (see Figure 1.2).

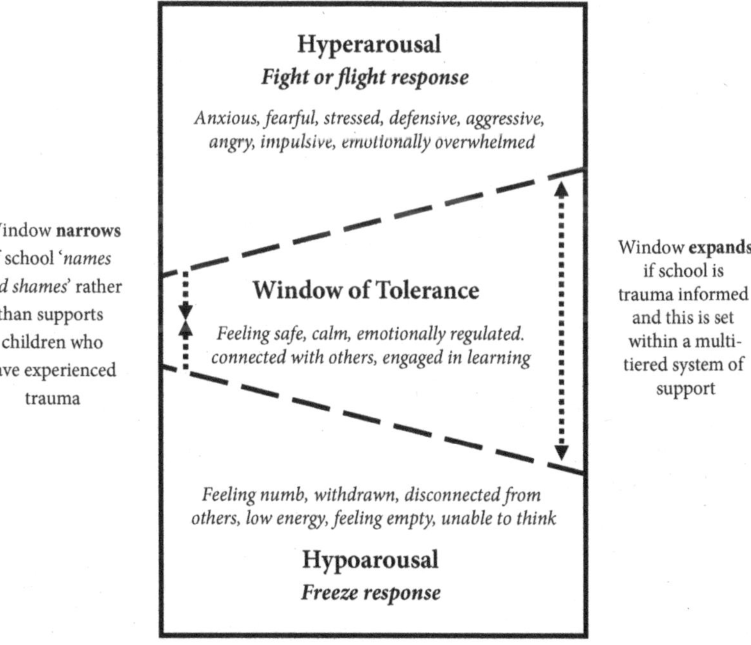

Figure 1.2 Window of tolerance.

Section I

Informing Ourselves about Trauma

2

The Concept of Trauma

Christine McKee

Key Ideas

This chapter will:

- introduce simple, complex and collective trauma,
- outline the potential impact of trauma,
- suggest why knowledge of trauma is important to the education professional, and
- introduce trauma-informed education.

Introduction

Given how often we casually use the word *trauma*, or *traumatized*, in our daily lives, we could be forgiven for assuming it is a concept that can easily be defined. That said, many of us are only too familiar with experiences which could be considered *traumatic*, not least those associated with the recent Covid-19 pandemic. In education circles and beyond we are hearing more and more about the need to be trauma-informed, trauma-aware and/or trauma-responsive. In this chapter, we will unpack the current thinking surrounding the concept of trauma and explore its relevance for education professionals in the twenty-first century.

Thinking Point 2.1

When you hear the word *trauma*, what do you think of?

Definitions of Trauma

Over the last twenty years, as knowledge and understanding of the potential impact of trauma has developed, an increased desire to appropriately assist those who have suffered adverse experiences has emerged. In response to this, the US-based Substance Abuse and Mental Health Services Administration (SAMHSA) assembled an expert group and produced the following widely accepted definition:

> Individual trauma results from an **event**, series of events, or set of circumstances that is **experienced** by an individual as physically or emotionally harmful or life threatening and that has lasting adverse **effects** on the individual's functioning and mental, physical, social, emotional, or spiritual well-being.
>
> (SAMHSA, 2014: 7)

These three E's of trauma highlight important aspects of our evolving understanding of trauma, namely that it is very much about how the particular event or circumstances affect the individual. The same event may be processed and felt quite differently by two individuals (SAMHSA, 2014; Chafouleas et al., 2016). As Mate states, it is not the event itself which is the trauma; rather, it is the 'inner injury' (Mate, 2022: 20) which happens as a result of the difficult event. It is 'not what happens to you but what happens inside you' (Mate, 2022: 20), the 'imprint left by that experience on mind, brain, and body' (Van der Kolk, 2014: 24). A number of factors both within and surrounding the individual influence the extent to which the scars of this inner injury endure, or indeed, if there is a scar at all. A focus on the number of Adverse Childhood Experiences (ACEs) (Felitti et al., 1998) a child has experienced then is perhaps an oversimplification of the issue (Lacey and Minnis, 2020). Divorce, for example, is not necessarily a traumatic experience in itself if managed sensitively and may in fact result in healthier living arrangements for the child. ACEs will be considered in more detail in Chapter 3.

Most commentators differentiate between simple (or type 1, big-T) trauma and complex (or type 2, small-t) trauma (NHS Education for Scotland, 2017; Howard, 2022; Mate, 2022). The former is described as a 'highly stressful experience … one time event' (Brunzell and Norrish, 2021: 28), and 'identifiable hurtful and overwhelming events' (Mate, 2022: 21) like accidents, natural disasters or violence in the family. While the consequences can indeed be devastating, the impact is often shorter term and there is less chance of the victim developing post-traumatic stress symptoms (Howard, 2022: 6). The latter, complex trauma, refers to multiple, ongoing, repeated traumatic experiences often at the hands of those who are supposed to love and care for us (Brunzell and Norrish, 2021; Perry and Winfrey, 2021; Howard, 2022). They often occur interpersonally and include, but are not limited to, sexual, physical and emotional abuse, neglect and ongoing family violence. Developmental trauma usually occurs early in life and refers to the significant impact that such negative experiences have on a child's social, emotional and physical development (Brunzell and Norrish, 2021). Mate (2022: 22) argues that this type of trauma is 'nearly universal in our culture' and that we must not discount seemingly lesser events like bullying or consistently harsh comments towards children from our definition of trauma. Similarly, trauma can occur as the result of 'good things not happening' (Mate, 2022: 23), while Perry and Winfrey (2021: 103) ask us to remember those 'quieter, less obvious experiences' like humiliation or marginalization.

The manual which is widely used to diagnose psychiatric diseases is the *American Psychiatric Association's Diagnostic and Statistical Manual of Mental Disorders* (DSM-V is the current one). Some have campaigned to have Development Trauma Disorder recognized here as a new category, for example, renowned psychiatrist Bessel Van der Kolk, but this has so far been rejected. It is Van der Kolk's (2014) view that the current system wrongly emphasizes behavioural control over recognition of the potentially wide-ranging impact of interpersonal maltreatment and distress (Van der Kolk, 2014: 191; Howard, 2022: 138) and as such interventions are frequently inappropriate or insufficient. That said, while it is useful to consider these *types of trauma*, reality often illustrates that the lines between these are often not so clear, and individuals may suffer from both these types to differing degrees across their lifetime.

A Paradigm Shift

What underlies all of the above is a reconceptualization of trauma in the hearts and minds of all who work and live with children and young people. It is a move away from a medical model and towards one which takes a biopsychosocial approach (SAMHSA, 2014: 5). In other words, an approach which considers the biological, psychological and social factors which lie behind behaviours and illnesses. Taking a more strength-focused view means moving away from 'pathologising to contextualising' (Greer, 2023: 32) and asking 'what's happened to you?' rather than 'what's wrong with you?' (Perry and Winfrey, 2021). Such an approach may allow us to begin to address the root causes of behaviours rather than just the superficial symptoms (Dolezal and Gibson, 2022: 3) and so move towards healing, repair and change (see Chapter 12).

It is also crucial to consider the sociopolitical and historical context (O'Toole, 2022: 115) within which trauma may occur. Palma et al. (2023: 8) challenge us to include racial trauma and to acknowledge that the 'source of the trauma may be a collective experience, as opposed to an individual one'. Saleem et al. (2022: 2508) define racial stress and trauma as 'frightening, dangerous, or upsetting race-based events or discrimination that can cause stress, death, or a threat to the physical or psychological integrity of self or others'. They note the 'cumulative impact of racism in smaller doses' and highlight its potential to 'illicit trauma symptoms' (Saleem et al., 2022: 2508). Acknowledgement of this and the implementation of systems and practices which address such trauma within our education systems are paramount if we are to fully meet the needs of all our young people.

Collective Trauma

So, what happens if we consider the Covid-19 pandemic through a trauma lens? At the time of writing, we can only begin to reflect on the lasting damaging impact this collective trauma may have had on many – though not all – children and young people. What is more certain, though, is that this unprecedented episode in our history has served to shine a light on factors which may mitigate the potential impact of trauma.

Collective trauma has been defined as 'a cataclysmic event that shatters the basic fabric of society' (Hirschberger, 2018: 1441), and 'experiences shared by a large number of people that pose significant challenges to the well-being of individuals, groups and society' (Wu, Y. et al., 2024: 116). Given that more than seven million people have now died as a result of the pandemic (World Health Organisation, 2024), it is no surprise that it has been viewed by some as a collective trauma (Wu, Y. et al., 2024). Indeed, many are still recovering from the 'shattered sense of safety' (Crosby et al., 2020: 2) which prevailed during the lockdowns and reports are increasing that young people's mental well-being has declined since then (Samji et al., 2022; Scott et al., 2023). The continued depth of feeling, and understandable sense of loss, of those directly affected was evident following the release of the first report from the UK's Covid-19 Enquiry in July 2024 (Hall, 2024).

It is clear that systemic inequities across many countries were exposed by the pandemic as minorities and those in deprived circumstances were disproportionally affected (Perry and Winfrey, 2021; O'Toole, 2022; Wu, Y. et al., 2024). This indeed warrants further attention but of more relevance for the purposes of this publication is the variation in experience reported by our children and young people. In an early study, Signorelli et al. (2021) suggested that the closure of schools and the resultant physical and social isolation meant that young people had to 'readjust their inner universe both from a cognitive and a social and emotional level' (Signorelli et al., 2021: 42). They were exposed to a narrative that told them the world is unsafe, and they were denied access to the social connections and environments which would have contributed to their resilience and emotional development. Parental responses may not have been as attuned during this time, for a myriad of reasons beyond their control, so for many children the pandemic disrupted the interpersonal foundations on which healthy emotional development is founded (Grady et al., 2022). Sadly for others, lockdowns led to further trauma in the form of increased domestic violence (Cowie and Myers, 2021) and unsafe living arrangements.

However, in spite of social isolation and the highly restrictive protective measures, not all young people felt that the pandemic was a negative experience – not all felt traumatized. Soneson et al. (2023) report that one third of the eight- to eighteen-year-olds they spoke to in 2020 felt that their mental well-being had improved during the first UK lockdown (Soneson et al., 2023). Better relationships with family and remaining connected with friends digitally helped, as did more flexible ways of learning and the absence of potential issues with peers at school. Enhanced sleeping patterns and more exercise also contributed to well-being. In another study based in Scotland, fourteen- to eighteen-year-olds enjoyed an increased sense of autonomy and personal agency, though they called for more training in mental health issues for teachers (McCluskey et al., 2021).

Poor outcomes from stressful events are not inevitable then, so it is imperative that we consider what buffers our young people from the worst potential effects of difficult experiences. The developmental age of the child at the time of the trauma is highly significant (Perry, 2009). As we will explore in more detail in Chapter 4, early attachment experiences will establish patterns and expectations in a child's brain. Genetic factors are also thought to be significant (Perry, 2009) but there is little doubt that the single most important factor is a solid network of supportive, responsive relationships (O'Toole, 2022; Nicholson et al., 2023). In the words of Bruce Perry: 'the presence of familiar people projecting the social-emotional cues of acceptance, compassion, caring, and safety calms the stress response of the individual' (Perry, 2009: 246). (We will explore the neuroscience behind this in Chapter 6.) In a study on the Covid-19 pandemic, feeling that we belonged and that we had a *sense of community* was shown to help individuals cope with the difficulties which arose (Mannarini et al., 2022). Similarly, a study on adolescents suggested that having trusted friendships protected against the development of depressive symptoms as lockdowns were implemented (Houghton et al., 2022). Children (and adults) also need a safe space in which to make sense of a traumatic event and process its implications (de Thierry, 2021). In the context of the recent pandemic, we must question if our education system has indeed provided this for our children and young people.

Thinking Point 2.2

How do you feel children and young people have been impacted by the Covid-19 pandemic, if at all?

The Potential Impact of Trauma

Awareness of the potentially devastating physiological and psychological consequences of chronic and repeated challenging experiences has increased considerably in the light of the original ACE study (Felitti et al., 1998). Ongoing adversity and trauma while a child's brain is developing can have – but does not always have – a long-lasting and far-reaching impact on their social and educational life. The stress felt by a child who continually finds him/herself surrounded by adversity is often described as *toxic stress*. Feelings of horror, helplessness and fear make this stress toxic in the sense that it 'is so emotionally costly that it can affect brain development and other aspects of a child's health' (Walkley and Cox, 2013: 2). The structure and function of the child's brain can be altered under these circumstances (Jacobson, 2021). Van der Kolk explains: '[i]f you feel safe and loved, your brain becomes specialised in exploration, play, and cooperation; if you are frightened and unwanted, it specialises in managing feelings of fear and abandonment' (Van der Kolk, 2014: 65).

Unpicking this last statement allows us to understand a vast array of behaviours we may see in the classroom, playground and beyond. A child who is constantly anticipating pain and suffering may be hypervigilant and reactive to even the slightest change in routine or environment. Their threat response system may be heightened activating 'powerful defence mechanisms' (Treisman, 2017: 17) in situations which others would consider innocuous, for example, unexpectedly another teacher walks into the classroom or assembly day is changed. They may fight, take flight or freeze. This may take the form of impulsive behaviour, aggression, inattention and other disruptive behaviour (Bland and Gershwin, 2023). Attendance may be affected. They may struggle to regulate their emotions. Hence it is not difficult to see how academic progress may be hampered. On another level, such a focus on survival means that the young person has limited access to the rational thinking part of the brain, their cognitive capacity is diminished, memory may be impaired. In effect, those executive functions like problem solving and planning just cannot get online because the brain is focusing on survival. It has detected threat – whether or not in reality there is real threat – so it is not stopping to think, it is reactive and impulsive. We can all relate to those moments when *we can't think straight*, where we can't find the solution to a particular problem because our brains are overloaded in some way. Only when a sense of calmness and safety return can we think, rationalize and plan. Threats of punitive consequences while a young person is dysregulated are pointless, as the young person's ability to process these and make a rational decision is severely impaired, albeit temporarily in some cases.

Another consequence of early complex trauma is relational; namely how children and young people build and maintain relationships with both their teachers and their peers. As we will examine further in Chapter 4, early experiences of need, and the extent to which those needs are met – or not – by our carers, establish patterns for how we conceptualize trust. That is, trust in our carers, in adults in general, trust that the world is a safe place. Without such trust, a fundamental element in positive relationships, children struggle to connect appropriately with their peers. Similarly, they simply cannot process that their teacher wants the best for them. Their reactions and behaviour are perhaps more understandable when seen through this lens. The early years also see us build the foundations of our self-image and sense of worth. Children who have been neglected or abused often view themselves as unworthy of love and attention (Brunzell and Norrish, 2021) and they have no faith even in those who show them abundant compassion. Again, when we consider a child's apparent indifference to their schoolwork or their frustrating lack of response to our pleas that they should care about their future, we must ask from where this is coming. Understanding that it is an in-built sense of worthlessness, for which they cannot be blamed, that leads to this debilitating state of mind is crucial if we are to even begin to address their needs in the education system. As Cozolino and Siegel (2013: 97) state '[w]hen we scan the faces of new students each fall, we see in their faces and expressions a reflection of the ways in which their brains have been shaped to experience and cope with the world'. The strategies we put in place to meet the varied needs of our pupils are the focus of much of this publication.

Alongside all of this is another aspect which cannot be ignored: the impact on our education professionals. Those who work on a daily basis with traumatized children have been found to often suffer from *compassion fatigue*, defined as 'the product of bearing witness to the suffering of others resulting in a reduced ability or capacity to be present with others, and feelings of powerlessness, isolation, and confusion' (O'Toole and Dobutowitsch, 2023: 2). In spite of often feeling fulfilled by their role and inspired by the opportunity to make a difference in a young person's life, teachers and other education professionals are often at the forefront of the challenging behaviour, resulting in them feeling emotionally exhausted and burnt out (Berger et al., 2021). Teacher absence rates and levels of attrition may reflect this phenomenon (McEnaney, 2024; Seith, 2024a). Later chapters will consider the role of reflective supervision as a strategy for mitigating the impact on educators (see Chapter 17).

Why Education Professionals, Why Now?

In July 2024, the United Nations Convention on the Rights of the Child (UNCRC) was embedded into Scottish law. Formalizing the right of every child to an education (Article 28) fits well with the focus on well-being and relationships which has underpinned policy across Scotland since 2008 in the form of *Getting it right for every child (GIRFEC)* (Scottish Government, 2022a). Such a focus has seen whole school nurturing approaches as well as targeted nurture interventions being embedded across Local Authorities in Scotland (Education Scotland, 2017a; March and Kearney, 2017). Relational approaches, as promoted by many and the National Trauma Transformation Programme (active across sectors of society since 2017), suggest we accept that trauma is 'everybody's business' (NHS Education for Scotland, 2017: 7) (see more on this in Chapter 15). In addition, a comprehensive review of the care system in Scotland resulted in the publication of a series of reports entitled, *The Promise* (Independent Care Review, 2020). This too asks all those who work and live with children to be trauma-aware and attachment-focused. Given this policy landscape and narrative, becoming trauma-responsive appears like the natural next step for education professionals in Scotland.

In our post-Covid-19 reality, we are perhaps more aware than ever of the potential impact of trauma as well as the inequities exposed during this international crisis. Writing about the Australian context, L'Estrange and Howard (2022: 4) suggest that there is 'increased impetus to re-evaluate education systems, educational policy, and school service delivery' to address these inequities. Indeed, growing awareness of the prevalence of trauma and enhanced knowledge of its potential impact corresponds with the agenda on inclusion and social justice for which many currently advocate. With reference to the US context, Van der Kolk (2014: 428) takes this even further and suggests that trauma is now 'our most urgent public health issue'. He goes on to remind us 'we have the knowledge necessary to respond effectively. The choice is ours to act on what we know' (Van der Kolk, 2014: 428).

For many, taking a trauma-informed approach in our classrooms and schools is not a choice; rather, they see it as necessary if we are to avoid continuing to harm our children and young people; 'schools need to increase their sensitivity to the complex developmental needs of their students by critically evaluating how their policies contribute to adversity rather than diminish it' (Downey and Greco, 2023: 4). SAMHSA's (2014) four key principles (the four Rs) of a trauma-informed approach notably include the need to actively *resist re-traumatization*. This comes in addition to realizing the widespread impact of trauma, recognizing the signs of it and responding to it (SAMHSA, 2014). Punitive consequences for dysregulated behaviour which exclude and shame may indeed do further harm as the pupil is denied access to positive attachments, restorative processes and that crucial sense of safety and support (Howard, 2022). In contrast, school staff could be considered key players in buffering the effects of trauma. The relationships they may establish with children can be critical in changing the view the child has of him/herself as well as of how they engage with their education as a whole. Hence there has to be some acceptance that the role of education professionals is expanding (Venet, 2023) and that 'mental health and wellness are integrally connected to students' success in the classroom and to a thriving school environment' (NCTSN, 2017: 1). That said, given the pressures on time and energy, this can often be a difficult balance. Support for our school staff, then, is essential if they are to embrace this approach. Some have indeed noted that their confidence and sense of effectiveness increase as they receive more training on trauma-informed approaches (Berger et al., 2021).

What We Mean by Trauma-Informed

Scotland's *Toolkit for Trauma-informed Practice* defines this as '[a] model that is grounded in and directed by a complete understanding of how trauma exposure affects service user's neurological, biological, psychological and social development' (Scottish Government, 2021a: 8). Applying this to the sphere of education essentially means a move away from behaviourist views of discipline and management of classrooms towards relational ones within which the importance of connection is recognized and prioritized (Howard, 2022). Compassion and restorative approaches should predominate within a trauma-informed classroom and school as strategies and practices are put into place to ensure that pupils not only are safe but feel safe (see Chapter 11). Venet asks us to place equity at the centre of our trauma-informed system as we seek to address the 'inequitable conditions within schools that cause, exacerbate or perpetuate trauma' (Venet, 2023: xviii). As such, ongoing racial stress and trauma must also be considered if we are to embrace a holistic view of our education systems. Equity and social justice cannot be achieved unless we are culturally responsive across our systems and practice (Saleem et al., 2022: 2516). This is not an approach to be adopted for particular children; rather, it is an ecological one which considers the interaction between classroom practice, institutional norms and systems-wide policy (Venet, 2023: 13) for all pupils and staff. Chafouleas et al. (2016: 147) discuss an *intraindividual lens* through which 'building self-regulation (resilience, coping) within the individual is emphasised, with external supports focused on creating safe environments and building positive connections and trusting relationships'. This adds a focus on prevention to our trauma-informed outlook and allows us to take a strengths-based, inclusive and hopeful view.

Implementation of trauma-informed practices in education should be underpinned by the five principles of safety (emotional and physical), trustworthiness (transparency of policy and procedures), choice (a voice in decision-making), collaboration (peer support) and empowerment (the sharing of power) (Scottish Government, 2021a: 11). There should be systemic alignment with these five principles and 'a profound paradigm shift in knowledge, perspectives, attitudes and skills that continues to deepen and unfold over time' (Scottish Government, 2021a: 11). Clearly, this is not a simple task but one which needs to be comprehensive and systemic if it is to be successful over time. Wassink-de Stigter et al. (2022) suggest three implementation drivers across which trauma-informed attitudes and practices must prevail: the competency driver, organizational driver and leadership driver. Through these there needs to be a focus on training and ongoing support for school staff, planning at a strategic level, and adaptive and engaging advocacy for trauma-informed practices across the leadership of an institution. Howard (2022) offers three key areas of support for learners: safety, relationships and emotional regulation. Of these she states that relationships are the most important as it is through these that felt safety will be achieved within an environment in which self-regulation is possible. To this she adds that there must be support for education staff as only if they remain regulated can they offer emotional calmness and support to the pupils.

A multi-tiered approach is also recommended for trauma-informed institutions (NCTSN, 2017; Berger and Martin, 2021; Bland and Gershwin, 2023). It is suggested that the first tier of support is universal and aims to build trauma literacy among practitioners, parents and children. In this lies the attempt to prevent further trauma and begin the healing process for those who have suffered. The second tier may target more *at-risk* children and young people with particular approaches or strategies, while the third tier may respond to the more intensive needs of a few pupils with targeted interventions, some of which may need to be carried out by professionals out with the school (see Chapter 10). At present, there are many different models and approaches across varied national contexts. In time, and with further research, the facilitators and barriers to each of these models will undoubtedly become clear. Prioritizing the key principles and remembering the underlying focus on relationships is perhaps what is most useful as we begin our journeys towards being truly trauma informed.

A final note here: every journey begins with the first small step and, for these purposes, that first step begins with our daily practice in the classroom. Every interaction with children and young people communicates the degree to which we care for them, love them, respect and protect them. It communicates the extent to which we see and hear them as vulnerable human beings who seek to connect and survive. It is in this consistent and hopeful behaviour, on our part, that we will begin the healing process with and for them.

Summary

In this chapter we have considered definitions of simple, complex and collective trauma. We have examined the potential impact of complex trauma, the focus of this publication, while remembering crucially that poor outcomes are not inevitable. As education professionals we occupy a pivotal role in ensuring that the manifestation of trauma in children and young people is recognized and that we take positive steps to prevent re-traumatizing them. Promoting a learning environment in which relationships are prioritized, and emotional safety is carefully considered paves the way towards being truly trauma responsive.

3

Adverse Childhood Experiences (ACEs)

Mike Carroll

Key ideas

This chapter will:

- identify a range of ACEs and comment on a lack clarity regarding the identification of ACEs,
- outline the link between adversity and negative social, educational and health outcomes,.
- outline some positive childhood experiences (PCEs) that help build resilience to trauma.

Introduction

Vincent Felitti and his colleagues introduced the acronym *ACE* for adverse childhood experiences (Felitti et al., 1998) in an attempt to describe the link between negative childhood experiences such as abuse, neglect and household dysfunction with future negative social, behavioural and health outcomes throughout a child's lifespan (Cronholm et al., 2015). In addition, Felitti et al. (1998, 250) found a discernible dose-response relationship between the number of childhood adversities and negative health outcomes. A variety of studies have replicated this dose response, with exposure to a higher number of ACEs linked to increased risk of poor physical, social and psychological outcomes (e.g. Andersson et al., 2021; Loveday et al., 2022). The critical 'dose' predictive of negative outcomes is taken to be four or more ACEs (Edwards et al., 2019). A cumulative ACE score does not necessarily suggest that all traumatic experiences make equivalent contributions to an individual's risk for negative outcomes (Briggs et al., 2021). Pairs of ACEs have been shown to interact to amplify negative effects beyond the sum (additive synergy) or product (multiplicative synergy) of the contributions of each ACE (Briggs et al., 2021: 243). Compensatory synergy (antagonism) 'also occurs in which one risk factor cancels out or reduces a second risk factor so that the total outcome is significantly less than would be calculated from the individual contributions of the risk factors to the outcome' (Briggs et al., 2021: 245). Nevertheless, although the evidence indicates that there is a dose-response linkage between ACEs and negative outcomes this should not be thought of as a fait accompli (Danielson and Saxen, 2019).

The 'impact' of this cumulative *ACEs score* has come to represent an urgent public health concern, a health crisis hidden in plain sight (Sonu et al., 2021: 517); consequently, research on ACEs has caught the imagination of policymakers and a range of professional practitioners in the UK (e.g. medical, educational, social work, criminal justice, etc.) and used to help inform the decision-making process, placing children at the centre, when considering resource allocation. It has been argued that the pattern of individual ACE scores and their link with negative long-term outcomes can assist with the development of evidence-based interventions aimed at mitigating the effects of ACEs, informing why, who, what, when, where and how to target resources (Edwards et al., 2019). However, the relationship between ACEs and negative long-term outcomes is best understood at a population level as there is an absence of empirical evidence for their power to predict problems at the individual level (Portwood et al., 2023). Furthermore, focusing on individual well-being, building the strengths and assets of individuals and communities, is helpful but ultimately may fail to address the underlying causes of negative long-term outcomes at the population level. A key finding of many studies on ACEs has been that they are more prevalent among the poor. Consequently, a *whole-child approach* linked to the notion of well-being needs to go hand-in-hand with policies that seek to address social and economic inequalities (Davidson and Carlin, 2019). In concluding this section, it is important to note that there is no one-size-fits-all solution to addressing the impact of ACEs; consequently, system-wide strategies involving multiple interventions are required to adequately prevent and reduce the impact of ACEs.

ACEs: An Ever-Expanding List

Much of the early work in this field drew on adults' retrospective recall of exposure to adversity using questionnaires. This is problematic as participants may well have difficulty recalling childhood experiences due to memory loss or by being reluctant to provide accurate information as a coping mechanism. This later finding may be the result of participants wishing to avoid interpretations of the data that could lead to intrusion from others attempting to resolve *problems*. Later studies combined recall with prospectively collected data (e.g. reports from siblings, official records from schools, hospitals, etc.) for comparison (Hartas, 2019). The main thrust of many ACE studies has been to determine causal links between the *cumulative score* of traumatic events, experienced before the age of eighteen, and long-term damage to physical and mental health (White et al., 2019: 458) with the cumulative score being taken as a proxy measure of the burden of childhood stress (Senaratne et al., 2024).

The original adverse childhood experiences identified by Felitti et al. (1998) included exposure to sexual, physical and psychological abuse; domestic violence; substance abuse, mental illness, and incarceration of a parent. Felitti et al. (1998) did not claim that theirs was a definitive list or indicate what should be considered potentially traumatic and what should not (Sonu et al., 2021: 518). Over time our understanding of the concept of childhood adversity has expanded to include a wide range of stressors that may have an impact upon children's well-being with the link between cumulative adverse experiences and child development being seen as a function of 'nature dancing with nurture over time' (Shonkoff and Garner, 2012: 234). Subsequent studies augmented the original adverse experiences with emotional and physical neglect, and parental divorce to form a set of ten adverse experiences across three categories of abuse, neglect, and household dysfunction (Portwood et al., 2023) (see Figure 3.1). The list of adverse experiences continues to grow to include: '(1) witness to a violent crime, (2) victim of a violent crime, (3) family financial problems, (4) frequent family conflict, (5) death of a parent, (6) death of a sibling, and (7) foster care or out-of-home placement' (Giovanelli et al., 2023: 4). The growing list of adverse experiences, rooted in maltreatment and household dysfunction, is largely interpersonal; however, we are all embedded in wider society within which community-level factors are thought to confer, an ongoing, contextual pressure within which the interpersonal adverse experiences are set (Sonu et al., 2021: 518). There is now a growing awareness that community-based events and experiences can give rise to community-based adversity (e.g. racism, sexism, intimidation, bullying and harassment, living in an unsafe neighbourhood, food insecurity, homelessness, etc.) (Cronholm et al., 2015). Often missing from these expanding lists is an examination of the role that economic hardship plays in predicting and amplifying the impact of clustering of adverse experiences (Asmussen et al., 2019).

Thinking Point 3.1

a. Use Figure 3.1 to reflect on your own life in order to identify your exposure to adverse experiences.
b. What were the sources of support that helped you overcome these adverse experiences?

The research does appear to indicate that there is an evidence base linking adverse experiences, which often occur together, with long-term negative outcomes in physical and mental well-being, educational achievement, social functioning, earning

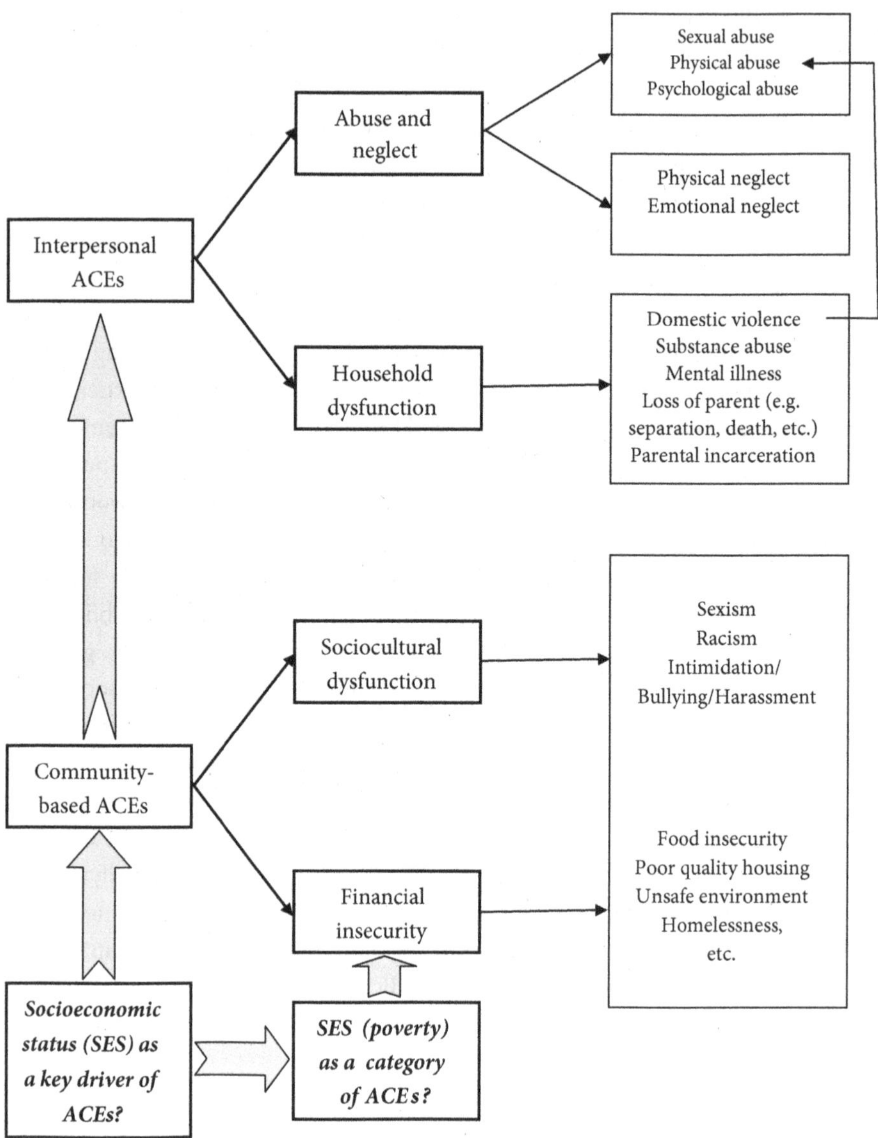

Figure 3.1 Adverse childhood experiences (ACEs).

potential, occupational stability, living standards, and the risk of limited lifespans (Steptoe et al., 2019: 416). Research looking at the impact of adversity on education indicates that 'children with histories of trauma exposure often experience challenges in school, including poor attendance, less engagement with the school system … increased risk for problems in academic performance, attention problems, social skills problems and aggression at school' (Conners Edge et al., 2024: 2). Clearly exposure to adversity hinders educational progress and as such they are a form of developmental trauma; however, the causal relationship between exposure to adversity and poor long-term outcomes is not straightforward as adverse experiences co-occur alongside compensatory physical, social and psychological processes (Asmussen et al., 2019: 427). For example, we interact and are connected with others outside the household, and this offers opportunities for support to overcome the impact of exposure to adversity within the household or community.

As stated earlier the role of economic hardship, or socioeconomic status (SES), in understanding and addressing adversity is largely missing from the research literature (Walsh et al., 2019: 1091). Arguably exposure to adversity is treated in a *decontextualized manner* as the societal conditions that may give rise to these experiences are rarely considered (Portwood et al., 2023: 39). To help explain adversity the focus is often on dysfunctional parenting with children seen as victims (Portwood et al., 2023) rather than the wider socioeconomic landscape. An *individual pathology* conveniently ignores research that points to 'clear associations between socioeconomic circumstances in childhood and adversity-related outcomes' (Walsh et al., 2019: 1091). Portwood et al. (2023: 38) argue that '[h]olding individuals responsible for their problems, is not effective for addressing the roots of these risk factors and reducing leading causes of morbidity and mortality at the population level'. Thus, considering poverty as an adverse experience would enable research to explore the complex relationship between adversity and the structural social context in which parents and children live with a view to develop 'population-based actions whilst avoiding the possible stigmatisation of families and children' who are often powerless to bring about change (Kelly-Irving and Delpierre, 2019: 453).

Exposure to Adversity

Exposure to adversity (e.g. parental separation, verbal and/or physical abuse, loss of a loved one, household domestic violence, etc.) is widespread with an estimated two-thirds of the US population having experienced at least one adverse experience before the age of eighteen (Giboney Wall, 2021: 119). Two population level surveys have shown that experience of adversity is widespread, with 48 per cent of adults in England and 47 per cent of adults in Wales reporting experience of at least one type of negative experience before the age of eighteen (Barnardo's Wales, 2022). As stated earlier, adverse experiences are also known to cluster with approximately one in four children experiencing four or more adverse experiences (Aytur et al., 2022). The Growing Up in Scotland (GUS) study indicated that approximately 65 per cent of children experienced at least one adverse childhood experience and 10 per cent experienced three or more by the time they were aged eight (Marryat and Frank, 2019: 3). Children who are most likely to experience adversity are those living in the lowest income groups as well as boys, having a mother with lower educational qualifications, having a mother who was under twenty or over forty at the birth of her first child and living in an area with higher levels of deprivation or in an urban area (Marryat and Frank, 2019: 4). In addition, studies in the United States have found that adversity disproportionately burdens populations of colour, indigenous communities and members of sexual minority groups (Champine et al., 2022), thus necessitating a trauma-informed social justice response. The vulnerability of exposure to adversity within particular social groups may well explain why studies have shown that it is not uncommon for adverse experiences to be transmitted across generations (Asmussen et al., 2019).

Adversity as a concept is difficult to define leading to a lack of consensus as to its meaning (Portwood et al., 2023). Indeed, White et al. (2019: 457) suggest that, more generally, adverse childhood experiences as a conceptual construct is somewhat confusing as they 'conflate[*s*] different issues, or divide[*s*] up indivisible processes, leading to problems in their explanatory weight and hence in developing policy and interventions on their basis'. Following on from the Adverse Childhood Experiences Study (Felitti et al., 1998), there remains a lack of consistency in determining what constitutes an adverse experience (Edwards et al., 2019: 413). In the early studies there was little by way of justification with respect to what childhood adversities were included and what were excluded (Hartas, 2019). As has previously stated, subsequent studies have identified a wide range of adverse experiences which are not always assessed or determined in the same way. Furthermore, it is unclear as the weight attached to different adverse experiences experienced by the same person and whether events are experienced in the same way by different individuals (Senaratne et al., 2024: 6). The lack of conceptual clarity is compounded as there are often few insights provided in terms of contextual information, for example, the severity, frequency and duration of childhood adversity; the age at which adversity was first experienced; the presence or absence of other risk factors (e.g. poverty) and/or protective factors (e.g. stable family support) (Hartas, 2019: 437). This conceptual confusion suggests that our understanding of the usefulness of adversity should be more nuanced (Taylor-Robinson et al., 2018). Despite some methodological issues adversity remains a useful conceptual construct at a population level; however, at an individual level we should be more cautious in attributing any exposure to adversity as inevitably leading to negative outcomes (Mersky et al., 2017: 67). At an individual level exposure to adversity should not be considered a determinant of poor outcomes merely a sensitizing concept. Indeed, White et al. (2019: 459) state that exposure to adversity 'cannot and should not be used to predict individuals at risk'. Adversity as a sensitizing concept indicates that it is important to become aware of the signs and symptoms of trauma as this may have a significant impact on the individual and as such practitioners should endeavour to develop a trauma-informed approach to their practice so that we are able to respond to any and all individuals who experience trauma (see Chapter 10).

To reiterate, at a population level there is an increasing body of evidence that links exposure to adversity with poor physical and mental health outcomes in adulthood (Steptoe et al., 2019). A wide range of risks have been identified including disease conditions in adulthood such as 'cancer, heart disease, stroke, obesity, diabetes, and chronic obstructive pulmonary disease' (Campbell et al., 2016: 344). There remains a question with respect to how robust this evidence is in predicting risk of long-term negative outcomes at the level of the individual; however, life is likely to be difficult if one were to be in receipt of multiple adverse experiences acting coterminously (Portwood et al., 2023). The profile of children exposed to adverse experiences could include academic underachievement, anti-social and disruptive classroom behaviour, and school suspension (Berger et al., 2021: 1041). A child experiencing multiple adverse experiences is likely to find the structured life of the classroom in sharp contrast with their chaotic and unpredictable home environment (Giboney Wall, 2021: 120). School policies and practice aimed at intervening to ameliorate the negative consequences of adversity need to start early (Giovanelli et al., 2023: 9).

Stress

Stress can be viewed both as a *friend* in that it promotes growth and development as well as a *poison* in that it can have a debilitating effect on development (NHS, 2018). There are three categories of stress responses in young children which include positive, tolerable and toxic stress (Gill et al., 2019: 107). Positive stress is usually brief and mild to moderate in magnitude. Positive stress can, particularly with support, facilitate development and is a normal part of everyday life. Tolerable stress occurs when the degree and duration of hardship or threat increases (e.g. bereavement in the family (see Chapter 7)) causing stress hormone levels to rise. Although such situations are also opportunities for growth and development, it is important that the individual experiencing the stress has access to a supportive interpersonal relationship with a caregiver. Such relationships help the child develop effective coping strategies that enable them to develop resilience to stress (NHS, 2018); however, the absence of a supportive relationship may lead to stress which can be debilitating.

Toxic stress changes the architecture of the brain (see Chapter 6) which affects the individual's ability to regulate their emotions and behaviour (Barnardo's, 2020: 4). Overactivation of the stress response, over a prolonged period of time, is linked to the development of toxic stress (see Chapter 2). The notion of *toxicity* is related to the severity, frequency and continuity of the stressful experience, particularly if the individual is exposed to multiple and coterminous stressors (Ximenes et al., 2019), compounded by a lack of support from a caregiver, aimed at developing coping strategies (Portwood et al., 2023). When supportive interpersonal relationships from a caregiver are at best inconsistent or absent, the likelihood that toxic stress will become entrenched increases (Shonkoff et al., 2021). The cumulative effect of adversity over time can also lead to toxic stress (e.g. the day-to-day reality of living in poverty) (Harris, 2020). When children experience chronic toxic stress, they experience high levels of stress hormones circulating in their blood stream leading them to be constantly in a state of 'fight, flight or freeze' (NHS, 2018: 35). An ongoing experience of toxic stress may affect an individual's ability to think and often leads to coping strategies that are focused on survival within an environment that is perceived to be threatening. These coping strategies include constantly monitoring the environment, being overly reactive to perceived signs of danger and social isolation. These are strategies which do not allow for successful integration within the classroom (Danielson and Saxen, 2019). Fortunately, research suggests that when protective factors or positive socio-environmental buffers are put into place (Srivastav et al., 2020: 526), children who have experienced toxic stress have the potential to recover from exposure to adversity (NHS, 2018: 36). The key is providing stable, and supportive relationships with caregivers to help children build resilience and life skills so mitigating the effects of trauma (Srivastav et al., 2020: 526) (see Chapter 12).

Thinking Point 3.2

Consider times when you have experienced stress as a 'friend' and/or as a 'poison'.

Pathology of Trauma

As seen in Chapter 2 trauma can be categorized in a number of ways and includes relational harm experienced by children, usually over prolonged periods of time, at the hands of those who should be protecting them. It is important in coming to understand the nature of complex, relational trauma that it is the nature of the act that is the problem and not the individual who has experienced the act as there is a risk that the *pathology of trauma* leads practitioners to centre the problem in the individual affected rather than within the person(s) or circumstances that perpetrated the trauma (NHS, 2018: 52). This is often the case with victims of abuse who turn inwards and blame themselves, overwhelmed by feelings of guilt and shame, as they think they are at fault rather than focusing on the perpetrator of the abuse. Another manifestation of the pathology of trauma is that parents and families are often blamed for 'exposing their own children to ACEs' (Hartas, 2019: 439); however, there is a history of trauma compressed in the present that needs to be considered. There is the notion that trauma can persist across generations, a form of historical or collective trauma (Danielson and Saxen, 2019). Intergenerational trauma refers to when caregivers with experience of adversity pass on the effects of their trauma to their children (Andersson et al., 2021: 2). Intergenerational trauma is often a feature in communities that experience long-term socio-economic deprivation. Within such communities a *cycle of poverty* is established over time, and this creates the conditions for a 'biology of misfortune' (Boyce, 2014: 107). To redress trauma in these communities, interventions across multiple systems, aimed at reducing structural inequality, are required (e.g. providing access to quality childcare and education, supporting families in accessing basic needs such as housing and nutrition) (Hartas, 2019). Exposure to childhood trauma begins early in life, even before birth, as a result of maternal exposure to adverse events (Ximenes et al., 2019) and this will have an effect on a child's developing brain (Hartas, 2019). Barnardo's (2018a) stress the importance of past, often negative, experiences amongst caregivers as these often manifest themselves in a reluctance to engage with a variety of agencies. Portwood et al. (2023: 37) raise another important consideration with respect to research on ACEs, namely that within the policy arena it can lead to the *privatization of risk* with individuals being seen as responsible for the problems they encounter; consequently, there has been a move away from understandings of social and economic injustice brought about by inequality to focus on 'biologised theories' (Macvarish and Lee, 2019: 474). Caregivers are seen as the cause of, and solution to, the social problems highlighted by exposure to adverse experiences. 'How can the parent be appealed to as the agent of change when they are identified so relentlessly as the cause of the problem?' (Macvarish and Lee, 2019: 468). The research on adversity should not be used to demonize caregivers but rather strive to illuminate the deleterious developmental impact of social inequality on children and young people (Kelly-Irving and Delpierre, 2019: 453). Everyday social inequalities in Scottish society, for example, income inequality, food insecurity poverty and child poverty, have all increased, albeit slightly since the Covid-19 pandemic (Scottish Government, 2024a). Edwards et al. (2019: 413) argue that policy in an ACE-aware Scotland should move beyond the rhetoric of individual culpability to one that seeks to change the circumstances that allows exposure to adverse experiences to flourish. To break the cycle of intergenerational trauma it is important to support caregivers in addressing the trauma they have experienced so that they may, in their turn, be in a position to support their children.

Positive Childhood Experiences (PCEs)

There are three domains of protective factors: individual (e.g. problem-solving skills), relational (e.g. a sense of safety and security provided through close relationships) and community (e.g. a sense that one belongs within different spheres of a community)

(Webster et al., 2025: 823). A layered approach of support, across these domains, is required to ensure that children develop resilience in the face of adversity (Srivastav et al., 2020: 526). The concept of resilience acknowledges that adverse and positive events regularly coexist in daily life (see Chapter 12). Although children and young people may experience adversity other, more positive childhood experiences (sometimes called *Angels*) (Briggs et al., 2021: 249) may be present acting to reduce the negative effects of ACEs (Wu, M-H. et al., 2024) as well as helping to build resilience (Crouch et al., 2023). Positive and adverse childhood experiences overlap with and operate separately from each other. Positive childhood experiences (PCEs) fall into five broad categories:

1 Nurturing, supportive and protective relationships that facilitate the development of adaptive capacities promoting well-regulated stress-response systems.
2 Safe, stable environments that are free from fear and within which individuals can engage without significant risk of harm.
3 Safe emotional spaces providing constructive social engagement.
4 Development of social and emotional competencies.
5 Sound and appropriate levels of nutrition which promote development and healthy eating habits (Crouch et al., 2023).

Social support from caregivers provides a protective effect or *social fund* that helps to compensate the negative effects of adverse experiences. Wu M-H. et al. (2024) suggest that an important aspect of this compensatory model is the contribution made by non-parent adults (e.g. teachers) along with peer support that help facilitate a sense of belonging within a school community. Schools can become a *safe base* to enable learning and healing to take place. Within such a community developing resilience is more likely through positive relationships with competent adults, who themselves are effective learners and problem solvers (Howard, 2019: 549). Developing a layered approach to support to manage and adjust their emotional responses when they experience adversity (Parameswaran et al., 2024: 189). With adult guidance in the classroom, Programmes of Social Emotional Learning (SEL) are designed to support children 'acquire and effectively apply the knowledge, attitudes, and skills necessary to understand and manage emotions, set and achieve positive goals, feel and show empathy for others, establish and maintain positive relationships, and make responsible decisions' (Barnardo's, 2020: 4).

Bethell et al. (2019: 8) suggest that as part of any strategy designed to address exposure to adverse experiences, society should seek to support the creation of positive experiences in the home, schools and the local community in order to promote resilience in response to childhood adversities. A key barrier to this is the chronic lack of services and family support in the UK (White et al., 2019). Initiatives could include promoting 'parent-child attachment, positive parenting (e.g. parental warmth, responsiveness, and support), family health, and positive relationships with friends, in school, and in the community' (Bethell et al., 2019: 2). After-school activities are another way that has been shown to promote well-being among children and young people (Crouch et al., 2023). The main barrier, for many caregivers, of such schemes is the limitation in financial resources. The role of supportive caregivers in helping children develop adaptive coping strategies and resilience to adverse experiences permeates the literature; programmes such as the *Strengthening Families Program* (SFP – https://strengtheningfamiliesprogram.org/) is one of the ways by which caregivers and parents can be supported. 'The SFP has been demonstrated to increase parental knowledge of child development, as well as build positive relationships and social capital among family members' (Crouch et al., 2023: 7). Facilitating involvement in community-based activities is another way to help children and young people gain a sense of belonging which will help them with developing adaptive coping strategies and build up resilience to adversity, all too often this is constrained by a lack of funding.

Thinking Point 3.3

Consider what skills, abilities and dispositions you have that could help you to effectively respond to a student's exposure to adverse experiences.

Summary

Since Felitti et al.'s (1998) seminal research, the list of adverse childhood experiences has expanded including adversities linked to abuse, neglect, household dysfunction and sociocultural dysfunction. The literature in this field provides useful insights into the probabilities of negative social, behavioural and health outcomes at population level. Indeed, Barnardo's (2018b: 3) assert that 'fundamental to making Scotland a trauma and ACE aware nation is raising awareness of the prevalence of ACEs in the general population'. However, exposure to adversity should not be taken as a determinant of future negative outcomes with respect to individual trajectories (Barnardo, 2018b: 1). There are a range of methodological complexities that suggest caution is warranted in the interpretation of the likely impact of exposure to adversity. For example, the clustering of adverse experiences assumes that the consequences will be the same for all (Kelly-Irving and Delpierre, 2019: 451). In addition, clustering provides little by way of insight into the severity, timing and duration of stressful life events all of which are likely to have an impact on how the individual perceives and reacts to these events.

There are a range of protective factors that can compensate for adversity with the presence of stable, supportive and nurturing relationships with caregivers being the most important. These will support children and young people to utilize adversity as an opportunity for growth through developing healthy adaptations to stress (Garner and Shonkoff, 2012: 225). In addition, there is a growing awareness that positive childhood experiences (PCEs) co-occur with and act to moderate negative outcomes associated with exposure to adversity (Bethell et al., 2019).

4

A Place for Attachment Theory

Christine McKee

Key Ideas

This chapter will:

- outline the origins of attachment theory the internal working model and attachment classifications,
- examine critiques of attachment theory,
- examine the teacher/pupil relationship, and
- discuss the place of attachment theory in our schools and classrooms.

Introduction

As education professionals we plan, teach, support and assess the progress of our pupils. We also care for and nurture the young people with whom we come into contact. But do we *love*? Indeed, what do we mean by love in our educational contexts and what role should it play? bell hooks offers a definition: [love is]

> a combination of care, commitment, knowledge, responsibility, respect and trust. All these factors work interdependently. When these basic principles of love form the basis of teacher-student interaction, the mutual pursuit of knowledge creates the conditions for optimal learning.
>
> (hooks, 2010: 159)

In Scotland, the independent review of the care system suggested that '[t]he purpose of the workforce must be to be caring above anything else' (Independent Care Review, 2020: 23). The actions promoted by the review's reports seek to create a Scotland in which children are 'loved, safe, respected and realise their full potential' (Independent Care Review, 2020: 4). In this chapter, we will explore attachment theory and the extent to which it offers a theoretical background to this focus on 'love' as well as consider to what degree it is relevant to those working in education in the twenty-first century.

Thinking Point 4.1

In your opinion, is there a place for *love* in our education systems? If so, what would this look like?

Bowlby

It is rumoured that the founder of attachment theory, John Bowlby, originally considered calling it a Theory of Love (Golding and Hughes, 2012: 26) as it is our first experiences of love within the relationship with our primary caregiver that lie at the heart of this theory. From the 1940s onwards, Bowlby's research reflected his interest in the bond between child and carer and the impact that separation and loss had on that bond (Bowlby, 1969; 1973; 1980). He asserted that a secure attachment meant that the child felt safe, protected and nurtured, while inconsistent, unresponsive care could lead to an insecure attachment. In his work, Bowlby differed from previous analysts in that he thought that babies attach to their carers not necessarily because they feed them but because they 'trigger the unfolding of infants' inborn disposition to seek closeness with a protective other' (Sroufe and Siegel, 2011: 36). Human beings, unlike some animals, are born to connect with others. They need another human in order to survive. As Perry and Winfrey (2021: 75) state 'we are relational creatures' whose 'lives consist of finding our place within the community of human beings' (Van der Kolk, 2014: 131). Our social and emotional needs are entwined with our physical ones. For a newborn child 'love is action; it is the attentive, responsive, nurturing care that adults provide', and, as we will see, it is these interactions which build the developing brain (Perry and Winfrey, 2021: 76).

Bowlby suggested that our behaviours are determined by our overwhelming need for proximity to our primary attachment figure as well as by the feelings of fear and anxiety we associate with enforced distance from our caregiver (Bowlby, 1982). This powerful and 'innately driven evolutional process' (Lawrence, 2023: 3) or 'biological instinct' (Van der Kolk, 2014: 137) is activated both towards caring and attentive parents as well as rejecting or even abusive carers. Edward Tronick's famous Still Face Experiment (Weinberg and Tronick, 1996; YouTube, 2022) illustrates some of those attachment-seeking behaviours. In this experiment a mother and baby face each other and engage in playful interaction. The mother is then asked to not respond to the baby but to maintain a *still face*. The baby tries all of the strategies at her disposal to gain the attention of the mother (e.g. arms waving, jerky movement, crying, screaming). Within seconds she turns away in distress, unable to console herself. Effectively, there is a mismatch between what the baby has come to expect of her mother, given her previous experience, and the mother's dismissive response. Dysregulation is rapid.

Finally, the mother is asked to return to her normal playful interaction and rectify the *mismatch* (Zuckerman and Tronick, 2023), in so doing regulating the child, and helping her to regain that sense of trust which was temporarily ruptured.

Secure Base and Internal Working Model

It was Bowlby's theory that repetition of such (less extreme) rupture-repair cycles via incidences in normal life builds resilience in children and shows them that they have a secure base in the warmth of that primary attachment relationship (Bowlby, 1988). When a child is nurtured and cared for, her cries responded to and her early emotions mirrored, she will develop a trust in others and in the world alongside a view of herself as loved and loveable. She will be able to tolerate separation from her carer and will feel safe to explore the world in the knowledge that she can return to a sense of safety and reliability (Bowlby, 1988). She will be able to form her own positive relationships as she progresses through life. And, most importantly, she will develop her awareness of herself, empathy for others, the ability to self-regulate and self-motivate (Van der Kolk, 2014).

In contrast, where needs are not met and cries ignored, the child is left in a state of confusion and distrust, unable to build a positive view of herself in relation to others. She may subconsciously assume that others are against her and that she does not deserve to be loved. Bowlby labelled this the child's internal working model and he suggested that this schema or template sets a pattern for the child's reactions and relationships throughout her life (Bowlby, 1973; 1980). For example, the teacher choosing Child A to answer a question over Child B may be misinterpreted by Child B as a statement that the teacher dislikes her. She may respond by angrily shouting at the teacher, illustrating a reaction which may appear to be out of proportion when viewed through secure lenses. The child's expectations of others as well as their confidence in their own worth will inevitably have an impact on how they behave both at home and in school. Much behaviour in the classroom could be attributed to how the child views the world and herself within it, and it is perhaps an understanding of this which will help us seek solutions. It has been suggested that 'the emotional quality of our earliest attachment experience is perhaps the single most important influence on human development' (Sroufe and Siegel, 2011: 36). While this may be true, the capacity for the brain to continue developing within new and more positive relational experiences is now uncontested (Kennedy, 2008; Webber, 2017). As we will see in Chapter 6, developments in neuroscience have served to confirm Bowlby's initial focus on the power of relationships. Change and healing are possible, and it is these on which education professionals must focus. This is what forms the theoretical basis for adopting relational approaches to distressed behaviour in schools (see Chapter 11).

Thinking Point 4.2

What strategies might you use to establish yourself as a *secure base* for a child in your class?

Attachment Classifications

A colleague of Bowlby, Mary Ainsworth, carried out research in the 1970s and took attachment theory a step further (Ainsworth, 1979). Through the Strange Situation Experiment, Ainsworth observed the interactions between a child and her caregiver – usually the mother – at play, then when the caregiver left the room, and finally how the child reacted when her carer returned. She classified the attachment strategies the child used according to the extent and the way the child tried to regain proximity to their caregiver. Three main categories were established: secure, insecure-ambivalent and insecure-avoidant. For the first category, the children visibly used their mothers as a secure base as they explored and played. They were distressed on separation and sought proximity to their mothers on reunion. The second group were anxious even during play, were extremely distressed when their mothers left but frustrated and difficult to comfort on reunion (Duschinsky, 2015). The third group did not get distressed on separation and on reunion they generally avoided their mother. Building on Bowlby's work, these attachment classifications were theorized to set the pattern for the child's future relationships, including those they would develop in school (Geddes, 2017).

Children who were found to be *secure* generally had caregivers who were responsive, warm and sensitive to their needs. Those who were *insecure-ambivalent* had perhaps had carers who were inconsistent with their responses and, as such, the child had adapted their behaviour in order to gain their carer's attention. Those classified as *insecure-avoidant* had lived with rejection and insensitivity so had learned that communicating their feelings could lead to rebuff so, again, had adapted their behaviour to maintain proximity (Duschinsky, 2015). A further fourth category entitled *insecure-disorganized/disoriented* was added following the work by Main and Solomon in the 1980s (Main and Solomon, 1986); children here had witnessed dissociative or frightening behaviour by their carers in the past (Duschinsky, 2015). Children with disorganized patterns of attachment exhibited often contradictory behaviours which suggested 'a conflict between simultaneous dispositions to physically approach and to flee the caregiver' (Duschinsky, 2015: 35). These may include overt fear, high levels of stress and anxiety or dissociation. However, while these categorizations offer considerable insight into children's behaviour, they should be applied with caution and flexibility. The dangers of the 'fixity and pathologizing implications' of assuming children fit neatly into these categories should be acknowledged (Harlow, 2021: 3).

Taking Attachment Theory Further

While many may consider the core aspects of attachment theory to be fundamental to human development, it is not without its critics. Many have called for a move away from the original *monotropy* (i.e. focus on the mother as one main attachment figure) (Rose et al., 2019; Jarvis, 2022) and towards a wider view of the principal attachment figure. These may be fathers or others with key parenting roles. Harlow suggests that 'the potential for change lies in relationships beyond the initial dyad' (Harlow, 2021: 3), and the internal working model is also not something which should be viewed as fixed or irreversible. Indeed, a deterministic view of a child's fate following 'diagnosis' of attachment issues was never Bowlby's intention, but such deficit thinking has been associated with attachment theory. The context within which a child develops is also crucial, and socio-economic, community and cultural factors will inevitably influence the health of the relationships the child has with others. Mate (2022: 126) reminds us that the 'quality of early caregiving is heavily, even decisively, determined by the societal context in which it takes place' and never has this been more true than in this age of social media and the myriad of tempting, often harmful, distractions associated with it. Others have lamented the 'relational poverty' of current times as we become increasingly disconnected from each other socially (Perry and Winfrey, 2021: 255).

The cultural context within which children are cared for merits further consideration and attachment theory has been criticized for imposing a Eurocentric view of parenting on cultures where multiple attachments are valued. For example, it is argued that traditional attachment theory is a 'stark contrast' to the multiple relational approach of indigenous people where elders, aunts, uncles, siblings and others play an important role in the caregiving, education and well-being of children (Choate, 2020: 35). Similarly, Maori society in New Zealand is founded on the interwoven concepts of *whanau* (family), *hapu* (extended family) and *iwi* (collective kin group) and it is a culture in which children can be equally attached to several parenting figures (Mikahere-Hall, 2019). In effect, few argue with the power and significance of early nurturing relationships but flexibility in our thinking around the direct application of attachment theory is needed.

Gordon Neufeld's work both reinforces this message as well as expands it. In an address to the European Parliament on the '*Keys to Well-Being in Children and Youth*' (Neufeld, 2012), he stipulated that true maturation allows a child to fulfil their potential but that there are four prerequisites for true growth. The first of these is that children need to attach deeply to the adult(s) responsible for them; they need a *context of connection* within which they will feel belonging and demonstrate loyalty and a desire to be *good*. The second prerequisite is that children need to rest from the work of attachment; that is, 'they must not have to measure up to find significance. To keep us close, they must not think that they have to be good' (Neufeld, 2012: 17). Not an easy task in the face of distressed behaviour but an essential role of the adult in Neufeld's view. The third is that children need to play, which is defined as 'relatively free of outcome, is differentiated from reality, and is expressive in nature' (Neufeld, 2012: 18). The final prerequisite is that children need to be allowed to feel their emotions, and these must be expressed and named. As educators we can take much from these suggestions as we move forward to consider what all of this may mean in our classrooms and schools.

What All This Means for Schools and Teachers

The behaviour of the children we teach is often a topic of heated discussion in the media. Levels of teacher stress and burnout are frequently associated with what is often termed 'difficult or challenging behaviour' (NASUWT, 2023). Policies on the 'management of behaviour' may focus on rewards and sanctions if influenced by behaviourist philosophies or, as is occurring more now, may concentrate on the establishment and maintenance of positive relationships (see Chapter 11). This latter suite of policies is influenced by nurturing approaches, trauma-responsive attitudes and attachment theory. Pupils' socio-emotional well-being is prioritized. Research has shown that the strength of the attachment relationship between primary carer and child has an impact on success in school (Bergin and Bergin, 2009). Furthermore, Bergin and Bergin add that evidence suggests secure relationships between teachers and pupils lead to higher attainment and greater motivation on the part of pupils (Bergin and Bergin, 2009: 154), particularly in terms of the achievement of at-risk groups (Bergin and Bergin, 2009: 163). So let us consider what happens if we consider pupils' behaviour through the lens of attachment theory.

The vast majority of the children in our classrooms will be securely attached enough to thrive or at least manage the school environment. We will notice these children's ability to co-operate, empathize, ask for help and engage in the activities presented to them. Geddes highlights the two factors which are necessary for successful engagement in learning as:

i. the ability and desire to attempt a task which perhaps involves something the child does not yet understand; and

ii. trust that the teacher will help and support him/her should they have difficulties (Geddes, 2017).

They will explore their world and the new learning freely as long as they feel safe in the learning environment. They will view their teacher as a *safe haven* to which they can return when distressed. As they mature, this feeling of security will foster their self-reliance and independence (Bergin and Bergin, 2009). Indeed, a sensitive teacher who is encouraging, who helps pupils and reassures, who is attuned to the pupils' needs and interests and who emanates warmth and trust will provide an environment in which pupils can flourish (Ainsworth, 1979; Bergin and Bergin, 2009).

In the absence of this sense of safety, we often see the paradoxical behaviour which exemplifies children with insecure attachments. They may simultaneously seek attention from education staff while also rejecting them via behaviour which provokes negative responses. 'Students who have learned not to trust or who view themselves negatively will express their views either through internalised or externalised maladaptive behaviour' (Kennedy, 2008: 222). As such, *attention-seeking* behaviour may then be re-imagined as *attachment-seeking*. While classifications of insecure attachment – as discussed above – illuminate the various different circumstances behind children's behaviour, few children fit neatly into those categories so it is more useful here to consider the broad range of behaviours we may see in the classroom. Maladaptive behaviour may include aggressive, hostile, unpredictable, controlling or impulsive actions and reactions. Others may withdraw, isolate themselves socially, be overly self-reliant or be excessively clingy. It is crucial that those working with these children understand that these behaviours are a 'reflection of underlying interpersonal inner experiences and intrapersonal relationship-history' (Rose et al., 2019: 164). In many cases, children are behaving in a manner which seeks to confirm their internal working model, that is, they are unworthy of positive attention. Sadly, it is in the familiarity of negative reactions where they find comfort and predictability. Safety, for many of them, lies in disappointment and punishment.

In addition, again as a result of not feeling safe, some of these children may demonstrate a hypervigilance – meaning they struggle to concentrate on their work. In effect they are guarding themselves against 'the unpredictability of perceived dangers' (Webber, 2017: 320). They are on high alert for anything out with their control and may quickly enter into fight, flight or freeze mode when triggered. They become dysregulated suddenly for reasons which are often hard to identify. Examples may include the classroom door opening, a particular smell or sound or a misinterpretation of the teacher's words or actions. They may appear excessively controlling as they desperately try to create an environment in which they can begin to feel safe. They may also be functioning at a lower social and emotional age and as such have not developed a full ability to self-regulate their behaviour and reactions (Treisman, 2017). If we ask what their actions may be communicating, we begin to see the often-terrified child behind hyperactivity and erratic behaviour. We may move away from viewing them as compliant or non-compliant and towards an understanding that this is a question of *can't* rather than *won't*. Immediately, then, we respond differently and begin to make changes which have real impact.

The Teacher-Pupil Relationship

Let us continue to examine pupil behaviour through an attachment lens as we explore the teacher-pupil relationship. It is appropriate here to recognize the potential power of this relationship. Research has shown that security of attachment for a child can change over time and that teachers may become protective figures (Kennedy, 2008; Bergin and Bergin, 2009). Indeed, increased attachment-awareness, for example, in the Attachment Aware Schools projects in England, has been reported to foster a more supportive, inclusive ethos within which young people's well-being and engagement are enhanced (Trivedi and Harrison, 2022). Schools have made systemic changes in order to take a more holistic, relational approach to children's education and early conclusions suggest that the pupils are *happier* and feel a sense of *belonging* to their schools (Kelly et al., 2020: 351). As Cozolino (2013: 93) suggests 'the brain is quite resilient and capable of reversing the effects of early negative experiences through positive ones'. He continues to highlight the pivotal role of teachers here. As they develop trust and demonstrate their care through listening, they become the child's secure base (Cozolino, 2013). An emotional environment which is safe and conducive to learning is created and growth becomes possible. New mental representations of relationships can occur within the minds of our young people as teachers and other education staff build positive relationships with them (García-Rodríguez et al., 2023). If deficit narratives around behaviour are replaced with this focus on the potential for change and healing, we begin to find compassionate, creative solutions for our schools and young people.

There is considerable recognition of the importance of relational approaches in Scotland as they are enshrined in education policy guidance. For example, the recent *Improving relationships and behaviour in schools* action plan (Scottish Government, 2024c) fully supports a preventative agenda in which relational approaches are prioritized. These are expected to be characterized by 'high warmth and support, high standards and high expectations of socially responsible behaviour' (Scottish Government, 2024c: 3). The General Teaching Council for Scotland's (GTCS) *Standard for Full Registration* as a teacher in Scotland stipulates that professional values should include '[b]uilding and fostering positive relationships in the learning community which are respectful of individuals' (GTCS, 2021a: 4). Added to this is *The Promise*, which states that '[a]ll of the workforce should access, at a level appropriate to their role, initial and lifelong learning that is grounded in attachment theory, trauma responsive care and the clear understanding and application of children's rights' (Independent Care Review, 2020: 108). Its ambitious vision for Scotland reflects a prominent position for attachment-aware approaches: '[s]ecure attachments, based on loving, consistent relationships, must be the bedrock of every decision made about children' (Independent Care Review, 2020: 72).

Accepting the validity and appropriateness of all of the above does not mean that it is always easy to put into practice amidst the tensions and stresses of everyday classroom life. Indeed, only with considerable reflection on our own practice can we fully understand our reactions to some of the behaviour of the children in our care. The work of Philip Riley is interesting in this regard as he has explored the teacher-pupil relationship from an attachment point of view. He asks us to more deeply examine the dynamics of relationships and comments that the need to gain affection from others is often a powerful albeit unconscious motivation in teachers choosing to be teachers (Riley, 2013). Therefore, the relationship between pupil and teacher is dyadic as opposed to unidirectional (Riley, 2009). This also makes the teacher vulnerable to rejection by the pupil (Riley, 2010). With this in mind, we may interpret a teacher's angry reaction to pupil misbehaviour and perceived distance in their relationship as 'an unconscious process aimed at restoring the connection by "protesting", sometimes aggressively, to the person perceived to have caused the increase in separation anxiety' (Riley, 2013: 116). Hence, knowledge and understanding of emotions and how attachment histories affect the display of these is crucial for teachers and other education professionals as they manage their daily interactions with children. As Riley suggests, this increased understanding may allow them to respond rather than react to challenging situations (Riley, 2013: 115).

Other researchers have examined the degree to which teachers or other education professionals can be *attachment figures* for children (Rose et al., 2019; García-Rodríguez et al., 2023). Clearly, teachers and others who work closely with children can offer the possibility of a secure base as well as a safe haven even where these concepts are not already established for the child. Their responsiveness and sensitivity to pupils' needs and emotional well-being is clearly paramount. Indeed, the relational, caring dimension of the role of the teacher is increasingly recognized. However, a teacher will never share the same level of intimacy as a parent; nor is it likely that the relationship will match the duration of a child's relationship with their primary caregiver. The role of the teacher could be said to be that of a secondary attachment figure (García-Rodríguez et al., 2023) or an 'ad hoc attachment figure' (Verschueren and Koomen, 2012: 206). Following detailed training and reflection on attachment theory as part of their course, one set of Initial Teacher Education students reported that they had gained enhanced insight into pupils' behaviour as well as an appreciation for their evolving role as nurturing figures whose role stretched beyond delivery of curriculum content (Kearns and Hart, 2017). They mentioned the *hidden curriculum*, an increased focus on the *pastoral side* of education and the significance of being a caring and trusted adult in order for learning to take place (Kearns and Hart, 2017: 520). Regardless of the terminology used, 'there is now a well-studied theoretical framework of teachers as "psychological parents" and of the key importance of the teacher-child relationship as a secure base and safe haven in children's school lives' (Verschueren and Koomen, 2012: 15).

Thinking Point 4.3

What do you think is meant by 'high structure, high nurture'?

Attachment in Action

As Howard (2022) suggests, safety, relationships and emotional regulation need to be prioritized both at systemic whole school level as well as at individual classroom level if we are to see attachment in action across education. Safety implies establishing clear boundaries for pupils but applying these without shame. Restorative approaches within a compassionate ethos in which mistakes are embraced as learning opportunities allow for safety to be established. The curriculum as well as daily classroom life must leave space for establishing and reinforcing relationships. Those working with children should learn the art of attunement: 'how we can tune into, read and then respond to someone else's state and needs at any given time' (Bombèr, 2020: 130). They should develop unconditional positive regard for all pupils (Rogers, 1967). Mentoring programmes may also help in this respect. Emotional regulation must be facilitated with access to safe spaces, calming corners, composed staff and activities which aid this. Yoga sessions, mindfulness and time outdoors are all examples of this. Naming and sharing emotions can build pupils' self-awareness and establish an environment where difficulties are shared and pupils' issues addressed without reproach. Alongside this, staff must be supported as they carry the weight of this emotional labour on a daily basis.

Summary

Cozolino (2013: 107) suggests 'the social agenda of the classroom must always be of equal importance to curricular content'. Understanding attachment theory and applying policies and practices which shine a light on the dynamics of relationships offer positive ways of addressing the distressed behaviour of our children and young people. In so doing, we are *loving* them towards a brighter future socially, emotionally and academically.

5

In Conversation with …

Part 1 Matthew Cooke, Former Chair of the National Association of Virtual School Heads (NAVSH)

Christine: Why did you agree to be part of this project?

Matthew: I'm a very passionate Virtual School Head Teacher (VSHT) and have been a VSHT since 2016. I was twenty-one when I started teaching, and I was not a disciplinarian. I had to raise my voice, and I was tested by a class, and I remember seeing certain senior teachers gain control through what was almost a ritual humiliation, in a way that really denigrated. I felt quite uncomfortable about this sort of power dynamic and how fear was used to create that culture and control. You learn from who you see, but it wasn't working for me. I just preferred life as a teacher who worked on relationships.

I look back on it now and, understanding trauma-informed practice and attachment, I realize that there are a lot of things that I accidentally stumbled upon. I didn't know the theory, but I had this practice that was really working. I realized just how powerful forming relationships is. I think, in schools, where obviously rules and structure are really important, delivered by someone who appears not to care, do not work. It has to be done in that landscape of care, by someone who wants children to do their best. Thinking about what I've learnt as a VSHT, I wish to apply some of that to give teachers a more enjoyable experience. When you're working with a very behaviourist approach and you are dealing with really strong sanctions and a very punitive way of working, it may work for 80 per cent to 85 per cent of the pupils but for the pupils I represent it does not work at all. They just end up falling out of the system and needing something alternative. And I know that this is avoidable. I know how you need certain structures in place. I just think there's a need to turn the tables on those structures; unless they are founded on relational-based practice, they don't work well. They work through fear, and on those that will be compliant. They don't create something I'm really passionate about, which is a sense of *fighting for the badge*. I think when you can get pupils really wanting the organization that they're a part of to do well, you've really cracked it. At school leadership level, I think there's something to be said for engendering that *fighting for the badge* culture, and it only comes through a relational-based approach.

Christine: Is there a misunderstanding that trauma-informed approaches have no boundaries?

Matthew: Yes, there is. There is a sort of a sense of it being diluted down to some very simple concepts. Certain teachers feel constrained by the fact they cannot shout. I also think that schools are fast-paced places. They're places where you have not got a moment to think, and you grab on to anything that works. You are less precious about the theory behind things. That's at leadership level and classroom practice level.

Christine: In Initial Teacher Education in Scotland, we try to get our students to look at themselves to counter the, 'so let's grab on to what works' approach.

Matthew: Absolutely. Yes. I think we're more psychologically informed. I think there's definitely a growing understanding that means we're applying better techniques as a result of knowing about brain science and neurodevelopment. I also think there is a sort of a challenge in that area as well, because a little bit of knowledge can be dangerous in the wrong hands. People can get quite focused on a diagnosis or practising in quite a simplistic way which is almost always going to have co-occurring issues, particularly when you're looking at children in the most challenging of circumstances. When a young person has had a really tough childhood and hasn't had their needs met early, sometimes that happens to someone who's neuro-divergent, sometimes they've got foetal alcohol spectrum disorder, and it kind of just morphs into some really different challenges and different requirements for intervention. It's one of those things where you can't know enough, you've got to constantly have that inquiring mind. I'm a big fan of just keeping that curiosity and of keeping things simple. Rather than asking, 'What are you doing?' it's asking, 'What happened to you?'

Christine: How would you define the term 'trauma informed'?

Matthew: I think it's a challenging term at the moment because it's become a bit ubiquitous. Obviously, it's predicated on the brain science around early childhood trauma having a physiological effect and manifesting in different ways, depending on all sorts of variables. The reason I struggle with it is because trauma is a really kind of quick and easy word to say. But it's about abuses, about neglect. It's about sexual abuse. It's about some really nasty kinds of aspects of someone's lived experience that we are just sort of tripping off our tongues. No one comes into care lightly now. The thresholds are really high, and they've had really damaging experiences. Trauma-informed practice as a term distances us from the emotional aspect of what we're dealing with. I'm moving much more towards talking about relational-based practice than trauma informed. If you talk about relational-based practice, everyone benefits from having good relationships. Relationships are really healing for those who need them.

Christine: Are we all talking about the same thing?

Matthew: You do need a common language. But I think a common language also creates a sort of an echo chamber, where I'm in the 'attachment and trauma informed' camp and someone else is in the 'real-world' camp where they're dealing with quite challenging situations. Language is really important, but it can also become a bit alienating. There's a danger that attachment and trauma-informed practice fall into that camp, which is why I'm quite interested in a new drive towards a sense of belonging. In the same way that we've seen behaviour policies moving towards being relationship policies, I'm hearing of attendance policies moving towards being belonging policies. Obviously, these things are dynamic, and when they become ubiquitous, they become less palatable. But what you're really trying to achieve is a sense of belonging, which will then increase attendance and engagement in a positive way, not through punitive measures. I don't think you can ever punish people into being better behaved, and I'm not seeing it work. In the same way, you can't punish people into school. You have to create that sense of belonging.

Christine: I suppose rewards don't work for the very same reason that sanctions don't work?

Matthew: There is something around needing to understand the psychology of children. The best thing you can do is create a space where learning is the reward. That happens when there are strong relationships in the class, when there's a strong sense of belonging, of self-esteem. I don't think we're there, but I am starting to see some practice that's encouraging in this area. When I was teaching, I'd put in groundwork and build relationships with the kids, who felt quite alienated in other parts of the school, and when they came to me, they felt like they belonged and a lot of it was about what I didn't do to sever that relationship as much as what I did do. Think of how much damage you do to the relationship between a school and a family when you write a letter to them saying we're going to go to court because of your child's attendance.

Christine: You're a VSHT. How significant is that role in this system?

Matthew: It's a wonderful position to be in. We're the bridge between social care and education. I'm lucky to have a very strong team who support me in that work. But that said, there are still some huge challenges. I've got 950 children, and I've got a team of less than fifteen full-time members of staff. That means trying to create the landscape that will support our children best. We work on a model of school improvement rather than being a pseudo service ourselves, and not just school improvement but also system improvement. The VSHT role is a very powerful position. There are things that I'm able to insist upon around school placements and school moves, keeping children in the same school, where it's possible. Our children are not homogeneous; they require every service that any child would possibly need. Trauma-informed practice is one of those key concepts, where if you can get relational practice right, you can lessen the demand in other areas because you will see fewer exclusions. You will see a greater engagement. The actual fact of the matter is that the vast majority don't really put their head above the parapet. They attend school very regularly. But they do underachieve in that context. And so, it's about looking at ways of raising the ambition for our children because education is going to be important. We know that if they're not in education, employment and training beyond sixteen, they've got significantly reduced life expectancy. We're not just talking about earnings; we're talking about the chance of making it to your thirtieth birthday.

Christine: What's the most successful intervention or initiative that you've implemented as a VSHT?

Matthew: There's a lot that we do. There isn't a singular silver bullet for this. We've got funding to support initiatives, and we've got a very wide variety of needs within our children. Some of our children arrive as separated minors from other countries who have very little English language. Obviously, their need is to learn the language, but also, it's to recover from the trauma of a horrendous journey where they would have witnessed some awful things. That's very different from our indigenous population who have a very different set of needs. You can't do it on your own. It's about supporting the teams. That's a really important principle of Virtual School Headship because what you really want is to strengthen their world so that it's good enough on its own. The best work that the Virtual School does is invisible to the child.

Christine: To what extent do you think national policy in England facilitates a trauma-informed approach?

Matthew: On the one side you do get a lot of support. For example, with this idea of 'belonging' – it's an evidence-based approach – the sense of belonging, works. That's what we need to be championing and quite a lot of the DfE (Department for Education, England) are in support of that. The policies that have come in have been driven quite hard with the fact that Virtual School Headship is statutory, the fact that's been extended again for children with a social worker, the fact that during Covid-19 children with a social worker became a new group who were understood to be vulnerable and required continued school attendance. So, there's a lot of policy that moves in the right direction. But you've also got a sense of policy needing to be tough on behaviour, almost like in the adult sense of being 'tough on crime'. That sometimes flies in the face of a strong sense of belonging as we also need to fine, and the fines grab media attention. I think recently, in England, the fines went up. What actually happened was legislation meant you cannot fine until you've completed a number of supportive steps beforehand. So, actually, the headline should have been, 'We're thinking much more about support before punitive measures and challenge'. You can't fine unless there's the evidence that support has been trialled first. That was a big policy change because, before that, you could just fine straight away.

Christine: I'm concerned that this perceived need to 'clamp down' gathers a head of steam really quickly.

Matthew: Yes, there is that rhetoric of 'othering' and 'distancing', and 'bringing the drawbridge up' so that 'anti-social behaviour' can't get in. And you've got a protected community. That's actually very understandable when you are leading a school, and you've got people being hurt as a result of the behaviour, so you've got a very challenging balancing act to make between knowing that those young people who are causing the challenges and maybe doing the hurting, they've got challenging circumstances, but you cannot allow them to cause harm and create the difficulties that they're creating. So, they do need a solution. I think what you are faced with is challenge when there's under-resourcing because if you haven't got the bodies in school, those things are going to spill out more. As a VSHT, I've seen a real reduction in the availability of peripatetic staff. The alternative model – like a pupil referral unit or bespoke programme – is a total postcode lottery as to whether or not you can get a young person into that. If they're not care experienced it really comes down to how challenging the parents are, which feels again a bit like a postcode lottery, and one that advantages anyone who's prepared to challenge and fight for their young person's needs. That creates a real unfairness because if you haven't got parents able to do this, the pupil will get what they get.

That is part of the Virtual School remit, to be the pushy parent for those that don't have pushy parents. Actually the best thing we can do is create a support mechanism that means that less children come into care. Numbers are increasing. Although it might feel good from a school perspective. When someone goes into care, there's often some really quick wins. Suddenly uniform's better, attendance's better, engagement's better; they feel comforted because they are being looked after. But the longer-term outcomes of particularly stranger care, coming into care with people you don't know, do not have a good long-term prognosis.

Christine: What's your vision for the future?

Matthew: I wish VSHTs didn't have to exist. The vision is improvement all the time. We want more of our young people to be successful socially and economically. The vision is to get as good as we are for our care-experienced children, to get as good for our children that we are now newly responsible for. We know that children who have a needs plan or children on a protection plan, their persistent absence in England is really high. It's over 50 per cent in some places. It's starting to go down, but it's at a really high level, much, much higher than any other group. And they are the children who are not safe at home. Social care has judged that they're not safe at home, and yet they're at home more than any other child.

The focus is on children having the protective factor of school engagement and of school achievement. Both are important. We understand how protective being at school is, but we need to move on to look at the achievement at school. Getting ourselves into a position where we've made as big a difference for children on the edge of care as we are for care-experienced children is the vision and ensuring that it is continuous.

Part 2: Larissa Gordon, Virtual School Headteacher (VSHT), Aberdeen City

Christine: Why did you agree to be part of this project?

Larissa: For me, first and foremost I care about people; I care about our children and young people and also those around them. I've also got a real interest in understanding the impact of trauma on brain development, and how the impact of that then presents in some of the behaviours that we see. It's about being able to support people to better understand brain development. While it's not necessary to have an extensive knowledge of brain development, I think it really does help to have some information to help see that it's not about our children choosing to behave in certain ways; it is about how their brain has developed throughout their childhood. I'm also passionate about ensuring that, collectively, we can create those environments that we talk about, where all of our children are thriving.

Christine: Tell me about your current role.

Larissa: I have been in post now since December 2015 and I'm the VSHT in Aberdeen City. I have an overview of all of our children who are care experienced. So that includes those who are living within Aberdeen City and those living and educated within other local authorities. I am working with children, families and wider partners including schools, social work, health and the third sector. The high number of different partners who can be involved with one child or family possibly demonstrates the complexities of need for some of our children and young people, and the necessity for the team around them to work collectively to get it right.

Christine: In your role, what do you understand by the term trauma informed?

Larissa: When I came into post that term maybe wasn't as widely recognized or used as it is now. While it is encouraging that there is an increased awareness, I believe there's a real risk it of it being overused or misunderstood. At times it feels as though its meaning is being lost in translation. For me, at the most basic level, it's about caring. It's being passionate and kind: really thinking about our actions, our words and the impact of them. It's more about how do we demonstrate being trauma informed? Taking a considered approach is really important, and I think that's innate for some. However, we can all learn and improve our understanding of the impact of trauma and, from there, how we present ourselves. Sometimes we say trauma sensitive rather than trauma informed. This just feels a bit easier for people to understand and relate to. It can be more helpful to think about the sensitivity needed around a child who has experienced trauma and why we are then seeing the distressed behaviours. I guess my concern with the term 'trauma informed' is that it can sometimes lead to box ticking, rather than real understanding or change. Sometimes practitioners come away from a single training session thinking; we are now trauma informed. The risk is though that it doesn't truly get embedded in practice and we don't actually see it reflected in day-to-day behaviours. The term 'trauma informed' isn't always fully understood. Once that kind of language starts being used, you'll hear people across services saying they're trauma informed, but then you have to ask, is that what we actually see in practice?

Christine: How would you describe a trauma-informed school?

Larissa: If I'm walking into a school that describes itself as being trauma informed, I'd expect to feel it right from the moment I come into the school grounds. It would come through in the positive interactions I witness, the warmth in conversations taking place and overall connection that is present. The conversations are really important. What do I see? What do I hear? Is it kind? Is it compassionate? If something has happened, am I hearing curiosity around that? I'm very much an advocate of PACE (Play, Acceptance, Curiosity, Empathy) (Golding and Hughes, 2012). As I come into the school (building), again I'm looking at how people interact. It doesn't matter who you are within the school. If you're in a staff room, how are children spoken about? What does that look like? What are we seeing within the physical environment? And is it calm? Looking at what's on the walls. What's being celebrated? The way you experience the walk through a school is really important; the interactions you see and feel are key. The ethos and culture of the school come through.

For children and young people, it would be about what they experience and how they experience it. Thinking about the physical environment, they may describe that as calm, something that's not going to be overwhelming for them. Physical spaces are important for our children and young people; however, providing calm spaces, especially within large mainstream schools, can be a real challenge. Thinking about relationships, they would describe what all staff are like with them – not just the teachers – and how they treat them, if they are accepting of them. They would talk about who is important to them or celebrates with them. Children know when someone is being genuine. They know if you are someone who is welcoming, and someone who takes time to find out about them in that curious way we mentioned. It's about being able to rebuild relationships or repair them if necessary and know that, actually, that's okay, because we're not always going to get it right, but taking time to rebuild when something has happened. Someone who doesn't give up on them, no matter what happens, that person is still there. We talk about 'stickability' because no matter what happens, a child needs to know that you are not going away and they are not their behaviours.

Christine: To what extent have you been involved in activities which you would consider to be trauma informed?

Larissa: We have taken a whole-family approach. This has been helpful in terms of how we support practitioners, families and how we think about a more relational approach through multi-agency working. This is then about more than just – the involvement of – education. It is about a team around that child and family. We also know from research and experience that trauma can be intergenerational, and that has a real impact on what we see in children. Unless we are working with the whole family, we're missing a key part of the picture and can't fully support healing and change for that child who is in our classroom. For me, being part of a multi-agency team and working together is vital.

Another activity is very much the work that I've been involved in with Scottish Attachment in Action (SAIA) (https://scottishattachmentinaction.org/), the extensive piece of research in 2022 (Scottish Attachment in Action, 2022). This was significant, because that gave us a clearer sense of what was happening across the country and where people were at in their thinking and practice. From that, we were able to form an understanding of the differences and what was needed. It gave us that sense of what it's like for new teachers coming out of Initial Teacher Education. If we consider what we are seeing in our classrooms now in relation to presenting behaviours compared to eight or ten years ago, there is a real contrast. More emphasis is put on understanding attachment now; however, this varies across courses and institutes in terms of time and content dedicated to it.

There is another activity that I am involved in, which I believe is important and that is the Virtual School Head Teachers Network. As a network, we consider what we can do more widely to support practitioners to understand trauma and specifically the needs of care-experienced children and young people. In partnership with myself as VSHT in Aberdeen City, the Centre for Excellence for Children's Care and Protection (CELCIS) convened a meeting with all local authority areas involved in developing the role of the VSHT back in 2019. Subsequently, the national network was established and is hosted and facilitated by CELCIS. That's been a network that's been and continues to be really important. We are closely linked as well with the National Association of Virtual School Heads in England as we have children who are being educated in both Scotland and England, across different local authorities. It is important for me, as a VSHT, to know that wherever my children are – and I talk about 'my' children in terms of me being their corporate parent – as it's important that I can be confident about what their educational experience is like and that it would be good enough for my child.

Christine: Do you think the VSH Network is working in Scotland?

Larissa: We've seen a real shift and we're sitting with around twenty VSHTs or someone in an equivalent role who are part of the network. The role has grown organically in Scotland, and there's been significant impact to date. This can be seen through case studies, research and practice papers published on the VSHT Network webpage (https://www.celcis.org/our-work/key-areas/education/virtual-school-head-teachers). We are fortunate to have the support of Scottish government and Education Scotland as part of the network. So in terms of that influence driving forward, for example, The Promise (Independent Care Review (ICR), 2020) within Scotland, there is really a strong impetus to support what happens within local authorities and beyond. It has also supported me in my role and how I approach what I do.

Christine: Do you think training on trauma-informed approaches has an impact on staff well-being?

Larissa: Absolutely. It is important to have support for staff in education and I am a great advocate of supervision. Other professions who are working with children and families who have experienced trauma receive supervision including social workers and our educational psychologists. We are seeing the impact of trauma on our children through their presenting behaviours in schools. It is important to be able to support staff to be able to continue supporting the children while maintaining their own well-being. So I suppose it's twofold. A better knowledge and understanding of trauma and attachment that sits alongside professional supervision.

Christine: To what extent do you think national policy facilitates this?

Larissa: We are fortunate in Scotland to have an enabling framework and vision, that is, The Promise (ICR, 2020), which drives policy development. We also have the commitment of Scottish Government to our VSHT Network supporting the direction of travel to become a trauma-informed nation. My belief is that we do have national policy that facilitates, and through the work with NAVSH we are able to work alongside our colleagues in England, learning from each other. We're on a journey and there are various factors to be considered but having that commitment from our leaders is vital. It is about how we take that and move from policy into practice.

Christine: Currently what are the barriers?

Larissa: It's not easy in schools. I'm fortunate enough to work with lots of practitioners across the country and, they are, really passionate caring practitioners, but it's tough. They want to be getting it right but there are challenges in relation to resources and time. We know that for our children, relationships are key. So, if we're not retaining staff or staff are moving, that again has a further impact in terms of breaking relationships. Our senior leaders work hard to foster a positive relationship-focused ethos within schools but building that kind of culture takes time. Resources are also limited, so it's about using what we have in the most effective way to create the greatest impact. For our children who are care experienced, it's about more than just considering what happens within the school. We know that there are times when they need to move home and be cared for elsewhere. This means a change of school and so connections and relationships are broken. When we have Virtual Schools across Scotland and England, we (VSHTs) are able to reach out to colleagues, and we know that they're working to try and deliver the best educational experience for our children and deliver on The Promise (ICR, 2020) (in Scotland), which means I can be confident that what I would want for our children is going to be sought with the same passion.

I think society can also present a barrier; the understanding of the wider general public, and I count myself within the general public, but again looking at that and understanding the impact of trauma. I believe that since Covid-19, people have a better understanding and some of the conversations I have, or I hear, look different now than maybe they did pre-Covid-19, because more people's lives have been impacted by trauma.

Christine: Have we still got a lot to see in terms of mental health issues like anxiety?

Larissa: I suppose this is where, for me, it's about trying to support that understanding that this is not just about care-experienced children within your classroom, because if we can take a trauma-informed relational approach, no child will be adversely impacted by this approach but many will benefit. There will always be children who absolutely have that stable environment. They come to school, they will thrive, and they will do well. And then you'll have, maybe a group of children who need a little bit of support shown through a nurturing, relational approach to help them to really achieve and succeed. Then you'll have children who will need far more in terms of intense support where we need to be making sure we get that right. We need to be thinking about our actions and taking a considered approach. If we do that for those children, nobody's going to suffer but many will benefit greatly. If we don't do that, then those children who need it most will not thrive.

Christine: So what's your vision for the future?

Larissa: Going forward it is about the consistency of experience for all children, no matter where they're educated. I don't mean just across Scotland but right across the UK. I value our partners and working closely with colleagues. What is needed is the recognition that it takes time for a child to feel safe and ready to learn and the length of time can vary between children depending on the impact of their lived experiences. We need to recognize and support those who really are striving to do this for our children. We should also look at how progress is measured and the value that's placed on the story of a child's journey. The worry is that people may revert to a more behaviourist approach which seeks to address behaviours that challenge the adults in a certain manner. Language used to describe those behaviours is also important. The way that the behaviour is described can shape the way the child or young person sees themselves and the way in which others interact with them. So, we need to get that across, and the understanding that when you're taking a relational approach, it's not about ignoring behaviour it's about understanding the underlying needs, emotions and experiences driving that behaviour and responding in a way that supports connection with the child to build trust. If somebody is working relationally, it's about accepting the person, not focusing on the presenting behaviours. So, coming back to a shift of language, people talk about behaviour management, but we should shift to behaviour support. I'm an advocate of reframing as well; we work closely with Each and Every child (https://eachandeverychild.co.uk/), and if we can reframe the language, then we can move some way towards changing how people think and approach things.

Section II

Understanding the Impact of Trauma

6

Understanding the Brain

Christine McKee

Key Ideas

This chapter will:

- outline the structure of the brain,
- examine how the brain develops,
- examine how learning occurs, and
- introduce polyvagal theory.

Introduction

If there is one concept which permeates much of the content of this forthcoming chapter, it is safety: physical and emotional safety, felt safety and perceptions of safety. This may come as a surprise in a chapter about the brain but, as we will see, it's a concept which underpins much of what we need to think about as education professionals in the twenty-first century. As Van der Kolk (2014: 63) states '[t]he most important job of the brain is to ensure our survival, even under the most miserable conditions. Everything else is secondary'. Here we will discuss how the latest knowledge about the architecture and development of the brain, as well as current theories around its functioning, arm those who work with children with invaluable knowledge and understanding which may indeed alter their practice in substantial ways.

The Architecture of the Brain

The complexity of the brain should never be underestimated but for the purposes of this publication, we will attempt to summarize key aspects and extrapolate those which are useful for those working in education. One useful model of the brain is the one espoused by Bruce Perry: the neurosequential model, originally known as the *Neurosequential Model of Therapeutics* designed for use in therapeutic settings (Perry, 2009; Perry and Winfrey, 2021). Perry suggests that the brain consists of four layers, each with different functions and roles and each with an ability to modify behaviour through different mechanisms (Brummer and Thorsborne, 2024: 59). And each, as we will see, tasked with keeping us safe from perceived threat.

The brain develops from the bottom-up (Perry, 2009: 242; Van der Kolk, 2014: 69), with the most basic layer being the brain stem. Fully developed at birth, this area connects the brain to the rest of the body via the spinal cord. Often called the automated or the reptilian brain (Curran, 2008; Van der Kolk, 2014), it is the oldest in evolutionary terms and is responsible for basic life functions like heart rate, blood pressure, breathing and swallowing. This part of the brain, along with the limbic system, dominates at birth as '[i]t's entire life aim was (and is) to preserve its own existence' (Curran, 2008: 7). It is hence also the home for our fight, flight, freeze responses, the instinctive reactions we have when faced with a threat to our survival. For example, without thinking as such, we jump out of the way of a fast-approaching car. This part of the brain could be considered to be *always on guard* (Brummer and Thorsborne, 2024: 61), its primary duty to mobilize us for survival. This compulsive (Brummer and Thorsborne, 2024: 61) and essentially protective aspect of this part of the brain is an important one to remember as we consider children and young people's behaviour in educational settings.

The next layer to develop is the diencephalon, which is situated just above the brain stem. Its role is to maintain internal balance in the body so it regulates motor skills, healing, arousal, appetite and sleep patterns as well as 'the body's ability to negotiate its environment' (Howard, 2022: 49). The hypothalamus is housed here and this releases hormones in order to maintain homeostasis. One example is cortisol, which is released in response to physical or emotional stress (Conkbayir, 2023: 118). As mentioned in Chapter 2, sustained elevated levels of cortisol can have significant consequences for the child's developing brain (Satchwell-Hirst, 2017: 51). We will further explore the brain's threat response system below.

The next part of the brain to develop is the limbic system, also known as the emotional brain (Conkbayir, 2023) or mammalian brain (Van der Kolk, 2014). This is in the centre of the brain and is where emotions like anger, anxiety, aggression, sadness, joy and envy are activated. Within the limbic system we find the amygdala and the hippocampus: the former is the 'brain's panic button' (Conkbayir, 2023: 118) or 'watchdog' (Siegel and Payne Bryson, 2012: 42) and it serves to activate the body's stress response system when it perceives impending danger and threat. The latter helps with memory storage and retention, working with the amygdala to process the degree of threat. As Howard (2022: 50) states, emotions are regulated here 'through complex interactions of perception, experience, memory, and body chemistry'. There is rapid development of this area between birth and the age of three years old so early life experiences and associations are crucial in shaping what is perceived as threat to that individual. For some, this may be as simple as the classroom door opening. Of note here is that this part of the brain is still relatively automatic. It acts in a 'mindless and reflexive' way (Curran, 2008: 139) as it was designed to allow us to react quickly to survive in moments of physical danger. In evolutionary terms this was clearly very useful. It is less useful if our reactive brain means we disproportionately react to a situation that is not in fact life threatening. For example, the classroom door opens and the child screams and runs round the class; fight and/or flight is activated. The *visceral sensations* that we experience if the limbic system detects danger or senses opportunity mean that 'the emotional brain initiates preprogrammed escape plans' (Van der Kolk, 2014: 66) before we can actually think and reflect on the consequences of our actions. Knowledge and understanding of this for those working with children is crucial if we are to fully comprehend both their behaviours and how we might help them regulate.

The rational capacities which we need in order to regulate our threat response and behaviour are situated in the final part of the brain to develop: the neocortex or the thinking brain (Satchwell-Hirst, 2017: 51). This is the outer layer of the brain and is thought to not be fully developed until we are in our mid to late twenties (Satchwell-Hirst, 2017: 51). It is this part of the brain which is responsible for more complex thought, for reason, logic and creativity as well as planning for the future and organization. Our executive functions are situated here. Our ability to use language to communicate resides here too, illustrating the higher level of development of this part of the brain in humans (Howard, 2022). When we are working with young children and adolescents, it is important to reflect on the age at which their prefrontal cortex is more engaged than their limbic system as this will vary between children, with those who have experienced trauma perhaps having delayed development of this upper part of their brain (Tobin, 2016: 10; Satchwell-Hirst, 2017: 51). As Nicholson et al. remind us, young children are less able to regulate their emotions and reactions because the 'neural connections that communicate information from the cortex to the limbic system are not fully developed' (Nicholson et al., 2023: 22).

The Left and Right Hemispheres

Another structural aspect worthy of consideration is lateralization, or the different functions of the left and right sides of the brain. While it is an over-simplification to consider ourselves *left-brained* or *right-brained* as the brain is a highly integrated system in which both hemispheres work 'in parallel' (OECD, 2007: 72), it is the case that each side specializes in different functions (Curran, 2008). The left side is considered 'logical, literal, linguistic …., and linear' (Siegel and Payne Bryson, 2012: 15), while the right side is described as 'emotional, nonverbal, experiential, and autobiographical' (Siegel and Payne Bryson, 2012: 16). Van der Kolk (2014) helps us understand this as he explains that the left brain 'remembers facts, statistics, and the vocabulary of events'; it allows us to talk about our experiences. The right brain 'stores memories of sound, touch, smell, and the emotions they evoke'; it reacts almost intuitively to gestures and voices (Van der Kolk, 2014: 53). The hemispheres are joined and communicate through the corpus callosum, connective fibres which link the two sides and, as Cozolino (2013: 27) describes, 'most brain functions are optimized by the interactive participation of both sides'.

When considering the potential effects of trauma, further comment about the right hemisphere in particular is relevant for education professionals. The right side of the brain develops first and dominates between the ages of the predominantly pre-verbal zero to three years old (Schore, 2000; Siegel and Payne Bryson, 2012: 16). It is in the right hemisphere that unconscious processes reside as it 'computes, on a moment-to-moment basis, the affective salience of external stimuli' (Schore, 2000: 31). In other words, it is this part of our brain which interprets gestures, body language and facial expressions before our more analytical left hemisphere develops. If we cast our minds back to the central tenets of attachment theory, we remember that those early interactions between primary caregiver and infant – in that pre-verbal stage – are crucial in establishing the early internal working models which determine our expectations of others as we move through life (Bowlby, 1973; 1980) (see also Chapter 4). Our reactions and regulation depend on those expectations. As such, neuroscience appears to reinforce Bowlby's theory (Schore, 2022). If there is repeated early adversity in a child's life, it is likely to disrupt the development of the right hemisphere hence potential future difficulties with emotional regulation (Nicholson et al., 2023: 41). As Schore (2022: 5) confirms 'the mother-infant attachment relationship impacts the developing right brain for better or worse. It can either facilitate a healthy resilience to stress or create a vulnerability to characterological affect dysregulation and deficits in social relationships'.

Therefore, an explanation for that lack of regulation, or apparent over-reaction, that we may see in our pupils may lie in an understanding of neurobiology. Dan Siegel and Tina Payne Bryson's seminal work *The Whole-Brain Child* asks us to focus on how we may foster the horizontal integration of children's brains (Siegel and Payne Bryson, 2012: 18). There is a need to balance the emotion of the right hemisphere with the cognition of the left. We may encourage awareness of feelings but also ask pupils to rationalize and regulate their feelings by processing them cognitively (Cozolino, 2013: 224). As such, we are hoping that they are 'well balanced and able to understand themselves and the world at large' (Siegel and Payne Bryson, 2012: 18), and that they 'avoid living in an emotional flood or an emotional desert' (Siegel and Payne Bryson, 2012: 18). There are many educational packages used across schools to develop pupils' emotional literacy which are founded on this knowledge. Siegel and Payne Bryson offer a number of strategies including:

a. connect and redirect – validating the child's emotions before explaining logically what can/needs to happen next,
b. name it to tame it – essentially helping the child to re-process and make sense of an experience by naming the potentially frightening emotions and sensations, and
c. teaching children about their brains so that they can begin to identify which *part* of their brain is dominating their thoughts and actions (Siegel and Payne Bryson, 2012: 22–33).

Thinking Point 6.1

What other strategies have you used/can you think of which help left-brain/right-brain integration?

The Upstairs and Downstairs Brain

Some of this echoes another form of integration which is required for healthy and regulated living, that between the upper and lower areas of the brain, sometimes known as the *upstairs* and *downstairs brains* (Siegel and Payne Bryson, 2012). The brain stem, diencephalon and limbic system are considered the *downstairs brain*, while the cortex is the *upstairs brain*. As mentioned previously, the brain develops from the bottom-up and the foundations (*downstairs*) need to be solid if the healthy development of the *upstairs* is to progress at a normal rate. If trauma impacts a baby's brainstem, for example, there may be delays with language development, social-emotional difficulties or cognitive impairments (Nicholson et al., 2023: 18). That said, as we will discuss below, the neuroplasticity of the brain means that repair and progress are possible if the relational environment around the child improves. For our purposes, as education professionals, we need to consider to what extent we rely on 'top-down approaches for bottom-up problems' (Delahooke, 2020: 14). To what extent do we expect too much of children whose brains simply *can't*, not *won't*, process what we are asking them to do? As Perry suggests, looking at children's behaviour through a neurodevelopmental lens allows us to address their needs appropriately; 'the idea is to start with the lowest (in the brain) undeveloped/abnormally functioning set of problems and move sequentially up the brain as improvements are seen' (Perry, 2009: 252). That all important concept of safety returns, as we recognize the need to calm a dysregulated brain before it will be able to hear any of our reasoning, including of course our threats of punishment or promises of rewards.

How Learning Happens

Let us now consider the brain in even finer detail, where learning begins. Let us consider neurons. Neurons are the brain's *building blocks* (Conkbayir, 2023: 102) and we have approximately eighty-six billion of them at birth (Nicholson et al., 2023: 17). More significant, though, is the connection between neurons. The synapse is the small gap between neurons and it is across this that neurons must connect with each other if they are to survive (Cozolino, 2013: 25). There are approximately 2,500 synapses at birth and 15,000 by the age of three (Nicholson et al., 2023: 17), a growth which highlights the enhanced significance of the early years. Neurons connect by transmitting information to another neuron along their axon – a bit like a tail coming out of the cell body of the neuron – via chemicals called *neurotransmitters* (Conkbayir, 2023: 102). Curran explains that nerve cells 'grow long, incredibly thin projections out from their cell walls looking for other nerve cells that are firing at the same time as them ....they actually go out looking for partners that are completely in tune with them' (Curran, 2008: 26).

This building of connections, or synaptic growth, is dependent on conditions and experiences (Nicholson et al., 2023: 17) or as Gaskill and Perry state, it is 'use-dependent' (Gaskill and Perry, 2012: 35). Cozolino explains: '[e]xperience sculpts the brain through the selective excitation and connection of specific neurons that come to form functional neural networks' (Cozolino, 2013: 28). *Repeated firing* of a circuit can lead to it becoming the most common pattern in the brain, be that positive or negative (Van der Kolk, 2014: 65), while a lack of reinforcement of a connection will mean it withers, in other words 'use it or lose it' (Conkbayir, 2023: 105). In physiological terms, as experiences are repeated the axons become covered in a substance called myelin, a kind of insulation (Curran, 2008: 131). This thickens and helps conduct information much quicker, and, as Sanders and Thompson (2022: 52) state, 'neurons that repeatedly activate each other increase each other's ability to communicate efficiently'. If we imagine a field of long grass and we take an initial walk through it, the path we create may be faint at first but if we continue to walk across that same path, it becomes more defined, clear and less likely to disappear. The connections in our brain are similar and this is what happens when we learn (Sanders and Thompson, 2022: 53). Our role as education professionals, then, must be to recognize the neuroplasticity of the brain – its ability to change according to new experiences – and continually strive to walk new pathways with our pupils. And it's no exaggeration to say that this could be life-changing for some children.

To some extent, this knowledge gleaned from neuroscience helps us understand Bowlby's work on attachment and the *internal working model* (Bowlby, 1973; 1980) of the child (see Chapter 4). Learning happens when there are changes in connectivity between neurons and *patterns* are formed (Cozolino, 2013: 222). Siegel and Payne

Bryson call these *associations*, and these are then what form memories (Siegel and Payne Bryson, 2012: 68). We base our feelings and reactions to something in the present on experiences in our past. We may also anticipate what is going to happen next based on such memories. Consider how certain songs or smells trigger particular emotions depending on the situation when we heard/smelled them. Curran describes this network of neural connections as templates and suggests that we view them each as 'a piece of information' (Curran, 2008: 30). When we learn, we add to them. He also highlights the significant role of dopamine in learning as the main 'synaptogenic chemical in the brain', meaning that it helps to make those connections between neurons (Curran, 2008: 61). The control of dopamine sits in the emotional/limbic part of the brain and it is often known as the 'feel-good hormone' (Baker and Simpson, 2020: 52). For example, when a child is praised dopamine is released, and they feel rewarded. Anticipation of that reward may then motivate them to repeat that behaviour. Learning, then, is intrinsically tied to the emotional/limbic system: as Curran states, '[i]f you have made good emotional connection with the person who is trying to learn from you – or from whom you are trying to learn – you have dramatically increased the chance of them learning that thing from you' (Curran, 2008: 61).

A further area of interest for education professionals is mirror neurons. While research on this phenomenon is ongoing, early findings and suggestions resonate with aspects of attachment theory. Mirror neurons refer to connections between one brain and another and were 'discovered' in the 1990s by Italian scientists who were studying the brains of monkeys. As they used electrodes to monitor the activity of particular neurons, for example, the ones which fired when the monkey ate a peanut, they discovered that the same ones fired when he saw the researcher eat a peanut even when the monkey himself was not eating (Siegel and Payne Bryson, 2012: 123). Therefore, the monkey's brain was influenced by the actions of the researcher and was 'vicariously mirroring' his actions (Van der Kolk, 2014: 68). Hence, it has been suggested that the roots of empathy, imitation and the ability to resonate and bond to others may lie here (Siegel and Payne Bryson, 2012; Van der Kolk, 2014). Therefore, we may also pick up on others' emotional states whether that be their joy, depression, anger or other state of mind. In summary, our brains really are 'biologically equipped to be in relationships, to understand where other people are coming from, and to influence one another' (Siegel and Payne Bryson, 2012: 125). As educators, it may serve us well to bear this in mind as we enter the classroom and the lives of our young people. How we manage our emotional state could be crucial to the learning environment for the children.

Thinking Point 6.2

As an education professional, what strategies do you employ to preserve your own emotional well-being?

Polyvagal Theory

As mentioned at the start of this chapter, one concept at the heart of a trauma-informed approach is safety. One theory which helps elucidate this is Stephen Porges' *Polyvagal Theory* (Porges, 2022), which offers a deeper understanding of the biology of safety (Van der Kolk, 2014: 90). As Porges himself states, 'Polyvagal Theory provides a neurobiological narrative that focuses on the importance of "safety" and the adaptive consequences of detecting risk on physiological state, social behaviour, psychological experience, and health' (Porges, 2017: 44). For him, our response to threat and sense of safety are not necessarily based on subjective, cognitive evaluation of a situation or environment but are rather routed in 'internal physiological states regulated by the autonomic nervous system' (Porges, 2022: 1). In other words, our body responds automatically to what we subconsciously perceive as threat or, conversely, the absence of threat. We are on a constant and enduring quest for safety in order to survive with our autonomic nervous system serving as 'our personal surveillance system' (Dana, 2023: n.p.). Our behavioural responses can therefore be seen as 'adaptive .... the human drive from our evolutionary history to survive and thrive' (Delahooke, 2020: 18).

The detection system at work here has been named by Porges as 'neuroception' (Porges, 2017: 68). In effect, it is 'an automatic and constant scanning and gathering of information from our outside world, inside world, and our relational world' (Desautels, 2023: 78). Deriving from the limbic system – discussed above – it is the part of us that is constantly asking, without us being consciously aware, 'am I safe?' We have certainly needed this to survive throughout history! Our nervous system is then alerted to the information gleaned via neuroception and prompts different responses. Faulty neuroception occurs when a person detects danger when there is none or thinks they are safe when there is actual danger (Delahooke, 2020: 20). This is the case for many traumatized children. As mentioned above, associations with previous traumatic experiences may skew what their brain perceives as threatening; the patterns established in the past set their bodies up for reactions which may be considered extreme. Let us now focus on those responses to threat.

The autonomic nervous system consists of two main branches: the sympathetic and the parasympathetic. Van der Kolk labels the former the 'body's accelerator', while the latter is the 'body's brake' (Van der Kolk, 2014: 89). It is the sympathetic branch which is responsible for energizing us for fight or flight when needed, while the parasympathetic branch slows us down. Within the parasympathetic branch we find the vagus nerve – hence Polyvagal Theory – one of the most significant in the body and one which joins all the major organs (Bombèr, 2020: 103). This nerve itself has two parts: the dorsal vagal pathway and the ventral vagal pathway. The first of these is the oldest in evolutionary terms and is responsible for our *freeze response*, where our body feels under so much threat that it immobilizes to protect itself – we may think of those animals which play dead in order to survive their predators (Desautels, 2023: 80). The ventral vagal pathway is where we feel safe, calm and connected to others, where we have access to our prefrontal cortex and where social engagement is fostered (Sanders and Thompson, 2022: 6; Desautels, 2023: 82).

Porges' work suggests that there is a hierarchy of responses to threat (Porges, 2022). Dana describes this as a ladder where the social engagement system is at the top – ventral vagal pathway – followed by the sympathetic branch where we begin to act and at the bottom there is the dorsal vagal pathway where we shut down and dissociate (Dana, 2023). When children are at the top of the ladder, they can play with others, listen, focus and learn. Further down the ladder they may be anxious, restless and eventually shut down as the brain is focused on survival. Consequently, access to the thinking *upstairs* part of the brain is limited (Delahooke, 2020). We know, therefore, that when the ventral vagal pathway is activated, we sense safety. In fact, it can only be accessed when we do not feel in danger (Desautels, 2023: 82). It follows, then, that social connection is what makes us feel safe: a kind word, a gentle tone of voice, a tender touch, friendship, love, being part of a team. These are all uniquely human signals that we are cared for and held in mind by someone else (Van der Kolk, 2014: 92). As mammals, we can only survive and thrive in packs so we need to collaborate with others (Van der Kolk, 2014: 64). We are indeed dependent on a trusted other from the moment we are born so it makes sense to conclude that 'social connectedness is a core biological imperative' (Porges, 2022: 7).

As education professionals there is much that we can do with this knowledge. Simply remembering that the threat response system is involuntary (Bombèr, 2020) leads us towards a more compassionate response to challenging behaviour. This label in itself is problematic and some have moved to use the term 'distressed behaviour' instead, arguing that this prompts us to comfort rather than confront. Our priority then is to regulate our pupils' nervous systems in order to shift them into the social engagement system rather than punish them into compliance. Sanders and Thompson suggest that 'creating safe environments and a felt sense of safety needs to be a primary goal of education' (Sanders and Thompson, 2022: 178) as they ask us to become 'polyvagal-informed teachers' (p. 177). In doing so we may introduce breathing exercises, music, a calming space, daily exercise or many other strategies but key to all of this is the ability of the education professional to remain regulated as well as remember that our systems are often 'cognitive-centric' (Delahooke, 2020: 10). Polyvagal Theory encourages both top-down approaches which promote connection to others and bottom-up approaches which seek to calm the nervous system (Van der Kolk, 2014: 101).

Thinking Point 6.3

a. How do you understand the term cognitive-centric mentioned above?
b. What strategies could be employed in nurseries and schools to move away from this?

Summary

At the heart of this chapter has been the concept of safety and how the body reacts in different ways to protect itself from perceived threat. This remarkable ability to adapt to situations and circumstances is perhaps our greatest strength. From the amygdala and the hippocampus to the autonomic nervous system, the complexity of the brain's workings as well as its lifelong plasticity is astounding. Behaviour is indeed communication of the *state* that the brain is in. Lori Desautels describes neuroplasticity as 'our human superpower' (Desautels, 2023: 34) as we hopefully consider how the traumatized brain need not be condemned to a lifetime of difficulties. In contrast, with the particular support of trauma-informed or rather brain-informed education professionals, change can happen, and healing begins. We need to be *intentional* about this (Desautels, 2023: 36), and take our time in the patient understanding that as we collaborate with each other we can effect true and lasting change in our young people.

7

Bereavement and Its Impact on Children and Young People

Mary Lappin

Key Ideas

This chapter will:

- examine definitions, concepts and the impact of bereavement,
- explore grief reactions and complications, and
- outline aspects of educational support.

Introduction

This chapter will explore some key definitions and concepts around bereavement and grief, and its impact on the individual and community. Some influential grief theorists will be emphasized, particularly those of relevance to an educational context. The chapter seeks to inform on the impact on well-being, particularly the well-being and learning of children and young people, and how the educator and professional can support bereft children and young people.

Beverly Raphael (1984: 29) in her handbook *The Anatomy of Bereavement* states that 'bereavement is the reaction to the loss of a close relationship'. This is an unambiguous and succinct definition that few would challenge. It is the nature of the reactions to loss that is of interest to the professional who works with, supports and educates the child. The word bereavement has its roots in the old English *bereafián*, the Latin word *reave* and the old Scots term is *beref*. Essentially the definition is a robbing or a deprivation of someone or something. It is generally used in reference to the death of someone significant. The significance of course is determined by the one who is bereaved. Mourning is closely related but not the same. One may mourn and engage in mourning rituals around the loss of a known, liked or disliked person, an esteemed colleague, or an international or local celebrity, but not necessarily be bereaved or suffer adversity and grief reactions.

Mourning and grief can be complicated, for some, steeped in ambiguity, disenfranchised or traumatic. It does not follow standardized chronology or predicted outcomes. Furthermore, grief differs in intensity and duration dependant on the nature of the loss, as noted in Worden's (2010) *Grief counselling and grief therapy*. It is important to note that bereavement is a feature of life, universal and unavoidable, and the chapter warns against pathologizing or adopting a symptoms narrative, locating grief solely within a physical and or mental health framework. This does not negate the suffering and distress that can be caused in experiencing the death of a loved one. Nor does it nullify the potential for complicated grief disorders, elements of trauma or the sheer toll that a loss, or multiple losses, can have on the individual, a family or a community affecting their sense of equilibrium, mental and physical well-being and the capacity to undertake the daily toils of life, family and work.

Impact and Reactions

Adversity of any kind provokes some cognitive and emotional response. This may be short-lived, temporary with minimal impact or bring considerable change, tough challenges, incertitude and some emotional insecurity and vulnerability. Adversity through bereavement can bring challenges in adjustment and adaptation. The death of a significant other, whether anticipated or unexpected, provokes response commonly known as grief reactions. Such grief reactions are generally experienced in five ways: cognitively, emotionally, physically, behaviourally and spiritually. Qualitative judgement is avoided; rather, the list above is a recognition of some common grief reactions without any notion of normality in grief or potential pathological features. Whilst it is unusual for a child to have prolonged upset and distress, there are emotional reactions and behaviours that are not dissimilar to those of adults. Indeed, children do suffer the common stressors surrounding significant loss such as anxiety, deep sadness, insecurity, anger, longing and vulnerability. In essence grief is an instinctive and intuitive response to separation from someone or something significant. This instinctive response upsets the equilibrium in the adult and the child. Reassuringly, research informs us that most children, with adequate care, support and information, will do well and make progress educationally, emotionally and cognitively (Haine et al., 2008). Nevertheless, we do a disservice to our children and young people if we do not acknowledge that bereavement has an impact, albeit that the impact will vary in nature and intensity. Its expression will fluctuate and vary as is commonly expressed in any bereavement support resource, that each person grieves differently. Furthermore, it is also a disservice if we do not give cognizance to the ongoing longing and prolonged grief experienced by some. Also, appreciation that the impact of secondary or resulting losses can be as demanding and arduous as the initial loss through bereavement is an important consideration, especially when the initial bereavement may have been forgotten in time by professionals. Such losses may include the relocation to a new neighbourhood, school, community or an altered social status due to financial constraints, leading to the loss of friends, neighbours, familiarity and an expectation of economic security and opportunity.

Potential reactions to the death of a loved one are well articulated in a myriad of work, including Raphael (1984), Worden (1996), Silverman (1999) and Drygrov (2008). In addition, many bereavement-support organizations outline the challenges to children and young people, such as Winston's Wish (www.winstonswish.org.uk), Cruse (https://www.cruse.org.uk) and the Childhood Bereavement Network (www.childbereavementuk.org). Silverman (1999) notes that at the heart of advisory networks and theoretical frameworks of grief support is a movement away from private or hidden grief but rather all should learn about grief and how to cope with its potential manifestations. Silverman (1999) makes a valid point: in learning about grief one may be better equipped to accompany and support a bereft friend, colleague, student or child.

Common grief reactions include some **emotional** responses such as shock, distress, vulnerability, numbness, anger, sorrow, fear and deep sadness that can impact on **behaviours** such as social withdrawal, irritability, bouts of anger, restlessness and/or inertia. Some **cognitive** engagement and disengagement are likely responses to a significant loss such as disbelief, bewilderment, confusion and preoccupation. Adversity such as bereavement can also have its **physical** manifestations, bringing disturbances in sleep patterns, appetite irritations and general feelings of low-level ill-health, anxiety, tension, headache, nausea and fatigue. Reactions within a **spiritual** realm are also a grief countenance, whether or not there is religious adherence. Spiritual reactions to loss include facets of identity, role, purpose, including existential crisis on the meaning and purpose of life, continued or discontinued belief in a deity and after-death destination. For disciples of a faith tradition there can be questions of the nature of the deity as merciful, benevolent or loving, yet robbing the deceased of life and the bereft of consolation. The aforementioned reactions are by no means an exhaustive list but provide some insight into the grief landscape of the bereaved as they wrestle with life that no longer contains the physical presence of a loved one or significant other.

Grief and Young People

Children and young people are not exempt from grief reactions. Indeed, all that the adult feels can be felt by the child. However, grief in the child can be masked in complaints of feeling a general unwellness, vague feelings of stomach-ache, headache and nausea. Daydreaming and lack of concentration, tearfulness and feelings of fear and insecurity can be present in the child who feels the absence of their significant other. Some regression to an earlier stage, most likely to a memorable or perceived time of security, is not unusual. All stages of childhood into adulthood share feelings of vulnerability with some anxiety about the remaining family, parent or carer leaving or dying. It is the remit of parents, health visitors and general practitioners (GPs) to look for signs of failure to thrive in the ongoing assessment of infant development and growth, with careful attention to weight gain or loss, sleep routines, preverbal responses and any lack in development as these are potential sources of concern, requiring additional care and monitoring. In addition, the classroom practitioner may notice some grief reactions paraded in and out of the classroom as the bereaved child navigates school life without their significant other. Familiarity with and knowledge of some grief theories can be beneficial, particularly for those expected to work with the bereft, thus enabling some sensitive support mechanisms, intuitive accompaniment and meaningful learning.

Grief Theories, Models and Interventions

Grief theories provide stage models, transition pathways and process paradigms through which thanatological deliberations (thanatology is the scientific study of death and dying), bereavement education and support networks are positioned. This chapter cannot provide an elucidation of all grief theories that have entered the practice of grief support and education in past decades. Rather the chapter gives due consideration to some familiar and contemporary theories that are given prominence in popular discourse and those used most frequently in education contexts. The work of John Bowlby (1969) and Colin Parkes (2008) on attachment and loss have played a significant role in the understanding of grief responses. Bowlby's research (1960) established that children are capable of grieving and recognized that absence from the parent or a significant loved one has an impact on well-being. Over fifty years ago, Bowlby and Parkes (1970) recognized that the bereaved may not only move through grief stages but also weave in and around these stages, revisiting a stage over time, as well as the emotional and cognitive impact of grief. The work of Stroebe et al. (1999) recognized that grief is an active process, requiring both the expression of feelings as well as the need to monitor and control. Stroebe and Schut (2010) proposed a dual process model of bereavement whereby the bereft oscillate between confronting and eluding their grief reactions. In other words, a model that tackles the discomfort of grief yet also recognizes the need for and practice of emotional regulation.

Stage model (Kubler Ross, 1969)

The work of Kübler-Ross is perhaps the most well-known and often quoted in popular culture. Her model suggests a stage-based process paradigm. Her notable text *On Death and Dying* (Kübler-Ross, 1969) is still influential in some grief counselling contexts and hospice work although a much decried and negated thanatology discourse. Nevertheless, the model seemed to resonate with the populace as a tool for grappling with bereavement whether as the bereaved or as the one in accompaniment. Kübler-Ross (1969) suggested a five stages of grief model, incorporating denial, anger, bargaining, depression and acceptance, whereby the bereft navigate through their grief experience. The model (Kübler-Ross, 1969) grew in popularity and was misappropriated in its adoption as a grief model for the bereaved. Her research, albeit lacking in empirical depth, involved listening to and observation of the dying who displayed common traits, reactions and patterns as they wrestled with their terminal status. Naturally a point of closure is to be preferred, namely that the terminally ill come to some state of acceptance about their imminent, or not-so-imminent, death. It is important to stress that the stage model was originally intended for and about the terminally ill and not a grief model for the bereaved. Perhaps its suggestion of structure and predictability provides some reassurance or consolation in the pain and bewilderment of grief. Regardless of intention, it joined the various twentieth-century grief models that provide some form of guidance and insights for clinicians, psychologists, health workers and undertakers for their work with the bereaved.

Kübler-Ross (1969) and other grief influencers, such as Freud (Fiorini et al., 2009), have posited a point of closure or endpoint in grieving, some kind of resolution, recovery or resignation, while other contemporary theories such as the work of Worden (1996, 2010), Silverman (1999) and Niemeyer (2001) challenge the assumption that there is any discernible end point in grieving, suggesting instead that the bereaved are engaged in an ongoing renegotiation of meaning over time. One such model, often used as a framework of basis for psychosocial and educational support, is that of the Harvard clinical psychologist William Worden.

Task model (Worden, 2010)

The work of Worden (2010) in the field of grief counselling and research advocates a task model, whereby the bereaved work through their loss experience and reach reconciliation and adjustment. The four tasks of mourning, as articulated by Worden (2010), are:

- **i.** to accept the reality of the loss,
- **ii.** to process the pain of grief,
- **iii.** to adjust to a world without the deceased, and
- **iv.** to find an enduring connection with the deceased in the midst of embarking on a new life.

In his previous work Worden (1996) articulated the fourth task as letting go and moving on or reinvestment of emotional energy. The notion of letting go is not always desired by the bereaved. There can be conflicted emotions and feelings of disloyalty if one feels a perceived expectation to, or indeed desires to, emotionally let go of the deceased loved one and move on with life and other roles or new relationships. Some kind of reinvestment of energy without losing a connection or bond with the deceased is preferable. Hence an amendment to his fourth task of letting go and reinvesting one's energy is articulated in later work as seeking an enduring connection whilst one embraces new experiences and relationships (Worden, 2010).

Worden (2010) is not alone in his attempt to articulate the notion of a relinquishment of emotional ties with the deceased loved one. For example, Niemeyer (2001) and Klass and Walter (2001) challenge mainstream assumptions within bereavement theories and death education, namely that the end point of grief is the letting go of attachment to the beloved deceased. They challenge the notion that grief work involves the navigation through adverse, uncomfortable grief reactions and thereafter a renunciation of any attachment or emotional connection. Traditional grief theories have assumed a Freudian view that successful grieving requires withdrawal of psychic energy from the loved one. Contemporary grief theories recognize that relationships and roles often adapt post-bereavement, in that the bereaved maintain some form of continuing bond with the deceased significant other.

One may assume Worden's (2010) fourth task leads to an end point or conclusion of grief work, having journeyed through the previous three tasks. However, they are not designed to be followed in a linear or specific order but rather recognize the cyclical and often unpredictability nature of grief. In other words, one can weave in and out of the tasks as required, although some kind of recognition or acceptance of the loss reality is generally required before one can progress through a grief process or any grief work. For some, acceptance of the loss can take considerable time. Such acceptance can be particularly challenging if the death is sudden or traumatic, such as road accidents, suicide or murder.

Worden's (2010) task model sits well within a socio-constructivist view of learning whereby the bereaved makes meaning and constructs new ideas based upon experience and knowledge. Hence education and psychosocial interventions often use Worden's model (2010) as a framework for exploring the grief experience. As the bereaved feel the acute pain of grief and seek to adjust to life and their roles therein, learning is focused on emotional literacy, health-giving expressions of grief and some agency in life choices post-bereavement as they move into new relationships or new roles.

Thinking Point 7.1

Consider Worden's four tasks. What learning may be promoted in supporting the bereaved as they seek to adjust to their new reality where the deceased is no longer physically present?

Continuing bonds model (Klass et al., 2014)

A continued relationship with the deceased is an important theme in bereavement work. Klass et al. (2014) define the phenomena as an ongoing relationship with the deceased. Like Worden's task model, a continuous bond model disputes the notion that grievers will at some point leave behind or break the emotional bonds with their deceased loved one (Stroebe and Schut, 2005). Rather the deceased is physically absent, yet the relationship continues, often through sharing stories, use of mementos, prayers, rituals, photographs and memories. Essentially the bereft can be consoled; their ongoing love and emotional tie are validated and integrated into daily life, rather than extinguished. Continuing bonds appear to benefit the bereaved by providing comfort, and a paradigm through which to accommodate the circumstances of the death. The loss and grief can be positioned within a coherent narrative or story supporting meaning reconstruction, self-identity and an affirmation of spiritual belief (Hewson et al., 2023). Features of coming to terms with loss and bereavement such as an openness to new relationships and reinvestment of emotional energy may suggest a certain relinquishing of the deceased; however, the continuing bonds model promotes integration as a healthy outcome. Integration thus is a key feature of bereavement support and any learning paradigm, stressing a healthy outcome. The child and young person, like the mature adult, can learn about and find ways to integrate the deceased loved one as they continue to live through their joys and sorrows of their earthly existence, while the deceased is no longer physically present.

Bereavement Work with Children and Young People in Educational Contexts

The needs of grieving children and young people are not difficult to list and are similar to any human need in times of adversity. They would include a welcoming and empathetic disposition, a capacity to listen well, supportive gestures, opportunities to talk, companionship, distraction, understanding, care and availability. In his influential book *Children and Grief* Worden (1996) proposes that there are ten needs in a young person who has experienced a family bereavement, including a need for adequate information and any anxieties they may have are addressed. Robust listening, clear messaging that they are not to blame and some help with overcoming feelings, or emotional turbulence, are requirements alongside some validation of the emotional response to loss. A continued routine such as the daily routine of school or weekly sport and recreations clubs can be helpful in providing a routine of familiar activities, persons and settings. While a familiar routine is helpful this cannot negate opportunities to remember the deceased. Such remembrance opportunities, such as formal and informal acknowledgement of the loss through conversation, rituals, religious services, cards and mementos, can enable good models of grief and a sense of involvement and inclusion which can provide some response to the pain and vulnerability inevitably felt when a loved one dies.

Teachers report bereaved young people to be more anxious, withdrawn and depressed than their peers (Dowdney, 1999). There can be difficulties with concentration and attention which unsurprisingly can result in reduced academic performance. However, consideration must also be given to improved performance, perhaps seeking to make the deceased loved one proud and satisfied with successful academic outcomes. It is not uncommon for the origins of school difficulties, resulting from a bereavement, to be forgotten by adults, especially when some time has lapsed and when school life is busy and demanding. This is understandable, yet awareness that the impact of loss can continue sometime after the initial bereavement can be helpful and assist the teacher and caring professional in identifying need and providing support.

The adolescent is often considered to be particularly at risk of adverse outcomes most probably due to the existing tasks associated with independence and transition. Furthermore, the disruption caused by the death of someone significant and its resulting changes and potential other losses can be a harsh blow on an emotional landscape that is already facing puberty, hormonal changes and challenges to the sense of the self of a young person who is leaving behind childhood and is en route to adulthood. Raphael's (1984) chapter in *Anatomy of Bereavement* on 'The Adolescent's Grief and Mourning' stresses that adolescence brings its own 'psychic upheaval [*and*] [t]he stress of bereavement is superimposed on these' (Raphael, 1984: 126). In other words, bereavement stressors add to any experienced or perceived turbulence that may come during the period of adolescence. It is not uncommon to witness adolescents engaging in risk-taking behaviours as an emotional outlet and coping strategy, a release from emotional unrest and bewilderment, albeit unsafe and potentially leading to trauma outcomes. The educator is concerned then with learning and teaching about appropriate and healthy coping strategies, and the adoption therein. Thus release, recovery and response can be expressed, respected and encouraged. The bereaved child and adolescent can face a life that is fundamentally changed in structure, family composition and routine, for some this change is welcomed for it brings relief and release from tension and conflict, while for others it is to be challenged and oppugned. Whilst an overemphasis on and presumption of trauma outcomes is to be avoided, similar pedagogical and emotional support is required for those living with adversity, for the stressors experienced are undoubtedly similar while intensity may vary. In other words, grief reactions, especially deaths that are sudden and unexpected or in traumatic circumstances, can be experienced as trauma, where the shock propels a chasm of challenges in identity, relationship, purpose and daily functioning as well as an inability to manage subsequent or future adversities.

Supporting Bereaved Young People in Schools

Educational establishments that support young people who have experienced some form of adversity including bereavement generally do so through psychosocial education programmes. Adversity through loss and bereavement support in Scottish, and some UK, schools is sometimes provided through intuitive teacher to child support or through curricula learning, with educational outcomes that focus on death, dying and grief. Occasionally guidance is provided by local education authority resources, initiatives and training. Most often, though, support is through evidence-based psychosocial interventions such as Seasons for Growth (SeasonsforGrowth.co.uk) or Rainbows (rainbowsgb.org). Educational and professional practice promoting researched, evidence-based programmes that have undergone robust evaluation and analysis could be considered a prerequisite of any trauma-informed practice or support. Such educational programmes often adopt Worden's (1996) four tasks, building in opportunities for young people to work through an acceptance of their loss, recognize the adversity and painful emotions that can arise as part of their loss story. In addition, opportunities to look at effective, healthy, coping strategies in working through painful memories and emotional turbulence, as the young person seeks to reinvest emotional energy without severing a continued relationship with the deceased, would be beneficial in processing grief. Working through the pain of grief can be prolonged and present barriers to any reinvestment of emotional energy if the grief is experienced as persistent, unrelenting or complicated.

Complicated Grief

One may assume notions of complicated or prolonged grief suggest elements of trauma, particularly in violent deaths, murder, war, road accidents and suicide. Undoubtedly such deaths can bring a period of mourning and grief that generates complicated emotions, intrusive memories and acute distress. In such experiences, grief may be intense, ongoing and debilitating. Szuhany et al. (2021) note that whilst most mourners find some sense of integration of their grief,

> a significant minority will experience unrelenting bereavement responses resulting in functional impairment beyond cultural norms, which historically has been labelled complicated, traumatic, persistent, or pathological; however, most recently, the consensus name is prolonged grief disorder.
>
> (Szuhany et al., 2021: 161)

Demarcation of a prolonged grief can be hard to determine for there is no prescribed time scale for mourning and grief. Individuals react uniquely to loss and responses can be multifaceted, in as much as our relationships differ in history, role and intensity. Clearly, a defined time scale is not possible because loss and bereavement seldom fit a tidy prescribed format, just as relationships seldom display uniformity. The result of a mourning period and grief responses to the death of a loved one is accommodation and assimilation, rather than recovery and full acceptance. A prolonged journey of distressing and turbulent grief response can cause concern for and about the bereaved. At times this may be articulated as being stuck in grief, and unable to move on.

Such observation of being stuck in grief or manifestations of prolonged mourning and distressing grief responses may trigger alarm or concern amongst professionals concerned for the well-being and educational progress of the young person. A first step is discerning through observation and careful listening to the nature and extent of the grief response. Worden's (2010) *Grief counselling and grief therapy handbook* highlights various 'Mediators of Mourning' (pp. 57–75) and provides helpful insights for anyone accompanying the bereaved, including guidance on discerning the needs of the bereaved person or the consideration of potential barriers to healthy grieving. Such mediators include the cause of death (expected, sudden, traumatic), nature of the attachment (parent, elderly relative, friend, pet) and experience of previous losses. Any concurrent stressors can impact the mourning process and the grief response. A nuanced but important principle is not only who the deceased was but also the nature and depth of the attachment to the person who has died. This is worth noting to assist in avoiding assumptions, or reaching unhelpful conclusions of complicated grief, while the bereaved is displaying deep sadness, distress and longing for someone presumed to be on the fringes of one's life. Such examples include an acquaintance or neighbour, not part of the inner circle of family, friends or carers, but mourned and grieved by the child, nonetheless. When grief is prolonged, and so brings potential complicated grief responses, medical intervention, psychological support or counselling may be required, particularly where there is a sense of being stuck unable to let go or suspend feelings of loss or oscillating between grief and relief. Multi-agency support around the child and family can aid professional discernment as to how to support the bereaved young person who is displaying signs of acute or prolonged grief.

Thinking Point 7.2

Consider an elderly neighbour with whom the child forms a strong affection and attachment who dies. The child mourns and grieves the neighbour, feels the force of the loss. What interventions may the educator initiate to support the child?

Summary

Death of a loved one can be a painful and distressing experience for child and adult alike. Pathologizing and/or the medicalization of bereavement should be avoided as it is one of life's adversities that all humans will experience. Emotional turbulence, sorrow, physical discomfort, cognitive bewilderment and a spiritual search for meaning are common reactions, while stressing that each bereavement is unique and each griever reacts differently depending on the nature of the loss, the circumstances of the death and the significance of the deceased.

Grief models such as Kübler-Ross' (1969) stage model and the insights of Bowlby and Parkes (1970) are highlighted in the chapter due to their familiarity in popular discourse. An emphasis on Worden's (2010) task model is stressed due to its contribution to educational and school-based psychosocial interventions. The educator is better placed to support the bereaved child, and to educate children and young people on death, dying and bereavement if there is some familiarity with evidence-based theories of grief and the skills, dispositions and knowledge base therein. Some familiarity with complicated and complex factors that may originate from or result in trauma due to the sudden or violent nature of the death is helpful to the educator who accompanies the bereft child or young person. It is important to note that whilst bereavement and loss can be painful, most children and young people adapt and oscillate between grieving and relief.

8

Pupils' Behaviours; Teachers' Responses

Clare Smith and Angela Curley

Key ideas

This chapter will:

- provide examples of manifestation of trauma through behaviour in schools,
- examine teacher responses to pupil behaviour,
- consider the impact of trauma-informed policies, and
- consider the perceived increase in 'behaviour issues' in schools.

Introduction

Trauma can be defined as an acute or chronic life event that overwhelms a person's capacity to cope (NCTSN, n.d.). Children and young people can be traumatized if overwhelming events happen directly to them, or if they witness or hear about them happening to somebody else. Responses to trauma in children and young people can include feelings of anger, anxiety, irritability, confusion. These feelings can become manifest in the school setting through distressed behaviour. Distressed behaviours can include defiance, aggression, resistance, withdrawal or lack of focus. Actions may include talking back to the teacher, refusing to follow instructions, shouting out or being physically aggressive towards peers or teachers. These behaviours can be referred to as 'challenging' but many people working with children and young people prefer to think of this as a young person signalling their distress. This chapter will focus on teacher responses to distressed behaviour and consider how policies on trauma-informed practice influence teacher responses.

Teacher Responses to Pupil Behaviour

Teaching can be emotionally demanding. This *emotional labour* has been studied to understand *how* and *why* teachers manage and express their emotions in class (Wang et al., 2019). Expended on a daily basis, emotional labour can lead to exhaustion and burnout (Bodenheimer and Shuster, 2019; Kariou et al., 2021). 'Challenging' pupil behaviour is cited as one of the causes of teacher stress and burnout (Dawes et al., 2024). How the individual teacher responds to pupil behaviour is a complex issue.

The common motivations for becoming a teacher include the desire to make a positive impact on young people and on society, a love of learning and/or their subject and the personal fulfilment associated with a rewarding career. Teachers do not come to the profession with a desire to confront or challenge children or young people unethically. However, on occasion, teachers can respond to pupil behaviour in a less than positive way. Negative teacher responses to pupil behaviour can be punitive, dismissive or confrontational. They can be manifested as voice raising or the use of inappropriate speech or body language. These responses can escalate the situation and the effect on the pupil is inevitably negative.

How teachers respond to distressed or challenging behaviour, and how they regulate these responses, is a growing field of study (Chang and Taxer, 2020; Frenzel et al., 2021). The key variables contributing to the teacher response have been identified as teacher self-efficacy, emotional responses and causal beliefs or attributions. These factors are interlinked, and all contribute to the complex make-up of teacher identity (Hanna et al., 2019). In terms of response to pupil behaviour, these can be considered individually.

Self-efficacy, as described by Bandura (1977) as how a teacher believes that they can handle the tasks, obligations and challenges associated with being a teacher, plays a key role in their response to pupil behaviour. Teachers with high levels of self-efficacy have been shown to build stronger relationships with students, allowing the creation of environments that are supportive, responsive and empathetic (Zee and Koomen, 2016). This correlates with studies that demonstrate that stronger efficacy beliefs in teachers lead to more positive attitudes towards inclusion in general (Mok et al., 2019; Savolainen et al., 2020).

The major sources of self-efficacy are theorized as mastery experiences, vicarious experience, verbal and social persuasion, and emotional and physiological states (Bandura, 1997), with mastery experiences proposed as the most powerful (Usher and Pajares, 2008). This suggests that if teachers working with young people affected by trauma are trained and receive ongoing support, they can improve their own self-efficacy. When teachers were provided with 'viable ways to process and create new meaning through their ongoing exposure to student trauma' (Brunzell et al., 2022: 9), they developed a greater sense of meaning at work evidenced through improvements in their own well-being and in their ability to engage students with learning.

The emotional response of teachers can be closely linked to self-efficacy. Teachers with low self-efficacy, or low agency in general, are more prone to negative emotional responses (Donker et al., 2025). When pupil behaviour is perceived as challenging, this can elicit strong emotions and impact the psychological well-being of teachers (de Ruiter et al., 2020). Theoretical models suggest that the occupational well-being of teachers is influenced by their everyday emotional responses to student behaviour (Chang and Davis, 2009; Spilt et al., 2011). Positive emotions in teachers are associated with their own well-being and decreased stress and burnout (Chang, 2013).

Weiner's (1985) interpersonal attribution theory suggests that individuals respond to actions or experiences based on the perceived behaviour or intentions of others. Causal attributions concerning pupil behaviour will impact a teacher's emotional and outward reaction to the behaviour. In a systematic review, Nemer et al. (2019) characterized teacher attributions along four dimensions: locus, controllability, stability and responsibility. Each of these dimensions has multiple facets; locus (the most cited attribution dimension), for example, can be described as a continuum of factors internal to the student to those external to the student. Furthermore, an aggressive action from a pupil could be attributed to the mood of the pupil (internal) or to a learnt behaviour from home (external). Controllability refers to the extent to which the teacher believes that the cause of a pupil's behaviour is within the pupil's control; the impact on teacher response to controllability is complex. For example, teachers may be more likely to attempt to promote self-regulation if they believe that a student can control the cause of their behaviour (Poulou and Norwich, 2002). However, if a behaviour is seen as controllable, teachers may exhibit less empathy and be less supportive. Wang and Hall (2018) reported that teachers tended to attribute distressed or challenging behaviour to student characteristics, both internal (e.g. effort, personality) and external (e.g. home dysfunction, lack of parental interest), rather than teacher- or school-based influences (e.g. instruction, teacher attitudes). The correlation between teacher attributions and emotional response is highlighted. The assessment of teacher attributions has significant implications for the implementation of trauma-informed practice. Teachers should be allowed to reflect on their causal beliefs in supportive environments in order to develop effective and empathetic responses to pupil behaviour.

Thinking Point 8.1

a. What form could/should the reflective space for teachers take?
b. Should it mirror the compulsory supervision provided to social workers?

Teacher Responses to Trauma

When working with children and young people affected by trauma or when undertaking training in trauma-informed practice, there is concern for the well-being of school staff who have experienced trauma themselves. The stress of coping with distressed behaviours can lead to staff becoming re-traumatized. The daily exposure to classroom situations that may be rooted in adversity and negated by exposure to trauma has been cited as a cause of burnout and even as a reason to leave the profession (Fazel et al., 2014).

It can often be assumed that teachers have the capacity to deal with and process trauma in their professional lives almost as if it were an annex to the curriculum which can be utilized whenever necessary. Just as teacher responses to pupil behaviours are complex, the response to dealing with trauma in a professional context is varied and is influenced by the lived experiences of adversity: including those stemming from school experiences and more influentially those stemming from personal childhood trauma (Robertson et al., 2021).

The ethos of a school and the individual classroom situations are important stabilizers or anchor points for building positive relationships with the key partners of a school community. This will strongly influence the success, or otherwise, of relational practices. Key partners are the pupils, teachers and carers who are part of a tri-partite educational agreement that sees each group interact within the mesosystem (Bronfenbrenner, 1979). When interactions are positive, then the development of the child academically and emotionally is positive. However, relationships within the school context are never uniform, and this is where silent societal influences such as socio-economic status, family breakdown and exposure to trauma can impact how pupils respond in the classroom environment. Unfortunately, these influences can pivot teacher responses and result in a crisis in confidence in managing indiscipline within the school setting.

There is an assumption that the *adult in the room* will always be able to control strong emotions using rational thought and learned strategies. Teachers might well be aware of how they should respond to pupil behaviour. The widely accepted basic rules of classroom management are included in teacher education programmes and are described in numerous single author books (e.g. see the work of Sue Cowley). Setting out clear expectations, positive re-enforcement, redirecting behaviour, consistent routines and ensuring that lessons are engaging are key classroom management strategies offered to novice teachers (see Chapters 10 and 11). Alongside these practical approaches, the forming and maintaining of positive relationships with pupils and the acceptance of the principle that *all behaviour is communication* has been integrated into the policies and practices of many schools, particularly in Scotland.

Trauma-Informed Policies

Since the pioneering work of Carl Rogers on the *person-centred approach* to teaching (1983, 1990), the importance of pupil-teacher relationships has been a focus of research into classroom behaviours and pupil outcomes. From these beginnings, the educational approach that places a strong emphasis on building positive and meaningful relationships between educators and students, known as relational practice, was developed. Positive teacher-pupil relationships have been linked to improved learning through enhanced engagement and motivation (Pinyu, 2024). Relational practices can help to redress the impact of trauma on children and young people. Internationally, trauma-informed practice has been advocated to support schools and teachers in understanding the nature and consequences of trauma and in building emotionally healthy classroom environments (SAMHSA, 2014; Overstreet and Chafouleas, 2016). These studies suggest that trauma-informed approaches can significantly enhance both the well-being and academic performance of students. However, being trauma and attachment aware is not always easy. The many complex factors that can result in distressed pupil behaviour are one critical element. However, the situation of the teacher will also significantly impact the relationship. How teachers instinctively respond to challenges in the classroom will also come from a complex mix of experiences, emotions and context, as described previously. These lived experiences are referred to by McMullen et al. (2020) as *sitting on a wobbly chair*, where we see a relationship between trauma, mental health and behavioural well-being. As knowledge about trauma-informed practice (TIP) has grown, the effect on pupils continues to be studied (Maynard et al., 2019). Jones and Harding (2023: 309) reported 'clear benefits to pupil outcomes' from attachment and trauma-awareness training in a range of specialist provision settings and reports from the Alex Timpson Trust (see https://www.timpson-group.co.uk/alex-timpson-trust/) evidenced positive outcomes in mainstream schools across several English local authorities (LAs) (Harrison, 2022). As the knowledge base grows, there are numerous, valuable texts and training materials that provide strategies that teachers and schools can use to help children and young people to reach their full potential.

A trauma-informed, or even a relational, approach to classroom or behaviour management is not universally accepted. In England, a debate on the use of behaviourist approaches to 'discipline' in schools is ongoing. The UK government publication on '*Behaviour in Schools*' (Department for Education, 2024a) (for use in England only) makes no mention of relational practices and includes behaviourist strategies such as the use of rewards and sanctions. Much of the debate on a *zero-tolerance approach* to behaviour is conducted on social media platforms. This government advice echoes the side of the debate supported by the UK government former 'behaviour advisor' Tom Bennett versus the voices advocating for a relational or trauma-informed approach. In Scotland there is a long history of child and young-people-centred approaches. In July 2024, the Scottish Parliament incorporated the *United Nations Convention on the Rights of the Child (UNCRC)* (Scottish Parliament, 2024) into domestic law. This historic moment was built on the foundations set by the principles of *Getting it right for every child (GIRFEC)* (Scottish Government, 2022a), a rights-based approach that recognizes the strength of relationships and human connections. Since 2008, Getting it right for every child (GIRFEC) has been the national approach to improving outcomes for children and young people taking a holistic approach to well-being (Scottish Government, 2022a). The landscape surrounding trauma and attachment-informed schooling in Scotland has changed dramatically in the years since the implementation of Getting it right for every child (GIRFEC).

Education Scotland (2018) articulated the need to integrate trauma-informed principles into established frameworks such as the nurture approach. This is a relational-based programme to support children and young people through a small number of trained personnel working within the school setting (Education Scotland, 2018). The first iteration of the nurture approach in Scottish schools was through the implementation of nurture groups based on the work of Margery Boxall (Bennathan and Boxall, 2000). Nurture groups are typically formed of a small group of children or young people, with one or two members of staff trained in nurture interventions. Glasgow City Council (GCC), Scotland's largest LA, set up their first nurture groups in 2001. Initial evaluation and feedback demonstrated the value placed on nurture groups by parents, children, young people, teachers and other professionals (Kearney, 2004; Gerrard, 2006; March and Healy, 2007). Further research evidenced improvements in attainment and in social and emotional skills for the children and young people included in nurture groups (Reynolds et al., 2009; McKay et al., 2010). These positive findings created the basis for a national evidence base on nurture groups. As the number of nurture groups grew in Glasgow, a whole-school nurture approach was promoted across the city. A framework to support the self-evaluation of nurture approaches was developed by Glasgow City Council that helped to inform the Education Scotland framework *Applying Nurture as a Whole School Approach* (Education Scotland, 2017a).

In Scotland, around 95 per cent of children and young people are educated in state schools which are administratively managed by thirty-two LAs. Each LA has implemented trauma-aware policies, in most cases through a nurture-based approach, but practice in this regard is still varied (Chapter 15 will explore strategies to change this). Informed by the *Children and Young People (Scotland) Act 2014* (Scottish Parliament, 2014), LAs produce Integrated Children's Services Plans every three years. These multi-agency approaches involve education, health and social work professionals working together to provide support for children, young people and families with nurture principles at the core (see Chapter 10). In recent years, the enactment of national directives in Scotland mirrored a shift from the traditional behaviour management policies to relationship-based policies. This evolution in school policies can be traced back to the publication of the *Better Relationships, Better Learning, Better Behaviour* report (Scottish Government, 2013), which emphasized the importance of positive behaviour support. Many Scottish teachers have been trained in programmes centred on nurture principles.

The Impact on Teachers

The impact of trauma-informed practice on children and young people continues to be studied across Scotland (Taylor and Barrett, 2022). However, empirical data on the impact on teachers and school staff is somewhat limited. In nations where whole-school, trauma-informed approaches have been legislated for some time, such as the United States through the *Every Student Succeeds Act* (US Department of Education, 2015), research is active, and results are eagerly awaited. Public Health Wales published one of the first evaluations of school-wide, trauma-informed training including control groups (Barton et al., 2018). Six months after the intervention, school staff expressed continuing favourable attitudes towards trauma-impacted students with an accompanying improvement in staff well-being. Another study involving control groups was conducted in Northern Ireland, and again, the impact of even minimal trauma-informed training on school staff was evident (MacLochlainn et al., 2022). Anecdotally, Scottish teachers have welcomed the adoption of relational approaches in their classrooms, particularly when they have been supported to implement the policies. Maureen McKenna, a former Director of Education for Glasgow City Council, was widely quoted stating:

> Teachers are much more knowledgeable now about the context of children's lives and behaviour is no longer looked at in isolation. One of the biggest achievements in Glasgow is that teachers don't see it as bad behaviour but as distressed behaviour. That all behaviour is communication is one of our big training focuses. Now they are seeing behaviour in a different light.
>
> (Seith, 2019: 1)

Across Scotland, and indeed, across the UK, *behaviour policies* are being replaced by *relationship policies* in schools. Guidance on developing such policies has been provided by Education Scotland (2024) and numerous examples of school policies can be accessed. The implementation of relationship policies represents a shift in practice for many teachers. There is little in the literature on the impact of this expected change in practice on Scottish teachers.

Thinking Point 8.2

How have individual teachers responded to the school level policy changes?

The Perceived Increase in 'Disruptive' Behaviour in Schools

Scotland enjoys a reputation as a trauma-informed nation and the policy landscape speaks to this. However, in reports from the Independent Care Review (Independent Care Review, 2020; Scottish Government, 2022b) and the *Support for Learning: All Our Children and All Their Potential* (Scottish Government, 2020a), evidence suggests there is still work to be done to strengthen relationship-based approaches in Scottish schools. The gap between policy and practice persists, but significant work is being undertaken to address the issue (see Chapter 15). This work is being carried out against the landscape of a perceived increase in disruptive behaviour in schools.

In 2023, the Scottish Government published their report on *Behaviour in Scottish Schools* (Scottish Government, 2023a). This was the fifth phase of research first undertaken in 2006. Educational professionals in schools and local authorities, including teachers, were asked about overall perceptions of behaviours – positive and negative – in three categories: low-level disruptive, disengagement and serious disruptive. While a significant proportion of respondents reported *generally good behaviour*, low-level disruptive behaviour manifested in talking out of turn and disengagement through withdrawal from interaction with others was reported almost on a daily basis. A *general worsening* in behaviour since the previous report in 2016 was noted as well as an increase in common low-level disruptive behaviour since the initial report in 2006 (Wilkin et al., 2006). These findings appear to confirm the narrative presented by sections of the media; see for example, the BBC commissioned survey of teachers in English schools (Moss and Dunkley, 2024).

As teachers report daily occurrences of low-level disruptive behaviours, there is accompanying evidence to support the theory that exposure to trauma can ignite these very behaviours in children and young people. Motta (2012) explored states such as anger, anxiety, startle and withdrawal from a psychological perspective as potential responses to secondary or vicarious traumas. With secondary trauma or secondary stress, the child has absorbed the primary stress from an adult who has been traumatized. Vicarious trauma relates to a significant alteration in the child's core beliefs which impacts on their personal security, and sense of self. However, both experiences of trauma have an overarching issue, which is the disturbance in emotions, leading to low-level negative behaviours in children and young people. Low-level disruptive behaviours were identified by 94% per cent of all staff questioned in the 2023 report as having the greatest impact on school ethos and atmosphere. Low-level disruptive behaviours which reflect Motta's (2012) theory emerge as the area to be addressed to improve outcomes for all. If the understanding, through education in nurture principles, is that *all behaviour is communication*, it could be argued that this is the area where further investment in teacher education – for pre-service and in-service teachers – is needed.

Whilst it could be argued that more work is needed, it would not be prudent to say that there has been a lack of development in trauma-informed initiatives. Globally, researchers such as Baker et al. (2016) have considered the sphere of influence from trauma and adverse experiences as a *public health epidemic* and describe the initiatives across multiple systems seeking to implement trauma-informed practices to help address the deep impact across the life span. While these initiatives have addressed the theory and the possible behaviours of those exposed to trauma and a wealth of writing on how schools should become trauma informed exists, a gap in implementation still persists. Baker et al. (2016) implemented a partnership-based approach developing a relevant attitudes measure of operational trauma-informed care (TIC), with a focus on staff working specifically in schools and human service settings. The psychometric evaluative Attitudes Related to Trauma Informed Care (ARTIC) scale targeted the human value of *informed care* in the affiliated settings, within a 7-point subscale to ensure that the central points of attitudes were fully represented. The subscales covered the themes: underlying causes of problematic behaviour and symptoms, responses to behaviours and symptoms, on-the-job behaviour, self-efficacy at work, personal support for TIC and system-wide support for TIC. To supplement the impact of low-level behaviour on daily classroom engagements, the NASUWT *Behaviour in Schools* report, published in September 2023, focused on trying to understand what was happening across schools in the UK in terms of behaviour. The published report indicated that the most common type of behaviour experienced by teacher respondents towards them was back-chat/rudeness (97.47 per cent) and being sworn at (80.61 per cent) (NASUWT, 2023). While these behaviours can be descried as 'low level', the frequency can psychologically be problematic for on-going teacher-pupil relationships. Applying these subscales to the findings from the *Behaviour in Scottish Schools* report, the theme of lack of self-efficacy in approach, conveyed in an additional finding as 'limited confidence in one's own abilities to respond', emerges (Scottish Government, 2023a: 9). The subscale measure of system-wide support, or lack of, is also noted. Relating back to the operational model of Baker et al. (2016), respondents from across educational settings indicated that there was a mismatch between the positive approaches espoused and the daily reality of working and supporting pupils with primary or secondary trauma.

While the attitudes subscale develops a person-centred approach to dealing with exposure to trauma, wider environmental factors must also be evaluated to contextualize responses. Documented by Nickerson et al. (2009) as reciprocal interactions, traumatic events and personal vulnerabilities can be underpinned by an environmental factor, particularly one which is unpredictable. Exacerbating or accelerating all types of behaviours, the Covid-19 pandemic provided an unpredictable landscape which changed personal environments. Reported by practitioners globally, the occasions of distressed behaviours, particularly low-level behaviours, increased significantly in the school setting. Removal of routine, disconnect with peer-groups, loss of access to supportive adults and fear of an inability to cope academically and mentally were present for many learners. Emerging from this unexpected shift in life was the reliance on technology, particularly mobile phones and social media platforms, for young people to engage in some form of communication. For a significant group of young people mobile phones also provided security, particularly if significant people in their lives were isolated or sick during the spread of the virus. However, the lasting impact of this need for security has manifested in mobile phone use as being identified as one of the most significant causes of low-level disruptive behaviour among pupils (Scottish Government, 2023a). Looking at this through the lens of trauma-informed care is this inability to be detached from a device part of rippling trauma, where being online provides security and a familiar environment?

Summary

This chapter explored the link between trauma and distressed behaviour in students, examining how teachers respond and how trauma-informed policies might influence these responses. Teacher responses are analysed through the lens of self-efficacy, emotional responses and causal attributions, highlighting the complexities of teacher identity and well-being. The chapter offers a contrast in approaches to behaviour management in England and Scotland, focusing on the Scottish emphasis on relational practices and trauma-informed care within a nurture-based framework. A perceived increase in disruptive behaviours, especially low-level disruptions, was examined, linking it to potential trauma exposure and the impact of factors like the Covid-19 pandemic. Finally, the chapter discussed the need for further research on the impact of trauma-informed practices on teachers and their daily practice.

9

In Conversation with ...

Part 1 Louise Pressley, Headteacher of Heathryburn Primary School, Scotland

Christine: Why did you agree to be part of this project?

Louise: The children are at the centre of it. I think it's something that we're quite passionate about as a school, making sure that our children feel welcome, that they are the heart of our school community, that they know that they're loved and valued. And it was just an exciting opportunity, to inspire others to have a slightly different look at things through a different lens.

Christine: Tell me what has worked for you.

Louise: I think we've been through such a massive journey, and to ask me what's worked really well, I can't say one thing in isolation. I think the biggest success story has been getting everybody on that same page, getting everybody to understand that behaviour is a communication. And that role in seeking connections with others is key; reframing behaviours, communication and attention seeking to see them as being about connection seeking, and that we're not going to have a one-size-fits-all solution, we're going to have to be adaptive. What will work one week will not work the next. But also, I suppose, giving staff that permission, that autonomy, that freedom and confidence to make decisions that are right for the children at that specific time. I wouldn't say there's one particular strategy, environment or room, but really just having faith in the power of connections and relationships, that they're the core for getting it right for children and young people.

Christine: And how did you manage to get everybody on board with that?

Louise: It took a long time. We started making sure that we had that shared vision – that everybody knew where we were working towards. Starting with the people that it was most difficult to reach, through understanding 'why'. Why were they not on board? Quite often it came from a place of fear, a place of a lack of understanding. So, we made sure that they were informed. We took all the worries and fears; we shared them. We were transparent, and everything was out in the open, but actually, making sure that people in that specific moment were open to learning and ready to learn, and being aware that some of our own staff and some of our own wider community were dealing with their own traumas and weren't in a place where they were ready to manage that and being accepting and understanding of that. Building that relational trust was key.

Christine: Is it as much about supporting the staff on their journey, as it is about putting things in place for the children?

Louise: To begin with, it was more about the staff than the children because the staff had to be in the right place to get the children to the right place. The way we looked at it is that we needed to be swimming instructors rather than lifeguards. That was the mantra that we used for the staff. You have to be in a place where you're ready to be proactive, and if you're not there, if you're constantly like this little duck paddling underwater, then you're not going to be able to be the best version. It was making sure that their well-being was key, that they were listened to, and when we got that right, it then became right for the children and young people.

Christine: Do you think as a country we support our teachers enough?

Louise: No! I think the intent is there. But I think the understanding of what it looks like day to day is different, and I don't think that can be fully understood without being appreciative of unique contexts and settings, because what support looks like for my team will look very different to the school that's just across the road. It's about being courageous as a leader in navigating through all of the information, policy and practice, and making sure that you're still aligned to the national picture. But you're making sure that it's right for your context and for your children.

Christine: What do you think about the term trauma informed?

Louise: It's quite negative. Trauma implies a one-off, a danger, a significant event. It's not necessarily that it can be *an* event; we know it can be a series of events. It's the same as when we speak about 'attention seeking', I prefer 'connection seeking'. So, to me, that narrative needs to be flipped. If we want staff to have a positive response, the way in which we're sharing the narrative needs to be positive. But actually, when you look into attachment theory and all the research, that is what it is. That's what trauma-informed practice is; it's attachment theory. For us, it's just been about making connections with the research and with what's going on.

Christine: What do you think makes a trauma-informed school?

Louise: I would say something like love, acceptance, understanding, unconditional forgiveness, that what happens one day is not forgotten but there's a reset the next day. It's making sure that everybody's got all the information they need; that we're sharing information, making sure that everybody has a voice, everybody matters, everybody's got that someone. One mistake doesn't ruin everything forever; we reset. We fix it and we move forward. And that kind of mantra that you might have to go one step forward and then three steps backwards. But that's okay, because wherever we're going, we're going together as one.

Christine: What made you start to look at things through a different lens?

Louise: If I'm really honest, the school was wild. We knew we weren't getting it right. The children's behaviours were speaking, physical violence, verbal aggression, just children not coping. We knew that we wanted to be self-sufficient. We knew we could outsource. We had other agencies coming in, but that was never going to bring about the change, because our need as a school community was greater. We knew that we were our own biggest resource, and it was very much about us sitting as a team accepting that we were not getting it right. We were driving the ship in the wrong direction. And we basically sat in my office one day and thought, 'What are we missing?', 'Where are we getting it wrong?' And I suppose the minute that we realized that actually they were communicating something through their behaviour, then we unpicked that. We looked at specific children as well. You know, the ones that we called our 'high tariffs'. Where are the commonalities? And actually, what we were finding was that their behaviours were because of their lived experiences and these experiences were making school life hard.

So, when we found that, then we basically realized that we had to find the golden thread. And how can we use it to make that difference? We had that shared vision. We knew what we were working towards. We didn't know what the end product was going to look like, but we knew what we wanted to give these children, and it just kind of grew arms and legs. We started with a really small army. We got a couple of people on board and got buy-in from that. And then when people started to see it making a difference, they were like, 'Oh, I was thinking, I could do this. And could we do this?' And it just kind of sounds really cheesy, but the love just grew. And people just seemed to get on board. It has actually been really interesting to watch over the last couple of years.

Christine: What would you say has been the impact on the pupils?

Louise: It's hard. I think, as a school community, it's just a different place to live and be now. So, the impact is they're safe. They're happy. And they know that they have trusting relationships. We still have real pockets of challenging instances. That also tells us the children feel safe to behave that way in our environment. And they're not hiding it anymore. I think the biggest impact has just been that we understand them. And because we understand them more fully, we can be their voice and advocate. Also, for us, we're able to identify key themes or key triggers ahead of time. Our children are more engaged. They're respectful.

Christine: Have parents commented on this?

Louise: I think their sense of community, their sense of belonging, they know that the door is always open. I think not just the parents have commented but also the local community. I think everybody just knows that it's about transparency; the door is open and if we can help, we will. I think it's important to be able to say, 'I don't know', or 'We're not getting it right'. Having that courage to admit such things, I think, has boded well with quite a lot of parents. 'We're not getting this right. We're not coping at the moment. But that's okay, because we will.' And it's also about not dressing it up with professional talk all the time but keeping it at a non-intimidating level and making sure that they understand that their voice matters, and that, if they're not happy, then we're advocates for them as well. I think those would be the bits that the parents would say have changed.

Christine: What was the role of the virtual school headteacher (VSHT)? How has that had an impact on you?

Louise: I think it is just knowing that there's someone else there to begin with, especially when we're supporting care-experienced pupils. Sometimes there's a disconnect between services. So, knowing that there's a middleman, so to speak, that understands education, but also can be there to draw on other services and support. I think the relationship there has been invaluable. I think we've been proactive in seeking support for those young people that we know need a little bit more. It's beneficial in making sure that we're doing everything by the book, for example, the way in which *The Promise* (Independent Care Review, 2020) has been implemented, and all the different legislation, etc.

Christine: Do you think national policy facilitates a trauma-informed approach?

Louise: I think it likes to think it does. But I think there are some barriers, that comes down to interpretation of policy. And actually, I say again, are you courageous enough to say, 'I know what that says, but this is what's right for us', and to challenge it? But I think it's shifting in the right direction.

Christine: I'm wondering if there's still a fear, that behaviour is worsening.

Louise: I worry that we're at a turning point, but for the wrong reasons, that we run the risk of behaviour being misunderstood. And I think we need to almost compartmentalize that absolutely there are some behaviours that are not okay. But are we really looking deeper through the correct lens to find out 'why'? And are we then making decisions based on that? I worry that we lose focus on the why of the behaviour and then just focus on the behaviours again.

Christine: I wonder if it's about a misunderstanding of a trauma-informed approach.

Louise: Yes, and that was a massive part of our work reframing. We don't have a Behaviour Policy anymore; it's a Relationships Policy, so we reframed that to be about boundaries and expectations as opposed to consequences. So, for our pupils, if they step out with boundary lines, we ask how our approaches help fix and mend those broken boundaries. It's not about being punitive but our pupils still have to be in a place where they're ready to learn and able to understand that. There is still right and wrong. There is still fairness, but it's about how are we navigating that that's different. That's taken a long time within our school community, and I would say there is a small population who still very much expect a punitive approach; if this happens, there should be a consequence. I suppose it's about how you navigate those conversations.

Christine: What barriers do you think we still have to it being embedded across the education system?

Louise: I think probably the financial restraints that come with education are barriers: we have the systems, we have the ideas, we have the structures, and we know what we need to put in place. We don't have the finances that need to come behind it. Although that is a barrier, I won't let it be a barrier in our school community. It's about being creative with what we've got. But I do think that for some communities there will be a struggle with the mindset. Resources are also a challenge. This approach relies so heavily on services working in partnership and not working in isolation, but so many services, for so many reasons, are stretched. Until there's that universal acceptance it is a challenge.

Christine: What's your vision for the future?

Louise: I'm thinking what's next for the ship, what direction is this ship going in? And I suppose for me it's about sustaining it, embedding that culture. I think it is embedded now, but actually I don't want to be taking that for granted because it's still going to need hard work. It's just making sure we are getting it right. As long as the children are happy, when they're coming through in primary one and they're leaving happy and going on to positive destinations. That's the vision for me.

What has been really lovely for us as well is when we speak about what's next. I've got four young people in my school building today who would all be school leavers but are all back, either volunteering or doing some kind of apprenticeship programme. That means that they felt safe and happy. And they want to come back. So, the bit for me around what's next is, how do we build on that? We've got a pupil who is care experienced and due to leave in Primary 7, due to leave this term. And we've planned what we call a backward transition. So, after they move on somewhere, they'll still be back to us one day a week, so they've still got the positive connections with the ones that they've had relationships with here. We've got to just be creative with thinking differently.

Christine: Is there anything else you would like to add?

Louise: Not to underestimate the impact journeys like this can have. It shaped me as a professional. I'm just so proud to be part of such an amazing community and see such amazing young people. And I think if you have high aspirations for them, then they will achieve more. I think that would be fair to say. If you were to ask my whole team in the last ten years, I would hope that that's what they would all say that it does. It just makes you appreciate life differently. It makes you accept people for who they are, but also makes you realize that you're not part of the problem. You're part of the solution. And if you view yourself as that, then it's about flipping that narrative.

Part 2 Stuart Guest, Headteacher of Colebourne Primary School, England

Christine: Tell me why you agreed to be part of this project?

Stuart: I think it's becoming increasingly apparent in schools, and particularly in primary education, that children's needs, and the complexities of those needs, are ever present, and we need to really understand and adapt to meet those needs if children are to be successful; ultimately it is about those children thriving.

Christine: What do you understand by the term trauma informed?

Stuart: I've moved from 'trauma informed' to trauma responsive. I think that's the biggest language change for me; 'trauma informed' is understanding and knowing the impact of trauma on a child, on their behaviour, on their body, on their neural development. But actually, that's only one part. The responsive element of it is, 'What are we going to do now?' What does this mean for us in terms of our practice, our interactions, our policies? Because, once we know all that, then we need to do something, because otherwise it's just knowledge. It doesn't go anywhere, doesn't change things, doesn't help children. For me, it's so much broader. When I first started going out into schools and training, it was very much on attachment and then it moved to attachment and trauma, and then it moved to attachment, trauma and disadvantage, because actually a lot of the things that we see presenting to us in working with children often come from disadvantage, as well as from trauma. It's that connected cycle of approaches. It's not just one thing. The child has got to be centre of that, with all their influences around them; there are all those different influences and what the inter-relational elements of those interactions might be. It's not simple but for me the simple thing that remains is compassion. Do we really want to understand this child, their needs and their circumstances? And do we want to attempt to put things in place that are going to support them to be successful?

Christine: So, it's compassion that comes first?

Stuart: It's CARE: compassionate, ambitious, respectful and engaged. Because that's ultimately what we want.

Christine: Have you been involved in activities which you would consider to be trauma informed?

Stuart: I've been working at the school for twenty years, eighteen years as the headteacher and as soon as we, my wife and I, adopted our children we realized that our typical way of parenting had to change. We had to learn more, through the process of adoption, but also actually having a child there, face to face with you, not responding in ways that you would expect of a typical child. So, you have to adapt approaches. When you start learning about trauma and attachment, then you realize some of the things that you do in a typical school are not great for children who have this background. And then you start to realize, many approaches that we use for children with additional difficulties and challenges are suitable as a universal offer. It's just a nicer way of being. Over the last fifteen years particularly, we've implemented change here at school reflecting that understanding of trauma and adversity, and thinking about how our procedures and policies can be nicer, kinder and not re-traumatize?

Christine: How do you see the role of the VSHT?

Stuart: I think it's a critical role, because they have the power to communicate with schools and put across the importance and understanding of why these children might have difficulties, and help schools understand the needs and challenges they have; and also, to educate the workforce. By educating the workforce, you can build compassion and understanding, and therefore when introducing trauma-informed approaches, there are more likely to be understood and implemented by staff. We know we want to do things to improve the lives of these children, but schools may need help to understand what to do. So, I think it's always about trying to understand these children, what they've experienced, build compassion and then develop provision from there. The virtual school have a lot to do, but there's a lot of success, particularly within England. When you look back to some of the exclusions data. The rate of permanent exclusions for care-experienced children is broadly the same as other children. Unfortunately, we do have the suspensions that for care-experienced children are significantly higher than all other children. So, there's still work to do on that. Schools are under a lot of pressure. To get things right and there are funding challenges. I think the education system needs quite a big overhaul.

Christine: How do you think pupils would describe a trauma-informed approach in your school?

Stuart: I don't think they would describe it as a trauma-informed approach. I think they would describe that they are cared for, listened to, respected, that they have a voice and that when they have difficulties there are people they can go to and support they can get.

Christine: Do you have any kind of key person system in place?

Stuart: We have a lot of systems in place. We've invested heavily in our pastoral and additional needs teams. We've got senior learning mentors. We've got other learning mentors dotted about as well. We've got a pastoral team, a SEND (Special Education Needs and Disabilities) team. We know that a lot of children with trauma, attachment and disadvantage in the background will often have additional needs as well. It really overlaps so we invest heavily in that big team. We also have things like a family support worker. It's just developing a culture of care and putting money into that.

Christine: And how have parents responded to that?

Stuart: Very, very well. We've got an exceptionally high satisfaction rate as a school, much higher than the national rates. We're one of the most popular schools in the area where other schools have got falling numbers; we are constantly oversubscribed. We've got a good reputation because we care. And we're nice and friendly. But we do drive standards. We do want our children to succeed but we do it in a way that they want to come to school because it's fun.

Christine: Have you managed to take your staff along with you?

Stuart: In the beginning, definitely a challenge, because fifteen to sixteen years ago, when this was started from a parenting point of view, you go with what you know. We were brought up in a Super Nanny era. You had people when I first started as a head who were of that mindset. 'No, children should just do that', 'They shouldn't be ... ', 'They shouldn't talk to me like that', and 'That's not acceptable'. That type of thing. Through training and building the understanding of why a child might react that way we show it's not personal. This is about their needs and what they're trying to communicate. And this is what you need to do to help support this. And this is what we will do from a senior leadership point to support you. We're not trying to leave you to it, there's backup here. Almost all of the people got on board with that. And you see the light-bulb moments. 'Oh, that's why they do that.' There were some that didn't get it. And they naturally moved on. But ever since then, when we've been doing these approaches, my recruitment process includes trying to identify the people that get it. Or have the capacity to get it. They might not have the knowledge yet, but they've certainly got that inside care and desire to do the best things for children, and I only then employ people that meet that type of profile. Often when I do training in schools, you see the colour drain from some people, who go, 'I've been doing this wrong'; 'I can see why it's not worked'. I always say to people, you have just got to forgive yourself. You can't hold on to that. You were doing things with a knowledge you had at the time, with the best interests of the children. Now you know differently. Now you may change.

Christine: Have you put anything in place for your staff?

Stuart: Absolutely. I mean all this idea of care; it's not just about the children; it's about the families and the staff. Then the biggest resource you have in a school are you or your staff. So, there's a couple of key things that we do. We ensure that we have as many support staff as possible and that is not common now. We prioritize. We also have massive well-being systems for our staff, twenty-four-hour doctor helpline that they can get prescriptions from. They can have free sessions at slimming world. They can access an online gym coach that we pay for because we know when the staff are okay; it's easier to be compassionate in a classroom when you are regulated yourself. But we also have professional supervision as well. Once a month we do have a supervision person come in, completely independent, an external professional who does supervision with staff that want it.

Christine: And are you seeing the impact of that?

Stuart: Massive impact. The general overall absence rate for our school is low. Teachers are generally happy within the scope of the profession which is really challenging. I've got massive retention of staff. I've got staff that been with me for many, many years. There are lots of knock-ons to a trauma-responsive approach in terms of your wider school ethos, your staffing, your budget.

Christine: To what extent do you think national policy in England facilitates that kind of approach?

Stuart: I think it's changing but I still think there's conflict. Unfortunately, you've got the behaviourist approaches, and then you've got the trauma-informed approaches, and it feels like these people are battling against each other, and it doesn't need to be a battle. Yes, you need strong routines, that's a given for being trauma responsive. It's different for each child, responses can be different based on their circumstances and their needs. It doesn't mean it's right what they may have done. But how you deal with it; you need to take into consideration the wider implications.

Christine: Do you think there's a misunderstanding of what trauma informed is?

Stuart: I think there is a lot of confusion. There are still the people that are making certain decisions that don't have a full understanding yet, and that is a risk. There's a risk there that the wrong messages are then given to schools on the approaches that they should take.

Christine: In the Scottish media, there's a big focus on how 'terrible' behaviour in schools is right now, and what are we doing about it?

Stuart: And that's my problem. Why is behaviour in schools a problem? That clamp down on it instantly goes to blame children, not blame the system. I'm not saying blame teachers or blame the schools; I'm saying blame the system. Is the system set up now for the complexity of needs that we're getting? We're talking changes in lifestyle, in technology, in access to early support and clubs and sports; all of these things, environmentally, will impact on how children present in school. So, I think it's all too easy to go, 'a child must behave'. But what do these children need? What does a school need to look like for these children? We're not pandering but if these children are not coping in a mainstream, typical secondary or primary school, why? What could it look like with the right support, the right funding, the right provision?

Christine: Do you think there's been a difference post Covid-19?

Stuart: Absolutely. We've seen a significant increase in speech and language issues, significant increase in general self-regulation and emotional skills. And it's ongoing. What's really interesting for me is a lot of families tell us that actually during the pandemic, during lockdown, actually, some of those children really thrived. Because the pressure of the school system for those children, it's really hard. A lot of them are masking during the day and just coping and then exploding when they get home. For the majority of children, schooling is okay. It works. But there's an increasing gap, there's a larger population of children where it's not quite fitting now. We're seeing it more and more. And we're seeing the mental health crisis in children.

Christine: So, what do you think still needs to be done?

Stuart: I think schools need to ensure as much as possible that each school has a variety of approaches for different children. So, children don't have to go from that school to a different school or an alternative provision. There's nurture, or there's a different pathway for those children. But that's also then accepted, acknowledged, respected and seen as a pro, not an against, when it comes to your results, when it comes to Ofsted. Rather than us having to argue, 'Well, this is why we're doing it'. That it's seen automatically as good practice. The children that are not attending school are the ones that are so distressed and there's so much anxiety that they can't attend school. It's completely missing the point, and therefore why are our school systems causing such anxiety? I'm not saying schools cause anxiety. I'm saying that for some children, the way the school's run doesn't necessarily meet their needs, but it's so much more complex.

Christine: What's your vision for the future?

Stuart: My vision is that anyone coming into the teaching profession has a really developed deep understanding of children's needs because they're so vast when it comes to trauma, attachment, autism. All the different special needs. We need to really understand them so that we can then meet those in the classrooms. We need to equip teachers with a set of tools, a toolbox of approaches that are recognized through research as the good ways to do it. So, if a child shouts at you, instead of your response being, 'Don't shout at me like that'; 'Who do you think you're talking to?', 'That's so disrespectful', there are scripts that we can all hold on to like, 'Wow! I can see this is really tricky for you. I know something is going on. I'm here to listen. Talk to me calmly. I will listen.' And we need to make sure that all of our teachers coming into the profession are equipped for what they're going to face and how to respond and have had time to practise it. My hope is that it becomes a general approach to being, so that that feeds through to parents who are struggling.

Section III

Responding to Trauma

10

A Trauma-Informed School System

Mike Carroll

Key ideas

This chapter will:

- outline some key principles underpinning the trauma-informed school,
- examine Australia's National Guidelines for Trauma-Aware Education, and
- outline some aspects of a Multi-Tiered System of Support (MTSS).

Introduction

Schools find themselves dealing with the negative impact of trauma on a daily basis as they are confronted with students failing to achieve their potential, a range of behavioural issues, reduced educational aspirations and ultimately a flight from schooling. Thus, students who have experienced trauma tend to place demands on the school system which, if not properly addressed, are likely to have deleterious long-term consequences as educational failure is likely to lead to diminished employment prospects and lower economic productivity (Monnat and Chandler, 2015: 726). In addition, research suggests that health care expenditures are likely to increase as experiences of adversity have been shown to be associated with unhealthy lifestyles (Shonkoff and Garner, 2012: 238).

Research suggests that there are tangible benefits associated with effective early childhood interventions that are then sustained throughout students' educational experiences (Shonkoff and Garner, 2012: 238). Unfortunately research evidence across the range of educational provision tends to be skewed towards elementary and secondary schooling (Zakszeski et al., 2017) giving us a limited overview of the potential impact of a trauma-informed approach (TIA) if adopted across a joined up educational system. This chapter suggests that if schools become trauma informed, this will enable them to meet the needs of students who experience trauma; in the longer term this can be seen as a 'preventative-spend approach' (NHS, 2018: 7).

Within the UK, trauma-informed care (TIC) has started to permeate thinking in mental health services, children's social care, residential care, police and prison services, care and justice services with a view to improve service quality. Implementation has been somewhat piecemeal with nation-wide strategies to promote joined up thinking in the devolved UK administrations only beginning to emerge. This chapter will take TIC to mean that

> all parties involved recognise and respond to the impact of traumatic stress on those who have contact with the system including children, caregivers, and service providers. Programs and agencies within such a system infuse and sustain trauma awareness, knowledge, and skills into their organisational cultures, practices, and policies. They act in collaboration with all those who are involved with the child, using the best available science, to maximise physical and psychological safety, facilitate the recovery of the child and family, and support their ability to thrive.
>
> (NCTSN, 2017: 2)

Principles Underpinning the Trauma-Informed School

In the United States the Substance Abuse and Mental Health Services Administration (SAMHSA) (2014) has set out four key elements that a school should incorporate into their organizational structure as part of developing a TIA. These elements are often termed the *4 Rs* (see Chapter 2):

- realizes the widespread impact of trauma and possible pathways to recovery;
- recognizes signs and symptoms of trauma in everyone connected with the organization;
- responds by integrating knowledge about trauma into all facets of the school; and
- resists re-traumatization by implementing trauma-informed policies, procedures and practices (NCTSN, 2017: 4).

To be fully effective these four elements should permeate all aspects of an educational system, rather than just a single school, so providing a continuous and consistent response to trauma (Conners Edge et al., 2024). That an understanding of trauma should permeate all aspects of an educational system does not mean that all practitioners within that system should have expertise, let alone provide trauma-specific interventions or therapies (Quadara and Hunter, 2016: 19). A central feature of the trauma-informed school (TIS) is that it engages in multi-agency collaboration with trauma-specific services who are able to provide trauma-specific interventions to meet the needs of students requiring support.

To become a TIS it is necessary to embark upon a journey of organizational change that will involve four stages: trauma-aware, trauma-sensitive, trauma-responsive and finally trauma-informed (Carter and Blanch, 2019). This describes a continuum of implementation, a process of change that represents a 'profound paradigm shift in knowledge, perspective, attitudes and skills that continues to deepen and unfold over time' (MDMHP, 2014: n.p.). Implementing a new initiative in schools is often problematic as there is often a lack of funding, a lack of time, a lack of knowledge and understanding as well as a reluctance amongst practitioners to *buy-in* to the new practice. Encouraging *buy-in* can be particularly troublesome as new initiatives often involve cultural change that challenges ingrained ways of thinking and working. Implementing trauma-informed practice in schools, such that it permeates the structures and culture of the school as well as the school's relationship with child-support agencies, is particularly challenging as the goal is to develop a fully inclusive practice that supports all students, staff and caregivers to respond to differing experiences of trauma (Howard, 2019). Taking time to ensure that the process of implementation is carried out thoroughly is crucial as there is an inherent danger that 'incomplete or ineffective implementation of trauma-informed approaches may be as bad as – or worse than – the status quo, since institutional betrayal can exacerbate the symptoms of preexisting trauma' (Carter and Blanch, 2019: 52). On a more positive note, many schools may well have already adopted initiatives that are a good fit with a TIA, for example, positive behaviour interventions and supports (PBIS), social emotional learning (SEL), restorative practices and mindfulness. These initiatives place learners at the centre of practice providing them with personal, social and emotional support, and a sense of connection and belonging as well as assisting their learning and providing support for trauma-exposed students (Thomas et al., 2019: 445).

Thinking Point 10.1

a. Reflect on your organization's position with respect to the 4Rs. Where do you see strengths and areas for development?
b. Identify initiatives that your organization already has in place that would be a good fit for a trauma-informed approach.

Unfortunately, the literature provides little by way of insight as to what each of these stages of organizational change looks like; indeed, there is no 'prescriptive roadmap for a one-size-fits-all approach' (NCTSN, 2017: 4). To facilitate progress towards becoming trauma informed, it becomes necessary to determine how thinking and understanding of these various stages is evolving in other educational jurisdictions

(Thomas et al., 2019). Becoming a TIS will require intentional leadership to bring about change in all facets of the organization: teaching and learning, flexible learning landscapes, interpersonal relationships, social, emotional and physical safety, maintaining positive relationships, community partnerships and the institutional environment, as well as connectedness between policy, procedures and practice (Lipscomb et al., 2024). To support systems-level change a collaborative endeavour between Queensland University of Technology and the Australian Childhood Foundation led to the development of *National Guidelines for Trauma-Aware Education* (NGfTAE) (Howard, 2021; Howard et al., 2022). These guidelines were developed for individual schools as well as for education systems. The guidelines provide a useful framework for the development of policy and practice linked to effective trauma-aware approaches. Contextual responsiveness underpins this process so no two school sites will implement the framework in exactly the same way; however, for progress to be possible all sites, through active, intentional leadership, will be required to develop collaborative working between educators, students and the wider community (e.g. caregivers, child-support agencies, health providers, etc.) (Phifer and Hull, 2016).

Several themes emerge from the guidelines which include the importance of professional development – knowledge and understanding of the signs and symptoms of trauma as well as how to respond – particularly with respect to school leaders (Wassink-de Stigter et al., 2022). Intentional leadership is critical in driving the process of implementation and engaging stakeholders (e.g. caregivers, child-support agencies, etc.). Inclusive practice is another theme, that is, developing teaching and learning, and disciplinary practice (e.g. anti-bullying, PBIS, restorative justice, etc.) that are responsive to all students, particularly those who may have experienced trauma. Creating a safe, structured and predictable learning landscape is more likely to reduce the risk of additional and unnecessary trauma (NCTSN, 2017) as these landscapes can help nurture regulatory capabilities for trauma-affected students. Creating a safe and nurturing space in which positive relationships are valued and can thrive and enabling all involved with the school to feel a sense of connectedness and belonging are critical components of the guidelines. Empowerment is a particularly important theme, with students given a sense of agency in how trauma-informed practice develops, as trauma-experienced students often 'experience trauma in situations of unequal power, whether interpersonal or institutional' (Carter and Blanch, 2019: 54). Providing students with a sense of agency will, for some practitioners, directly challenge ingrained ways of thinking and working in terms of relationships based upon unequal distribution of power; consequently, leadership is crucial here to 'avoid institutional betrayal and retraumatization' (Carter and Blanch, 2019: 54). A sense of agency can be promoted through student brainstorming activities, perhaps at the beginning of an academic session or unit of work, focused on exploring reasons for heightened arousal (e.g. when, where, how, why) as well as looking at steps that can be taken to de-escalate. The outcomes of such brainstorming activities can then be used to assist the teacher and student design individualized safety plans to facilitate de-escalation (Brunzell et al., 2016). The emerging understanding of trauma-informed practice should be incorporated into a school's policies and procedures such that these become *lived documents* as they describe what actually happens in the school on a day-to-day basis; policy rhetoric corresponds to the actuality of practice. The guidelines also acknowledge that responding to students' traumatic experiences comes with a cost to practitioners in that they can experience secondary or vicarious trauma, particularly given that they often have limited scope to change the students' circumstances (Thomas et al., 2019). As part of ensuring practitioners' well-being, it is essential that schools encourage practitioners to reflect on their experiences through participating in peer-support meetings with the purpose of preventing secondary trauma. Such meetings provide an opportunity to remind practitioners that a TIA is a 'process and not a product' (Thomas et al., 2019: 428) within which they play an integral part. The final element of the guidelines is to encourage ongoing and honest self-reflection on all aspects of policy and practice related to the school's TIA (Conners Edge et al., 2024).

Thinking Point 10.2

Create a mind map highlighting steps that your organization could take to move forward from its present position towards becoming trauma informed.

Multi-Tiered System of Support (MTSS)

In meeting the needs of all students, many of whom have experienced complex trauma, policies and practice should envision a multi-tiered approach with the level of support increasing across the tiers. According to Champine et al. (2022: 467) a trauma-informed school (TIS) actively promotes the development of skills to respond more effectively to those who have experienced trauma by offering a continuum of support. Within a TIS it is possible for healing and growth to be simultaneous processes (Keyes, 2002). To achieve this a TIS seeks to provide training, resources and solution-focused interventions to meet the needs of students who have been exposed to trauma. A Multi-Tiered System of Support (MTSS)

(Garcia et al., 2023: 2) is a structured approach to addressing trauma that recognizes that many students will be affected by trauma to differing degrees of severity and duration often compounded by an absence of interpersonal supports that otherwise would help them navigate the traumatic event(s). In a multi-tiered approach, there are three interrelated levels of intervention: low-intensity, intermediate-intensity and high-intensity (Zakszeski et al., 2017: 318).

Scotland's Additional Support for Learning (Scotland) Acts 2004 and 2009 provide a legal framework for the identification, support and review of the Additional Support Needs (ASN) of students who experience barriers to learning. Education authorities have developed a staged-intervention approach to meet their legislative duties. This approach sits within a vision of a professional learning framework for a trauma-informed and responsive workforce (see Chapter 15). The staged intervention approach (see Figure 10.1) consists of the following:

- **Stage 1** – (Support for All) support provided by everyone who works with students (e.g. classroom teacher, support staff in schools, etc.) with no or *mild* adverse circumstances. This utilizes internal school resources.
- **Stage 2** – (Early intervention) more specialist support provided by those who have direct and/or substantial contact with students who may be experiencing *mild-to-moderate* adverse circumstances (e.g. pastoral care teacher as key point of contact with other agencies, support for learning teacher, home-school link worker, etc.). This utilizes internal school resources and some external community services.
- **Stage 3** – (Additional Support) support provided by those who provide specific evidence-based supports or interventions, under clinical supervision and/or who direct or manage services (e.g. school leadership team, school nurse, educational psychologist, social work, etc.). This utilizes external community services, often linked with a cluster of schools, who will engage in collaborative dialogue with individual schools focused on meeting moderate to severe adverse circumstances.
- **Stage 4** – (Specialist Support) support provided by those who, by virtue of their specialist training, are directly involved in delivering one-to-one clinical interventions, and evidence-based psychological interventions or therapies (e.g. medical practitioners, Child and Adolescent Mental Health Services (CAMHS), etc.). Specialist staff take a lead role in offering consultation, coaching and supervision to others involved in meeting the disparate needs of students experiencing severe adverse circumstances (NES, 2021: 14).

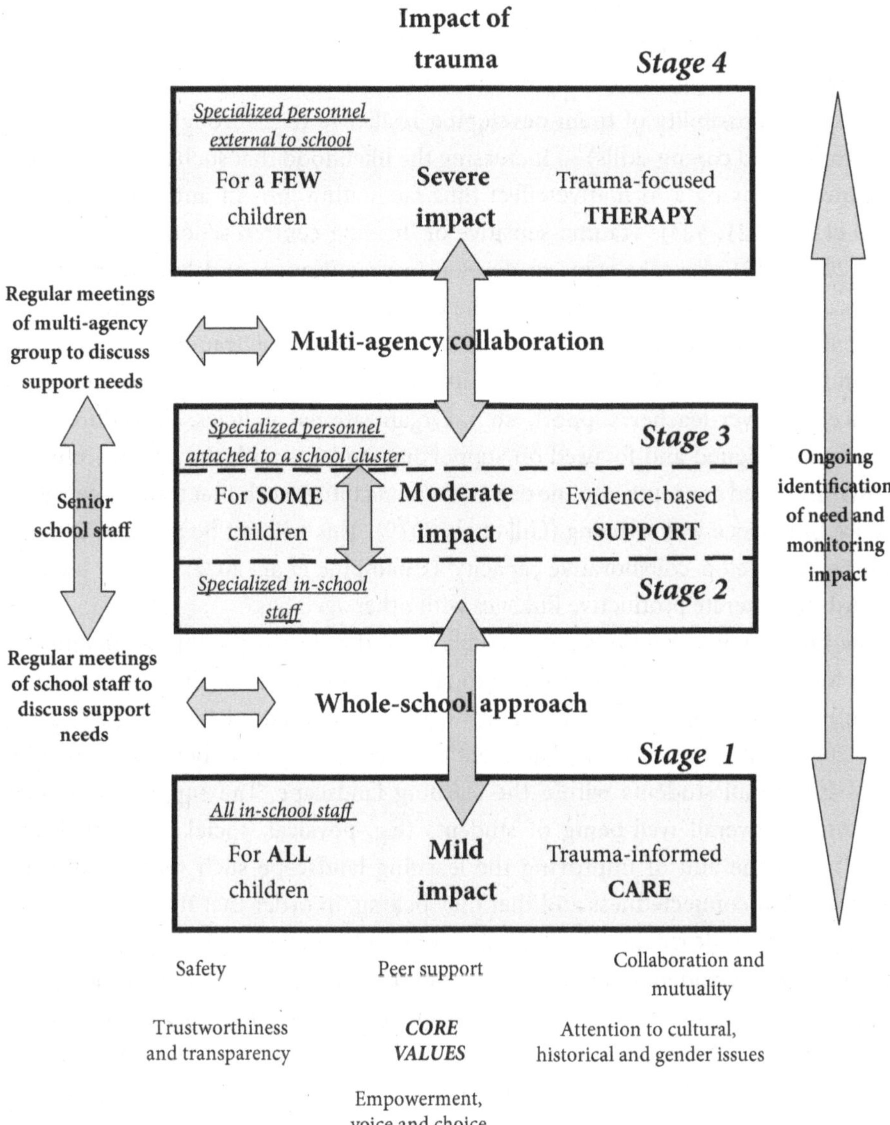

Figure 10.1 Staged intervention: A multi-tiered system of support.

Trauma-Informed Care

Universal or low-intensity trauma-focused interventions (Zakszeski et al., 2017) focus on developing trauma-sensitive relationships as these are seen as being crucial in terms of how we prevent any given traumatic experience or set of experiences from becoming debilitating. Low-intensity interventions can be proactive by adopting a preventative approach that anticipates and seeks to reduce the possibility of distress/

harm arising from a traumatic event(s) (e.g. anti-bullying programmes, promoting physical activity, restorative practice linked to discipline, etc.) (Matlin et al., 2019). Providing students with safe, stable and nurturing relationships with adult caregivers improves the possibility of them developing resilience (e.g. through instruction in classroom-based coping skills) so increasing the likelihood that such experiences are re-framed as having a formative effect thus facilitating growth and future success (Sonu et al., 2021: 523). Trauma-sensitive or 'healing-centred schools' (Chafouleas et al., 2021: 218) also take steps to develop in practitioners and key stakeholders, such as caregivers, an understanding of the impact of trauma, as well as a heightened sensitivity in recognizing the indicators and symptoms of trauma (e.g. through staff and caregiver workshops on adversity, strengthening home-school linkage to enhance caregiver-teacher support, etc.). Organizational policies, procedures and practices are aligned and focused on supporting students with the goal of infusing trauma-informed concepts into the organizational culture such that trauma-sensitive practice becomes a way of being (Gill et al., 2019). This will not be possible without the drive to develop 'collaborative capacity' (Champine et al., 2022: 470) by looking outwards to generate productive linkages with other agencies.

Low-intensity interventions are available to all the students within an institution with a focus on creating a positive relational space aimed at enabling recovery and preventing traumatization or re-traumatization becoming debilitating (Higgins et al., 2022: 208). Low-intensity interventions involve supports being provided by school staff to all students within the learning landscape. The supports provided focus on the overall well-being of students (e.g. physical, social, emotional and mental) with the aim of improving the learning landscape such that all students have a sense of connectedness and that they belong, in order that they may achieve their potential as learners. The school is often the most stable and predictable environment in a student's life as distinct from their unstructured, often chaotic and stressful existence beyond the school; consequently, the school has the potential to be a healing environment (Stokes and Brunzell, 2019). Structure, consistency and predictable classroom routines are important features of a trauma-informed school environment. It becomes important to involve students when changes to these routines are perceived as necessary so that they have a sense of control (Chudzik et al., 2025). In addition, allowing time for transition to modified routines is critical so that students can re-adjust to change so helping to re-assure them that change will not be a source of increased anxiety (Giboney Wall, 2021).

Learning Environments

There are a variety of approaches to teaching and learning that assist in developing regulatory capacities within students, especially trauma-experienced students. These approaches could include the following:

- Decompression (check-in) activities at the beginning of lessons attending to how students feel rather than what they know. These activities, which initially address students' feelings, contribute to building strong classroom relationships. These activities also alert teachers to whether individual students are about to begin lessons with a heightened state of arousal that needs to be addressed otherwise this will act as a barrier to learning. Awareness of an increased arousal state will enable the teacher to step-to-the-side of the student and to proactively engage in taking steps towards de-escalation. Interventions aimed at de-escalation set within the context of a calm, routine and predictable classroom environment along with genuine relational attachment are more likely to enable the student to regulate their emotional state. In addition, such activities allow students a period of transition to learning so that the time they devote to scanning for signs of danger (Giboney Wall, 2021) does not clash with the time they need to pay attention to the instructional set.
- Planned periodic pausing of instruction – providing brain breaks – utilizing mindfulness techniques such as breathing exercises or physical movement exercises can facilitate opportunities for respite from the pressure of academic performance. Periodic pausing also allows for decompression by providing students with an opportunity to physically regulate as well as focus on their affective state. In addition, these activities can sensitize teachers to heightened states of arousal which may require individualized interventions to facilitate de-escalation. Decompression activities can form part of lesson planning as well as being called upon when teachers detect that students are displaying decreased capacity for effective learning (Brunzell et al., 2016: 262).
- Students' traffic lighting (Green – good to go; Amber – need to slow down/ pause; Red – need to stop) their readiness for learning during the course of a lesson will allow them to express their affective – arousal – state and assist the teacher to determine whether there is a need for a brain break activity or, in dialogue with the student, the enactment of an individualized intervention to facilitate de-escalation.
- The instructional set could include in-built support by breaking down tasks into a series of sequential micro-goals in the hope that progressive achievement of linked micro-goals will raise self-esteem and spur students onto further achievement.
- Setting cognitive goals within a co-operative learning frame could enhance the development of positive attitudes such as encouraging 'sharing, taking turns, cooperating, considering others' needs, expressing gratitude, or considerately managing conflict' (Jensen, 2000, cited in Giboney Wall, 2021: 126). These are transferable life skills that will help students navigate social environments.

- Utilizing varied teaching methods and providing opportunities for choice are more likely to accommodate the learning needs of trauma-experienced students (Crosby, 2015; Chudzik et al., 2025), particularly when the classroom forms only one part of a more flexible understanding of learning landscapes.
- Flexible learning landscapes could include *sensory spaces* and/or *safe spaces* for trauma-experienced students to use within classrooms as well as elsewhere in the school. These spaces linked to individualized safety-plans, co-created with the student, will help assist the process of de-escalation (Brunzell et al., 2016).
- Providing real-time feedback (feedforward) on their progress will enable students to feel secure in their learning as they will be able to understand what they are doing well and what they need to do to improve (e.g. knowing when to ask for help, using an alternative strategy or resources, etc.) whilst engaged in the process of learning (Burns et al., 2019).
- Providing opportunities for deliberative practice to facilitate consolidation of learning as this is likely to reduce any anxiety associated with rushing through curricular content.
- Opportunities for formative assessment during and at the end of lessons may help students develop a stronger understanding of their own strengths and areas for development and encourage them take greater responsibility for their own learning (Black and Wiliam, 2018).
- Periodic production of escalation maps, as a form of formative assessment, will allow students to identify moments during a lesson or in their school day when they feel heightened arousal and/or periods of calm. These maps can help inform future teacher curricular planning focused on retaining optimal states for learning (Brunzell et al., 2016).

Evidence-Based Support

Intermediate-intensity interventions, often linked to more complex and prolonged experience of trauma, are required when some, but not all, students have been affected by traumatic experiences that are hindering their development. These intermediate-intensity interventions seek to address trauma symptoms, or other responses, individual students and groups have after they have experienced exposure to trauma. Skill-building workshops in schools (e.g. PATHS and Social and Emotional Learning (Barnardo's, 2020); Personal, Social, Health and Economic Education (PSHE Association, 2022), etc.) delivered by educational practitioners are examples of targeted interventions aimed at developing life skills to help promote resilience. Another example is psychoeducation interventions (e.g. anxiety, depression, PTSD, etc.) that are often delivered by educational psychologists or qualified health educators working within educational authorities often as time-constrained inputs and/or in group settings (Sharkey et al., 2024).

As the complexity of needs increases this progressively requires collaboration between teachers and specialist personnel working in the school and the wider educational system (e.g. Additional Support for Learning staff, Pastoral Care staff, school counsellors, educational psychologists, home-school link workers, social workers, etc.). Traumatized students are often unable to control or regulate their emotional responses which results in them becoming disengaged with learning through externalized (e.g. confrontational) or internalized (compliant, withdrawn, subdued) behaviours, both of which result in poor social, academic and emotional outcomes (Avery et al., 2022). Pastoral care teams and school counsellors have a degree of specialized knowledge and expertise that makes them best placed, following professional dialogue with classroom colleagues, to support those students whose experience of trauma is compromising their academic, emotional and social progress (Howard et al., 2022). Senior pastoral care staff take responsibility for creating a 'Culture of Care' (Lipscomb et al., 2024: 653) which seeks to integrate a variety of approaches to help support those with experience of trauma, including programmes of social and emotional learning (SEL). Senior pastoral care staff have a significant coordinating role – internally and externally – in ensuring that SEL plays an important role in a school's trauma-informed approach. SEL involves students acquiring skills, knowledge and attitudes that will help them understand and manage their emotions, develop and maintain positive relationships which includes developing skills in conflict management, as well as setting and working towards achieving positive goals as part of responsible decision making (Barnardo's, 2020). One example is the *PATHS® Programme* in the UK which supports schools who are incorporating a trauma-informed approach by providing resources, training and ongoing support (Barnardo's, 2020). Emotion coaching, based on the work of John Gottman (Gus et al., 2015), and the use of *PACE* (Playfulness, Acceptance, Curiosity and Empathy) (Golding et al., 2021) comprise other approaches which seek to help pupils identify, understand and manage their emotions.

Thinking Point 10.3

a. Engage in a confidential discussion with a member of the Pastoral Care and/or Support for Learning team(s) to ascertain the different forms of support available to students with experience of trauma and how these fit within the tiered approach described in Figure 10.1.
b. As part of this discussion determine how this support is identified and implemented.

Trauma-Focused Therapy

High-intensity interventions are required for those students for whom the impact of trauma is so severe that they require individualized help from specialist trauma therapists and trauma-specific services (SAMHSA, 2014). For example, the programmes of support such as play or art therapy, dyadic developmental psychotherapy or trauma-focused Cognitive Behavioural Therapy (DeCandia et al., 2014) are all examples of high-intensity interventions. For some students specialized clinical care is the most suitable way to 'contextualize an individual's choices and circumstances in terms of the experiences they have had, and to respond with solutions that are compassionate and humane' (Danielson and Saxen, 2019: 5).

For those students who are the most traumatized by their experiences it becomes necessary to facilitate access to more intensive interventions for which the school does not have the necessary expertise. The starting point for this consists of a combination of gathering and evaluating evidence that points to a student's social, emotional and academic progress being stymied by exposure to traumatic experiences. Part of this evidence building will involve engaging sensitively in trauma-informed conversations. These conversations are not necessarily aimed at ascertaining details of the trauma; it is for the student and/or caregiver to determine whether this is something that they wish to disclose (Higgins et al., 2022). Rather, these conversations provide the student/caregiver an opportunity to articulate how they perceive their social, emotional and academic development is being impeded as a result of exposure to traumatic experiences. The outcomes sought from gathering and analysing the available evidence include: (1) finding ways to limit exposure to adverse experiences; (2) supporting the development of coping strategies, (3) assisting students in making tangible progress with positive social, emotional and academic outcomes; and (4) seeking ways prevent future exposure to traumatic experiences (Zakszeski et al., 2017). To access the necessary support, senior staff engage in multi-agency collaboration to draw on support from external professionals (e.g. healthcare services, social work services, CAMHS, etc.) (Phifer and Hull, 2016).

In order to facilitate access to clinical care, senior school staff require knowledge and understanding of how to navigate mental health service provision, including screening and referral procedures (Garcia et al., 2023: 6). One of the ways by which senior school staff acquire this knowledge and understanding is through participation in multi-agency collaboration. Trauma-focused therapies identified, through multi-agency working, may involve some students being *targeted* for intensive one-to-one support out with the school setting which can compromise their sense of connectivity with their wider peer group. It is important that schools maintain a trauma-sensitive focus on these students so that they do not inadvertently re-traumatize them by *emphasizing difference.*

Summary

There is a growing body of research that indicates that the impact of trauma may be lessened by trauma-informed approaches, particularly in the educational sector (Matlin et al., 2019). Unfortunately, there is no easy or quick path to assist schools seeking to engage in organizational change towards becoming trauma informed. A key component that appears to help a school on its journey to become trauma-informed is professional development designed to support practitioners in becoming aware of and acknowledging the impact of trauma as well as recognizing the signs and symptoms of trauma in students. In addition, the trauma-informed school is outward looking seeking assistance through multi-agency collaboration in order to meet the disparate needs of students. A trauma-informed school provides a tiered system of support by integrating a variety of whole-school, trauma-informed approaches with the aim that all students are supported whilst being treated with compassion and understanding (Overstreet and Chafouleas, 2016).

11

Approaches to Behaviour

Tracey Stewart and Mary Wingrave

Key Ideas

This chapter will:

- examine theories of behaviour,
- look at theory in practice, and
- examine relational approaches.

Introduction

This chapter explores behaviourist and relational approaches to behaviour which, on first examination, seem to be theoretically in opposition but which we would suggest are symbiotic. We first examine theories of behaviour and outline their overarching assumptions. We then outline critiques of these approaches in terms of the trauma-experienced child.

Whilst the behaviourist practice of sanctions, time-out and humiliation are now seen as outdated and ineffective in the long term, it could be argued, with supports in place, that there is still a place in today's classroom for behavioural approaches such as the use of praise, in-the-moment recognition and socialization. In this chapter we seek to highlight the move away from the *management* of behaviour to *understanding* behaviour, towards an appreciation that practitioners need to be better equipped to respond to children's needs, rather than simply reacting to their behaviour. The aim would be to see children as *attachment needing* not *attention seeking*. This will be followed by consideration of relational approaches which stress the importance of understanding each child. We hope to show the necessity of building relationships to better understand and support individualized interventions to facilitate self- and co-regulation for each learner, consequently boosting learners' self-esteem and their identity as valued members of the school.

The effects of trauma on a child can severely impair their ability to self-regulate and sustain healthy relationships (Brunzell et al., 2015). There can also be long-term physiological effects of toxic stress and children may be constantly fluctuating between states of hyperarousal and hypoarousal (Schore and Schore, 2008; Conkbayir, 2023). Trauma can manifest itself differently in how a trauma-experienced child may behave, as such trauma should be considered an additional support need. McKee and Breslin (2023) highlight that we need to understand what has happened to children and respond with interventions which support self- and co-regulation. Consistency of adult behaviour is seen as the cornerstone of relational approaches (Dix, 2017). Relational approaches will be developed later as we consider how they can be used to provide a supportive environment for all.

Perspectives on Behaviour

Understanding theory supports the implementation of practice. Applying theory to practice, and justifying the approaches used, is the aim of the tables below. We have utilized an early-level setting; however, the discussion is applicable at any level throughout the school life of a child. Within each theoretical overlay, we give an assumption of previous understandings and critique these in relation to supporting the trauma-experienced child.

The *Behaviour in Scottish Schools 2023* (Scottish Government, 2023a) report highlights that while staff in Scottish schools experience a wide range of positive behaviour, there are significant reports of *low-level 'disruptive' behaviour*. There has been a perceived decline in pupil behaviour since 2016 with school staff reporting decreases in positive behaviours and increases in 'negative' behaviours (Scottish Government, 2023a). Implicit in this analysis is that children should leave their *emotional baggage* at the school gate and be ready to learn. The focus here is on low-level disruptive behaviour and the example used to illustrate practice is of a six-year-old child who refuses to sit on the mat with their peers at story time. The tables demonstrate how each perspective may be adopted in practice, to further highlight alternate ways of considering behaviour.

Thinking Point 11.1

How often do you reflect on the approaches you use and how often do you observe outcomes/impact before changing tack?

Behaviourist Approach

A practitioner utilizing a behaviourist approach may begin by rewarding the child for sitting on the mat with a smiley face sticker, a smile or the invitation to go first for snack after the story. The assumption is that the child learns that by adopting the preferred behaviour – of the adult – they will enjoy being in the class and derive pleasure from successfully achieving the 'prize': 'Do this and you'll get that' (Kohn, 2018: 4). However, an approach based on providing extrinsic rewards linked to observable behaviours provides no insights as to the inner life of the child. Furthermore, the trauma-experienced child is unlikely to behave in line with the expectations of others as their early development has resulted in coping strategies focused on survival in unsafe environments. Arguably an approach based on extrinsic rewards and/or the withdrawal of 'privileges', such as 'golden time', is unlikely to promote the development of intrinsic motivation (Kohn, 2018). The idea that children can be empowered by having a choice is also called into question as arguably this approach seeks to exert pressure to ensure compliance and control over the children's behaviour (see Table 11.1). As has been discussed in Chapter 2, the impact of trauma can dysregulate emotional responses and hamper rational decision making. A more relational approach of within-the-moment recognition of the child's efforts could have a more lasting impact on their self-esteem, showing them that their efforts are being noticed.

Table 11.1 Behaviourist approach

Perspective: Behaviourist	Assumptions
The behaviourist approach is based on classical conditioning theory developed by Pavlov and operant conditioning theory developed by Skinner (1993). Here the intended outcome is to change behaviour as rewards outweigh the attraction of 'problematic' behaviour. This approach aims to establish expectations of cause and effect and re-assure the child that they can anticipate consistent responses from the practitioner.	Children can be conditioned to learn appropriate responses either by rewarding such behaviour or by sanctioning unwanted behaviour. The assumption is that the child wants the reward or does not want the sanction and is made to feel they are making a choice in their behaviour. Theorists have criticized the idea of sanctions emphasizing that by humiliating an already stressed child nothing of lasting benefit can develop. (Brunzell et al., 2015; Dix, 2017; Conkbayir, 2023).

Socio-constructivist Approach

A practitioner advocating the socio-constructivist approach would talk to the child about why they do not want to sit on the mat and ask about the kind of story they like, what they think about story time, in order that they can be encouraged and, when appropriate, reminded, 'remember you liked hearing the funny story'. This supports the changing of the child's self-cognition, where they may have previously held the identity of a *fidgeter* or *bad listener* to a more positive view of themselves. By taking the time to converse with the child, perhaps seeking to determine if they would like to participate in a different way (e.g. sitting on a chair beside the mat or at their home desk), the practitioner is demonstrating an interest in their thoughts and therefore in them, not just responding to 'problematic' behaviour. By facilitating dialogue, the practitioner can help support the child in their socialization, as 'the practitioner has a crucial role to play by designing appropriate activities and experiences that involve social interactions' (Carroll, 2023: 60). *Moving to the child's side* and *listening to their voice* demonstrates concern for them as individuals. In so doing the practitioner is beginning to take a tentative step towards a more relationship-based approach.

Table 11.2 Socio-constructivist approach

Perspective: Socio-constructivist	Assumptions
This builds on the behaviourist perspective to take account of intrinsic factors such as perceptions, attitudes, expectations and beliefs – the thinking processes that influence behaviour (Vygotsky, 1978; Bandura, 1986). Knowledge is co-constructed through collaborative social engagement. (Spodek and Saracho, 1999). This theory proposes that a child's culture and environment is responsible for teaching children not only what to think but how to think. Vygotsky 's zone of proximal development (ZPD) describes, peer or adult guidance as critical in supporting learning.	A person's knowledge and behaviour are learnt through social collaboration, therefore the idea of 'how to behave' in particular situations is socially constructed. The trauma-informed practitioner must consider what behaviours a child may have already observed or be continuing to observe. Within the education setting socialization is considered by McCulloch and Stewart (2023) as the art of inclusion (or exclusion), and children are adept at perceiving who and which behaviours within the school are valued. For the trauma-experienced child, their ability to recognize this (or be in a state to recognize this) may be compromised and therefore their awareness that certain behaviours are 'problematic' may be limited.

The assumption here is that the child is encouraged to tap into their own intrinsic motivation to want to sit on the mat for the story and is choosing to do so because it makes them feel safe and good about themselves, and possibly also supports their identity as part of the group. By encouraging the child, listening to what they have to say and promoting the benefits of the activity they may view themselves differently. Later, the child can be encouraged to self-identify what they like about activities that they were previously reluctant to become involved with. This helps build a sense of self-worth and resilience and, alongside a broader approach to building trust, can slowly support the trauma-experienced child to feel valued as an individual and as a member of the class (see Table 11.2).

Eco-systemic Approach

Conversations with colleagues may reveal that the child's family has a particular negative, confrontational or fearful view of the school due to previous experiences. The child therefore may have an unconscious, responsive behaviour to avoid or defy teacher instruction. The trauma-experienced child lives within a wider 'relational, structural and cultural-ecological context' (Gose, 2025: 408) which serves to shape the behaviours manifested within the school context. The eco-systemic approach would encourage dialogue with the family, and to develop harmonious and co-operative relationships. Through dialogue practitioners may grow in awareness that the child has experienced trauma and be mindful that certain behaviours by the adult may trigger involuntary responses in the child (e.g. eye contact may act as a trigger).

Conversations with the child may reveal that they find the mat itchy, or that the radiator is too loud and therefore the physical environment is a deterrent to their participation in story time. The solution would then be to alter the physical environment which then may help to encourage the child's participation. The physical environment may also trigger responses in relation to past trauma, for example, being down low whilst an adult is looming above, being in the shadows rather than the light. Involving those within a child's microsystem in understanding their experiences and collaborating to create consistent strategies to support their learning will lead to a more holistic and consistent approach to positive behaviour. However, a multi-agency approach will be required to help understand and address the causes of trauma within and beyond the school. However, being aware that adult behavioural patterns and the physical environment can detrimentally impact upon a trauma-experienced child should underpin all practitioner actions (see Table 11.3).

Table 11.3 Eco-systemic approach

Perspective: Eco-Systemic/Ecological	Assumptions
Each child is influenced by others, for example, the family, peer group and school. It examines the roles and ways of behaving within each sphere of influence. Bronfenbrenner (1992) has expanded this thinking, inviting further consideration of the social, cultural, economic and political systems that exert an influence over the child. When considering the impact of trauma, we must be aware that trauma can be inflicted within any one system and be either supported or intensified within another.	Behaviour can be viewed as a 'dance' that is adopted when interacting with different people. This is where behaviour is altered. How each system interacts also impacts on relationships. The interconnectedness of these systems is the focus when considering interventions. Bronfenbrenner also considered the more practical aspects of the physical environment – the actual resources within the school. Although practitioners may not know what has happened in any one system, they must be aware that aspects in the educational environment may trigger responses from the child. Consideration of space, noise, routine and ways in which adults act can all impact upon a child's fight, flight or freeze responses and their ability to participate in learning. The initial emphasis should be on providing a safe and calm learning environment in which trust is built through positive relationships.

Psychodynamic Approach

Here the practitioner might consider that something about the environment or the activity is triggering the response. In this situation the practitioner may observe the child over a period of time to identify possible triggers. This may reveal, for example, that the child feels complete disregard for the adult's instruction, perhaps because they do not trust the adult's response and therefore prefer the more predictable responses of laughter from the other children. As discussed above, they may perhaps be subconsciously triggered by sitting on the floor, whereby the adult's size is magnified and makes the child feel threatened. They may even find the experience of being 'herded' into a small space distressing.

Through observations and dialogue with the child over time the practitioner may be able to identify patterns of behaviour which can be addressed through changes to the environment, their choice of words or the time of the day when an activity is carried out. This may help to ameliorate the child's response and alleviate some of their anxiety. For the trauma-experienced child significant support may be needed to repair damage to their psychosocial development and it is possible, at this juncture, that the practitioner may require professional support from outside agencies (see Table 11.4).

Table 11.4 Psychodynamic approach

Perspective: Psychodynamic	Assumptions
This perspective stems from the psychoanalytical thinking of Freud and Freud (1991) and theories of attachment (Bowlby, 1978) whereby a child's behaviour stems from an unconscious reaction to previous experiences. These concepts are explored further within Chapter 3.	The child is seen as attachment needing, rather than attention seeking (Ayers et al., 2015). Previous experiences will subconsciously influence reactions. The idea is that there are key figures within a child's life, with whom they can build safe, positive reciprocal attachments and in turn enhance their sense of self-worth.

Each of the above approaches present practitioners with the tools to support children to achieve positive outcomes. However, schools often adopt traditional behaviour management strategies founded on punishments and rewards, which foreground the changing of unacceptable behaviours (Ayers et al., 2015; Carroll, 2023). However, Head (2007), Dix (2017) and Conkbayir (2023) suggest that such approaches often lack long-term success. As discussed above, for the trauma-experienced child they may impact negatively. According to Avery-Overduin and Poed (2023) these approaches do not always consider the individual circumstances, and the strategies implemented are often without consideration of other issues that may impact the young person's life. Further, they can be counterproductive to some children, who require a balance of empathy, understanding, and direction (Smith et al., 2015). Trauma-informed practice advocates for *time-in* rather than *time-out*, whereby the practitioner supports the child through co-regulation (Dix, 2017). Unfortunately, Head (2007) notes that many schools adopt the use of separate provision, which does not lead to a longer-term understanding of behaviour, as the approach ultimately fails to address the cause of the child's disillusionment with education (Head, 2007). For example, nurture rooms can be used to support a child's pro-social skills and self-regulation (see Chapter 8). However, adopting approaches that allow trauma-experienced children to be supported in class with their peers is more likely to promote long-term inclusion and self-regulation.

Relational Approaches

Short et al. (2018) propose that by strengthening relationships with children, learning can be improved and developed, and difficult emotions and experiences can be explored with a view to moving forward. As noted by Olson (2009: 4) 'children's learning lives develop primarily outside of, or in opposition to, their experiences in school'. A relationship-centred approach can offer a more holistic and sustainable way to support students' social, emotional and academic development (Smyth et al., 2010).

The fundamental benefit of a relational approach is the reframing of how behaviours are understood with a move towards more supportive practices and away from deficit models (Spurling et al., 2013). The creation of a relational environment is helped by practitioners' consideration of transitions and by Daniel Siegel's (1999) *window of tolerance.* Siegel (1999) identified the window of tolerance as being characterized by each individual's ability to regulate and respond to life events. This window is distinctly different from person to person and can be viewed as a zone of tolerance for life's stresses. Children who have experienced trauma can find their zone of tolerance limited, resulting in them often responding with what others may perceive as antisocial behaviour: anger, numbness, aggression and withdrawal. A relational approach seeks to help and support children to expand their window by gradually developing resilience to cope and ultimately to expand their window of tolerance. Further, practitioners need to be cognisant of their own window of tolerance when supporting distressed children and seek support themselves if required. Through consistency in the classroom and across the school, children can feel secure in a predictable shared environment with strategies used to signal changes in routine. Planning transitions, sharing and discussing them with the children also helps staff consider what routines are necessary and how they should be managed. These relational practices endeavour to keep children included and engaged, thus leading to positive learning and participation (Munford, 2022).

Relational schools set out to engage with children's lives not just with learning goals (Smyth et al., 2014). Payne and Welch (2018) claim that restorative approaches reduce exclusions, improve attendance and attainment. Restorative practices emphasize the importance of building positive and supportive relationships between teachers, children and other school staff (Payne and Welch, 2018). Whole school practices are used to develop and restore relationships. The individual's development is considered, and dialogue is used to help resolve conflicts, not just between practitioner and the child but also between children themselves. Bryk and Schneider (2002) state that a relational approach recognizes that the learning environment can be the most constant and reliable setting that some children experience in which to build *relational trust.* This is where a nurturing approach can be developed so that children can recognize and regulate their conduct, build resilience, and develop attachments. In turn, the child's feeling of being safe in a supportive classroom is created, leading to effective learning and positive social interactions. Once the school has provided the children with a secure base and built a relational context within which there are interventions in place to support self- and co-regulation, it will be possible to address thinking and feelings about behavioural choices. It is only then that dealing with matters of discipline is likely to be effective.

Attachment and Nurture

While in Scotland, exclusions from school have reduced considerably, as noted by Wingrave (2011: 92), '(i)nclusion has to be seen as more than sustaining the presence of a child' in school and it is necessary to ensure that the child's needs are met'. Nurturing approaches were developed by Margery Boxall (Boxall, 2002), who argued that if children were given the opportunity to develop trusting relationships they would settle and engage with learning and build resilience (Wingrave, 2011). Nurturing approaches are built upon Bowlby's attachment theory (Bowlby, 1969) (see Chapter 4). Bowlby contended that for positive emotional bonds to be developed, a child must attach to a caregiver who provides the necessary comfort and support. If attachment does not develop, the child could develop a lack of trust towards adults and others. Subsequently, the child's behaviours could present as remote, hostile, disruptive or unhappy. Attachment theory provides insights into the attitude and concerns of children and signposts behaviours that require interventions and support (Kennedy and Kennedy, 2004).

Bennathan and Boxall (2000) suggest that poor attachments can signal the need to provide children with targeted interventions where they feel valued, respected and connected to their teachers and peers. For children to access learning opportunities and experience a sense of achievement, the education professional should increase their responsiveness and sensitivity through consistent, appropriate responses and positive interactions (Tsappis et al., 2022: 192). Kural and Kovacs (2021) found that recognizing fractured attachments could be relevant in identifying and supporting the development of resilience (see Chapter 12).

Relational Approaches in Practice

In order for the relational approach to be successful, a strong teacher-child relationship is key as it fosters trust, respect and communication. When a positive relationship is created children are more likely to feel safe, valued and motivated to engage in learning (McCulloch, 2018; McKay and Macomber, 2021). Schools and practitioners need to make time and space for conversations and reflections on what approaches work for the individual. Staff should prioritize emotional and physical safety, including managing changes and transitions (Hart et al., 2004). Classroom settings ought to offer predictability, consistency and *unconditional positive regard.* Hence avoiding children developing the belief that their worth is solely dependent on their ability to conform to particular standards (Kohn, 2018).

Rather than focusing on the child's failings, practice is driven by successes and is receptive to what the child deems relevant and of interest to them as individuals

Table 11.5 Key practices to support a relational approach

Create a safe and inclusive environment	Establish clear routines and expectations for behaviour, act to resolve conflicts and promote a positive culture of respect, understanding and kindness.
Build Positive Relationships	Take time to get to know each child demonstrating empathy and creating opportunities for meaningful interactions, inside and outside the classroom.
Teach social and emotional skills	Teach children how to manage their emotions, resolve conflicts calmly and peacefully. Model effective communication and demonstrate how it can be used to resolve situations.
Use restorative practices	Avoid punishments. Discuss behaviours, repair situations, promote accountability and reconciliation among children. Adopt a 'clean slate' approach to previous behaviours.
Provide individual support	Recognize and respond to children's diverse needs, offer individualized support and interventions to allow children to experience success both behaviourally and academically.

(Woodcock and Woolfson, 2019). Thus, the learning experiences can be engaging, challenging, meaningful and enjoyable. Aspelin (2021: 594) claims that 'teaching means bonding; without a bond between teacher and student, there can be no teaching'. Following Morgan (2018), teaching and learning is reciprocal where the child is not passive in the process but can take ownership of the experience based on what is relevant and of interest to them leading to positive learning experiences and greater independence.

These practices are proposed as an alternative way to support children in schools and are intended to challenge traditional thinking about teaching, learning and behaviour. Professional dialogue and solution-focused approaches support practitioners in building resilience in children. Education professionals who adopt a relational approach focus on getting to know children as individuals, understanding their unique strengths, challenges and interests. By showing empathy, compassion and genuine interest in children's well-being, teachers can create a nurturing and inclusive learning environment where children feel supported and understood. Investing in relational approaches and nurture principles not only benefits individual children but is essential for creating a thriving school community grounded in care, compassion and collaboration (see Table 11.5).

Thinking Point 11.2

Do you feel your school/setting has a preferred approach to low-level disruptive behaviour and if so, how is this communicated to all staff?

The Way forward

If children are to become *successful learners* (Education Scotland, online) and truly feel a positive identity as learners, then their experiences within the classroom are crucial. The nurture principles highlight the significance of transitions in children's lives, for example, the transition from home to school or transitions from one setting to another, as well as everyday transitions, where children must learn how to be part of that class and cope with changing expectations and approaches. The practitioners' aim is to create a sense of safety and positivity and an understanding that the adult can be trusted to behave calmly, consistently and do what they say they will do, which may not be the experience children have previously had (Roffey and O'Riordan, 2001; Porter, 2006; Roffey, 2011; McCulloch, 2018). In this context, and indeed throughout their school lives, it is important to understand that children bring with them their own internal emotional lives, their own perceptions of themselves and of others and their own experiences of school (Education Scotland, 2018). Self-esteem and resilience make the difference between one child's minor upset and another's catastrophe. Practitioners should be cognisant of the variety of behaviours and explanations for this behaviour.

If practitioners are to maintain a sense of self-efficacy, positive purpose and control of their setting so that learning can occur, then they need to reassure themselves that behaviour can, to some extent, be learnt and therefore changed and that there is potential to address disruptive behaviours. However, they need also to understand that the trauma-experienced child may be unable to respond to reasoning in a moment of distress and that building self-esteem and trust takes time. The potential impact of previous and current events out with the educational setting may mean that children cannot focus on learning until they are within their window of tolerance and feel safe (Roffey and O'Riordan, 2001; Porter, 2006; Ayers et al., 2015). Furthermore, children 'with a history of trauma typically have a more difficult time remaining in their window of tolerance' (Gose, 2025: 404).

Summary

Within settings there are certain appropriate contextual behavioural responses that children do need to learn, for example, the routine of the school day, how to conduct themselves at the snack or lunch table, how to share the attention of the adult in the room and the resources provided for them. This may be very different from their previous experiences, but these boundaries reinforce the sense of safety that children require. Enforcing these boundaries need not be done punitively. Practitioners should be mindful that through their consistent behaviour they are reassuring children that they can expect certain behaviours from them, the adult in the room, and this is key to the nurture principles (Boxall, 2002). By offering consistent, calm responses and remaining positive, practitioners can show that whilst certain behaviours are not acceptable, the child, themself, is still a welcomed member of the classroom. Treisman (2017: 28) states that these behaviours provide a means of communication:

> Rather than taking behaviours at face value, it is helpful to view behaviours as forms of multi-layered communication that tell a story and often provides us with a map of and clues about the child's inner worlds and unexpressed needs.

Children need to be continually offered a *clean slate* ensuring that they feel safe within the school and that their needs are addressed through interventions designed to support self- and co-regulation.

Greater funding for improved adult to child ratios would help provide effective support for 'time in' and co-regulatory practice for children with additional support needs, including trauma-experienced children. This would support practitioners to feel equipped to implement trauma-informed practices (Joyce et al., 2023) and remain within their own window of tolerance as discussed above. Tolerance and understanding of human individuality must be at the heart of any setting, and positive interactions between all those in the setting should be equally considered in order to support everyone in a safe, nurturing and inclusive learning environment.

12

The Concept of Resilience

Joyce Nicholson

Key Ideas

This chapter will:

- explore developing understandings of resilience,
- outline social ecology approaches,
- outline social (justice) approaches, and
- examine paradoxical resilience.

Introduction

Exposure to adversity is not uncommon in the lives of children and young people in Scotland. Research over the past fifty years has shown that some young people have good outcomes despite exposure to risks (Rutter, 2006; 2013). The construct of resilience has developed across a range of disciplines to describe the processes and sociocultural conditions for resilience to develop despite the challenges young people have experienced. In this regard, resilience approaches are a more positive and strength-focused approach in comparison to more deficit framings of young people's experiences of adversity. Resilience has been centred in Scottish education policy, research and practice developments in addressing well-being, inequalities in education outcomes and academic attainment, as well as in responses to Covid-19. The concept of resilience is a central element in the Getting it right for every child (GIRFEC) approach in Scotland's National Practice Model (Scottish Government, 2022a). The approach embeds resilience-focused responses to improve the well-being and outcomes of children and young people. Rooted in the work of Daniel and Wassell (2002), who argue there are three *building blocks for resilience*: a secure base, self-esteem and self-efficacy. Davidson and Carlin (2019) critique the approach for lacking recognition of, and responses to, structural determinants in young people's outcomes and well-being, leading to *steeling* young people to adversity rather than challenging inequity and striving for social justice.

Resilience is then a complex and contested concept. Resilience is not something that individual young people possess; rather, it may develop over time, it is temporally and contextually specific, and it is a result of relational, social and environmental conditions. Psychological models tend to focus on internal factors, individuals' well-being, self-esteem and protective factors that may mitigate risk. Social and ecological models acknowledge structural and systemic issues and challenges in developing resilience and have implications for the role of schools in making *resilient moves*. Critical voices have argued that it has become 'meaningless', and wide adoption has resulted in *iatrogenic harm* (Fisher and Jones, 2024) which responsibilizes individuals and is devoid of sociocultural contextualization. The mechanisms that promote resilience remain challenging to understand. Despite these critiques and limitations, the strength-based focus of resilience as a concept in children and young people's well-being is important to examine. This chapter will review these approaches and critiques and consider the role that schools can have in working meaningfully with resilience.

Resilience is related to the significant range of responses that people have to adversity or risk (Rutter, 2006). Adversity has become synonymous with research on ACEs (Felitti et al., 1998), discussed in Chapter 3. Adversity in the context of this chapter also includes structural challenges experienced by young people, including homelessness, disability and child poverty. In 2022–3, 24 per cent of children in Scotland were living in child poverty (Scottish Government, 2024a) and poverty has been strongly linked to the so-called attainment gap in Scottish Education (McKinney et al., 2023). Experiences of adversity may be acute, chronic, and/or complex and temporally short- or long-term, one-off incidents or chronically repetitious and so in our attempts to conceptualize resilience-focused responses, we must always be mindful of the wide range of experiences and impacts on young people. Not all young people who experience adversities will be traumatized. Adversities also crucially involve social-economic, political and sociocultural contexts, including child poverty.

Developing Understandings of Resilience

Resilience appears in fields as broad as ecology, psychology, workplace stress management, structural engineering, mental health and well-being, education and within policy spaces managing responses to emergencies, including pandemics. Definitions then vary, though the most straightforward suggests an individual – or group – ability to *bounce back* after adverse events. Such simplistic outcome-focused definitions, however, fail to recognize the complex mechanisms involved in responding to challenges. It may be easier to define what it is not. Resilience is neither a trait nor a characteristic of an individual. It is not fixed, meaning that a young person may be resilient in one circumstance and not in another, and can develop across the life span (Masten, 2001; Rutter, 2006; 2013). There are a range of definitions and approaches to resilience which will be broadly discussed as social-ecological approaches and critical social justice approaches. They have different implications for educators about how best to understand, respond and provide opportunities for responding to risks and challenges experienced by young people.

The conceptualization of resilience has developed from an initial focus on individuals who had better than expected outcomes in response to risk, to social-ecological models that focus on factors that facilitate the development of well-being under stress and, more recently, social justice-based approaches. In the 1970s and 1980s psychologists and psychiatrists researching individuals who appeared to have internal qualities despite exposure to risks and significant challenges suggested that some individuals were 'invulnerable' to adversity. This view was increasingly challenged by researchers such as Masten (2001), and the deepening understanding of the range of factors, both internal and environmental, that shape individuals' responses in adapting to stress and risks. Crucially, as recognition developed that resilience is dynamic and not an individual trait or characteristic, it is not possible to describe individuals as a *resilient child* or *not resilient*. Indeed, resilience has been conceptualized by Pietrzak and Southwick (2011) as a continuum, which may be present to differing degrees across multiple domains throughout life. At distinct stages of an individual's development, these internal and environmental factors may be present at some stages and not others and so this is a dynamic concept.

Rutter, a child psychiatrist, conducted a wealth of seminal research including institutional deprivation, comparative school studies and adoptees in the UK and Romania. He suggests that resilience is 'an interactive phenomenon that is inferred from findings indicating that some individuals have a relatively good outcome despite having experienced serious adversities' (Rutter, 2013: 474). In his view, resilience is an ordinary response to risks and is dependent on protective factors and the resources needed to support this. Rutter (2006) argues a range of factors impact the development of resilience including genetics, social relationships and good family functioning with an absence of discord and conflictual relationships. Resilience, with the processes that engage multiple risk and protective factors, leads to positive developmental outcomes over the longer term. It may be that what Rutter (2013) terms 'maladaptive responses' are protective in the short but not long term. For example, a young person may respond to abuse by emotional withdrawal, which may be protective in the short, but not longer, term. Protective factors include good parent-child relationships, temperament, family support, positive school experience – not necessarily academic outcome – and, self-efficacy and self-esteem.

Bronfenbrenner's (1979; 1995) bioecological theory conceptualizes children's development as a process of bi-directional and reciprocal relationships between an individual and their immediate environment, their relationships with parents, family members and teachers (microsystem), with local communities (mesosystem), with services and institutions (exosystem) and with cultural and media systems (macrosystem). Bronfenbrenner (1995) later added the chronosystem to reflect lifetime system changes. These would now include technological changes and such as young people's interactions with social media, the impact of events such as the global pandemic and the climate emergency. While this model has received significant critique, it is still a dominant framing approach in resilience literature, particularly for education.

Ungar (2013) offers a multi-systemic, social-ecological theory of resilience, arguing that resilience is not an internal psychological state of well-being, and instead 'in situations of adversity, resilience is observed when individuals engage in behaviors that help them to navigate their way to the resources they need to flourish' (Ungar, 2013: 256). Ungar suggests that the more adversity a child experiences, the more resilience is dependent on the external environment and the resources available to the child to sustain well-being and facilitate growth (Ungar, 2013). Cultural differences in risk and protective factors are also important in this approach, for example, in some community cultural contexts, caring and providing care for relatives may be viewed as positive and expected, whilst in others it may be viewed as 'maladaptive' family functioning. The emphasis then is on family relations, social and community structures, services, including education, and culture as resilience resources. Ungar (2013) emphasizes the need to change the environment and ensure access to resources available to children who experience complex adversities. Schools are therefore important to *navigate and negotiate* resources of support for the well-being of young people. It is then the social and physical ecology that aids processes that protect against risk and not the individual qualities or attributes of a child that responsibilizes them for their responses when faced with adversity. Within these approaches, teachers and schools can offer opportunities for young people. Rutter (2013: 479) suggests that schools should offer opportunities to ensure that 'children must be able to take responsibility, exercise a degree of autonomy and have the opportunity of learning from their own mistakes'. Rutter's work underlines that good interpersonal relationships are significantly associated with resilience. Social-ecological models suggest that to strengthen ecological systems:

- teachers should develop positive relationships with children and their parents;
- schools should provide opportunities to learn, change and grow self-esteem and efficacy;
- whole school approaches to nurture and belonging in school are key; and
- schools should maintain a focus on strength-focused responses to challenges and facilitate access to resources for young people.

Thinking Point 12.1

a. How would you define resilience?
b. Do you agree that resilience is an interactional process rather than an individual trait? What implications does this have for your practice?

Social (Justice) Approaches

Critics of the conceptualization and application of resilience have challenged the focus on individuals as responsible for adapting well to challenges and adversity, including the structural determinants of well-being. Joseph (2013) argues that resilience has become *embedded neo-liberalism* that places responsibility squarely on individuals and has become a *shallow and shifting concept*. Harrison (2013) does not reject the concept but invites us to carefully reflect on our use of resilience to consider power relationships, including normative gendered roles, and the toll and cost that resilience brings to individuals and family groups, particularly women and girls.

In her study of young girls in a public housing estate in Syndey, Australia, Bottrell (2009: 335) asks, '[h]ow much adversity should resilient individuals endure before social arrangements rather than individuals are targeted for intervention?' In developing social theories of resilience, Bottrell (2009) suggests foregrounding young people's resistances to adversity, understanding the practices that may be protective for particular social groups, rather than what in other views may be deemed maladaptive.

Hart et al. (2016), and Aranda and Hart (2015) argue for a social justice approach in resilience research. This, they suggest, would be far from the internal, individualized focus of most resilience-focused research because, grounded in relations of risk, this new wave of resilience research would focus on structural inequities and work on *changing the odds* for young people. A social justice approach encourages and supports practitioners to be fully engaged with work on inequalities. 'We propose that it is time for resilience to go beyond understanding how individuals cope with adversity, to challenge the structures that create disadvantages in the first place' (Hart et al., 2016: 6). Hart et al. (2016) argue this approach, which they call *Boingboing resilience*, has *emancipatory potential* in that it is concerned with both overcoming adversities and challenging the conditions of adversity itself. In their work with stigmatized and marginalized groups, they challenge stigma and discrimination in their own practice, that of colleagues, with and alongside local communities. They argue for the co-production of research with those experiencing adversity and marginalization. In a school context they suggest, ensuring that the school has a supportive and positive school culture that reflectively challenges discrimination, together with targeted work to build resilience strategies for young people to manage stigma and bullying (Hart et al., 2016). Teachers are advocates for young people experiencing a range of challenges. Teachers and other professionals, Hart et al. (2007) suggest, should focus on making *resilient moves* for young people. Resilient moves are everyday steps or actions that people can make to help build resilience. Aumann and Hart (2009: 11) define resilient moves as

> The kinds of things we need to make happen (e.g., events, parenting strategies, relationships, resources) to help children manage life when it's tough. Plus, ways of thinking and acting that we need ourselves if we want to make things better for children.

These moves are grounded in four principles. Firstly, *Accepting* where children and families starting points are; secondly, *Conserving* positive or good things that already are happening for children and young people; thirdly, *Commitment* to engaging and working with children and their families; and lastly, *Enlisting* relatives and appropriate others to help while moving on from those might have let them down in the past. These, Hart et al. (2007) call the *Nobel Truths*. Hart and colleagues have developed the Resilience Framework (Hart et al., 2007) working with communities in Blackpool. The Resilience Framework has five sections which contain forty-two potential interventions and versions are free to use for young people and for families. The sections cover the following:

- Basics: food, shelter, safety, etc.
- Belonging: good relationships and people you can count on.
- Learning: opportunities inside and outside school.
- Coping: skills for managing the everyday ups and downs.
- Core self: developing self-identity, self-esteem and confidence.

(see https://resiliencepathway.co.uk/resilience-framework)

Thinking Point 12.2

a. What is your view of Social Justice theories of resilience?
b. Have a look at the resilience pathway at https://resiliencepathway.co.uk/
c. How could you use this in your practice?

Young People Experiencing Multiple Adversities: Parental Substance Use

Resilience is dependent on exposure to risk and adversity including poverty, family conflict and violence, and substance use. Indeed, Mahdiani and Ungar (2021: 149) in their paper '*The Dark Side of Resilience*' pose the issue of the resilience paradox, namely 'that more resilience may actually create more vulnerability in some contexts'. Resilience may not always be viewed as a positive adaptation to risk. As many as one in three young people under sixteen years of age in the UK and across Europe live with a parent regularly using substances (Manning et al., 2009; Olszewski et al., 2010). Manning et al. (2009) estimated almost a million children in the UK, around 8 per cent, were living with an adult who had used illicit drugs within the previous year. All classrooms will have young people whose caregivers use drugs. Many, even most, young people will be cared for well by parents who use substances. However, for some young people there is likely to be a range of potential harms to children affected by parental substance use, including effects on infant and child development, emotional and physical harm, and neglect (Cleaver et al., 2011; Roy, 2021), lower academic engagement, performance and outcomes (Lowthian, 2022), emotional and behavioural problems (Gorin, 2004), family conflict and domestic abuse (Cleaver et al., 2011; Barrett et al., 2024) and increased likelihood of substance use (Velleman and Templeton, 2016).

Young people who live with parents who use substances experience stigmatization (Muir, 2024) and often experience isolation and bullying in school. Backett-Milburn et al. (2008) highlight the management of stigma through the concealment of issues outside the immediate family, including in school. Concealment led to constraints on the identification of their needs and the support they received in school. School is the space where young people can engage in social and physical activities they enjoy, and for those who are experiencing complex challenges at home, school may be the only space they are able to see friends and socialize.

In my small-scale study with six families who used illicit drugs and their day-to-day experiences of school (Nicholson, 2022), most of the young people did not belong to clubs or youth clubs outside of their school. Young people agentically managed school by enacting several strategies, including self-exclusion from school and managing stigma. Self-exclusion was used both as a short- and long-term strategy in responding to challenges due to constraints such as caregiving responsibilities, the need for predictability and routine, and as a response to bullying. Caregiving by young people for themselves, their parents and siblings has been a central feature of research on young people's lives affected by parental substance use (Bancroft et al., 2004; Backett-Milburn et al., 2008). Caregiving impacts attendance, engagement with and self-exclusion from school. Care is a complex shifting of boundaries between parents and children. Self-exclusion also has links with bullying (O'Brien and Dadswell, 2020) and was experienced by most young people in a study by Nicholson (2022), underscoring the need for resilient moves to address bullying as highlighted earlier by Hart et al. (2016).

The management of stigma by young people was central to interactions with school. Young people discussed the complex navigation of the relational risks of disclosure with friends and teachers and other school staff in order to ensure the maintenance of their family life. Young people 'experienced multiple, complex stigmas including parental illicit and prescribed drug use, the absence and or incarceration of birth fathers, parental mental health issues, domestic and sexual abuse, and the stigma of being removed from parental care' (Nicholson 2025: 8). They also did not disclose issues and challenges to teachers. Young people living with complex family issues discern who and when it is best to disclose information. One young person, aged fifteen years, stated that they 'don't want to stick out. I want to be under the radar' (Nicholson, 2022: 180).

Young people living in complex family situations are then navigating and negotiating a host of constraints and relational tensions. Their experiences demonstrate the range of responses to managing school, driven by a desire for hiddenness and careful management of disclosure of the realities of their day-to-day lives. Their management strategies are protective mechanisms against further harm and a demonstration of their agency. These strategies may be assessed by professionals as problematic and may more usefully be viewed, according to Callaghan and Alexander (2015), as *paradoxical resilience* as highlighted in their work focusing on children's experiences of domestic abuse. Callaghan (2023: 18) explains:

> When power imbalances are so stark, and when children's relational experiences are characterised by coercive, controlling, and manipulative behaviours, their resistances to those behaviours are shaped by the context in which the violence and abuse takes place. What appears to be 'dysfunctional' and difficult is often the way that children have found to cope. Resilience is inherently paradoxical and inherently reflects the oppressive practices that it is responding to.

Berridge (2017), in his mixed-methods study on educational experiences and attainment that included twenty-six young people in care in England, found a similar range of demonstrations of agency in young people's relationships with school that resulted from their differing contexts and their assessments of support offered. He concludes that there is a need to both acknowledge and develop a deeper understanding of how agency is expressed by young people.

Case Study

This case study is a composite story from doctoral research with young people who have lived experience of parental substance use (Nicholson, 2022).

Alexis is ten years old. She lives with her mother and younger sister, who is two years old, in an area of high multiple deprivation. She has occasional contact with her father. Both her parents have long-standing substance use issues, primarily illicit drug use, and her parent's relationship is conflictual and often violent. She says she 'likes' school and has, in the past, had teachers who she felt supported her. She has a small number of friends. The school is aware that she has been bullied in the past by peers, as she self-excluded from school during this time. The school worked alongside youth workers to address bullying by peers. She lived with her gran when she was eight years old due to the impact of domestic abuse and drug use by her parents. At that time, she received additional group support at school as a young person who was living in kinship care, which she found 'helpful and supportive' and something she could engage in 'for myself'. She enjoys dancing and art.

Thinking Point 12.3

a. Thinking about the above case study, what concerns do you have and how might you respond?
b. What resilient moves/actions could you/the school take to support Alexis?

Summary

This chapter has explored approaches to understanding resilience for young people who are growing up experiencing a range of challenges. Whilst this chapter has highlighted some of the ongoing debates about the definition and application of resilience, it remains an important concept in responding to young people experiencing trauma and adversity. We should be mindful in working to support young people of the warning offered by Mahdiani and Ungar (2021: 151) that 'resilience can be wrongly deployed as an inducement to tolerate disparity and inequality, accepting the deferral of demands for change, or as an excuse to assign individuals who lack power the responsibility to change their lives'. A critical understanding of the moves we can make, recognizing paradoxical resilience, avoiding responsibilizing young people for the social and individual challenges they face, and challenging stigma and discrimination in schools, seems crucial in supporting young people to thrive in a world of increasing inequity, to respond to marginalization.

Thinking Point 12.4

a. How would you now define resilience?
b. How do you understand your role in making resilient moves for young people?
c. What resources could you draw on to make these moves?

13

Fictitious Places Provide Safe Contexts for Learning

Pauline Cooney

Key ideas

This chapter will:

- explore why story matters,
- examine Story Drama,
- outline the role of the teacher, and
- explore distance as a safe place.

Introduction

The aim of this chapter is to examine the ways in which the use of story drama can support *emotional being* for young children who have experienced adverse circumstances when the world in which they inhabit feels unfamiliar and/or unsafe. Story drama is defined as 'improvised role play stimulated by a story' (Booth, 2005: 8). Its strength lies in its multifaceted nature, enabling learners to 'become the co-constructors of a story, the story itself, and the characters living within the story' (Booth, 2005: 8). The concept of well-being permeates current educational discourse, and for children who have undergone trauma, this sense of *being* can be particularly heightened as it is shaped not only by their experiences per se but also by their perceptions of these experiences (van Gulden and Vick, 2010). This nuanced *sense of being* is values driven and important to explore as it acknowledges the authenticity of their feelings, voice and identity.

Thinking Point 13.1

a. How can story be used as a means of exploration within a classroom?
b. How can a teacher facilitate learning when working from within a story?

What Kind of Drama?

The chapter will develop an argument for moving beyond talking about and/or around a story, to using stories which the pupils and teacher inhabit (Booth, 2005). The overriding perception around the discipline of drama is that it can be difficult to implement and challenging to manage; indeed its educational value is often questioned (Baldwin, 2008). Yet this is a product-orientated view of drama that centres around performance such as the school nativity play or improvisational games. Rather, it is the process of drama and associated pedagogy that captures its true essence. The drama considered in this chapter aligns with story drama, a contextual learning process where learners are engaged in fictional worlds through role play and dramatic conventions (Neelands and Goode, 2000). This way of working offers a unique opportunity for children to learn within the realms of *pretend*. When an adult enters this fictitious context alongside the children, their intervention can support and enrich the learning experiences that evolve from the emerging fiction. When teachers and children explore a theme or issue within the boundaries of a make-believe world, reflection must be woven throughout. It is this reflective thread that affords the children the opportunity to safely explore, reframe and refocus their own understanding of the world in which they live (Miller and Saxton, 2011). Learning in and through drama creates a safe space where learners can be simultaneously engaged and detached. Engagement occurs within the realms of the fictitious context. Detachment occurs when participants suspend disbelief, allowing them to reflect on the meaning that is contained within the fictitious context. This distinctive feature enables the children to make meaning from the stories they encounter; it is through engaging in these narratives that children can find their authentic voice safely.

Let us start with a story …

The teacher of a Primary 2 class (aged 6) has a piece of material wrapped around her shoulders to indicate to the children that she is *in role*. This is her first time using the drama technique *Teacher in Role (TiR)* (Neelands and Goode, 2000: 40). She has adopted the role of a dragon. The children are in role too, representing members of a small village they have collectively imagined. The village is situated at the bottom of a *fictitious mountain*, with the dragon's cave situated halfway up. The villagers have trekked along the mountain path to meet the dragon. They are apprehensive but curious to discover why the dragon appeared to be crying when he flew over the village square as they were setting up for festivities to celebrate the festival of light! The villagers gingerly approach the entrance to the cave, calling on the dragon who emerges cautiously to meet them. The dragon and the villagers engage in conversation. 'Why do you frighten us?' 'Why were you crying?' 'Can we trust you?' The villagers discover that they had misunderstood the dragon, discerning that the dragon is, in fact, lonely. One child, in role as a farmer, looks at the dragon and says,

'I know how you feel. I feel lonely too.' The dragon (TiR) questions this, as every time he swoops down to watch the villagers, he notices that the farmer is always working surrounded by with his fellow farmers. 'How could he possibly be lonely?' The farmer replies, 'Yes, but there is always a part of me that is lonely.'

Thinking Point 13.2

a. What do you think was the teacher's intention here?
b. What might the children gain from this learning experience?

The child in the story shared above had been in the care system. Their capacity to build and sustain positive relationships with the teacher and fellow classmates was limited. The teacher was seeking ways to reach out to and make connections with the child. Working in role provided an opportunity for the child, alongside their peers and teacher, to think, *to be* and to reflect from a distance. Miller and Saxton (2011: 121) write of the power of such story drama scenarios; thus 'they unravel the issues and challenges of being human through the metaphor of story'. Previously, the child had resisted or was simply unable to articulate or share their personal thoughts and feelings during more traditional class discussion activities such as circle time. Whilst the child was speaking from the perspective of the imagined role, the story drama struck a chord; the sentiments it evoked resonated with their lived experience. This transformative exchange was the building block for reciprocal understanding, helping to nurture the child-teacher relationship in the real classroom thereafter.

Stories Matter

Stories allow us to discover ways of knowing self, knowing others and knowing the world in which we live (Booth and Barton, 2000). Drama education facilitates this, offering creative, stimulating and rich contexts for stories to unfold and, crucially, for emotions, attitudes, beliefs and empathy to flourish. Story drama matters because it offers *all* participants the opportunity to engage *within* a story. Booth and Barton (2000) explain that young children 'can find "self" inside the act of storying, as they try to order and communicate their thoughts, constructing both the story and their identity in the process' (Booth and Barton, 2000: 15). Engagement is facilitated by the teacher who works both *in* and *out* of role. The imaginary context of the story drama provides the children with an opportunity to explore issues, examine situations and even to take risks; this is deeply reflective. Children enter imaginary situations and contexts which allow them to 'test the fire without getting burned' (Kukla, 1987: 76). As children navigate through an unfolding story, they are invited and encouraged to react, respond and enact authentically rather than simply talking around possible emotional content. An opportunity is created which allows the children to reimagine rather than simulate or reproduce, often one-dimensional dramas. This reimagining involves the type of role play advocated by Bolton and Heathcote, one that 'is making of meaning for contemplation' (Bolton and Heathcote, 1999: viii). Teachers and children unravel meaning and gain understanding through the artistic medium of role work. This, Taylor (2000: 112) argues, 'provides experiences which change and transform us, experiences which provoke good and sometimes unsettling questions, experiences which both please and educate'. Given the open-ended, unscripted and unpredictable nature of this approach some teachers may feel a sense of unease at the thought of relinquishing control. Yet this way of working provides space for each child's creativity of thought and agency. It is, ultimately, social constructivism in action where teachers invite and listen actively to children's responses in a 'different way' (Killen and Cooney, 2017: 10).

Developing a Sense of Self

Positive relationships lie at the heart of effective learning and teaching (McCulloch, 2018). Attachment theory tells us that insecure early attachment experiences can have implications for relational connections (Geddes et al., 2017) (see Chapter 4). When children enter the classroom, they bring with them their lived experiences, coined by Esteban-Guitart and Moll (2014: 31) as 'funds of knowledge/funds of identity'. Identity – one's sense of self – is in a constant state of flux, evolving as individuals grow, develop and interact with the world around them. Yet an additional layer of complexity emerges when 'developmental trauma' (Bombèr et al., 2020: 68) comes into play; in this scenario identity and self-worth are highly fragile as the child views themselves, 'through the lens of their own feelings of worthlessness and shame' (Bombèr et al., 2020: 68). The heightened sense of constant anxiety is the common thread weaving through the child's funds of knowledge/identity.

For those children facing early adversity a wide range of characteristics can manifest, and these necessitate sensitive and informed intervention. Geddes et al. (2017: 46) advise that '[i]nterventions need to be consistent and led by the fundamental need for these children to feel safe'. This sense of security and safety can be achieved through a range of interventions: visual timetables, use of transitional objects, and breaking activities down into manageable, achievable steps. These all contribute to building a compassionate learning experience for the children. Van der Kolk reinforces the significance of cultivating a safe environment as follows:

> More than anything else, being able to feel safe with other people defines mental health; safe connections are fundamental to meaningful and satisfying lives. The critical challenge in a classroom setting is to foster reciprocity: truly hearing and being heard; really seeing and being seen by other people.
>
> (Van der Kolk, 2014: 423)

The challenge for educators can be that for vulnerable children, their safe space is invariably to withdraw and to compartmentalize their authentic feelings and emotions. Their safe place is not to be seen, not to be heard and not to share. How do teachers truly listen, truly notice and foster reciprocity with children who carry with them trauma and appear not to engage?

How a child feels personally, socio-emotionally, physically and cognitively affects their capacity to learn and all this is linked intrinsically, to positive health and well-being (Education Scotland, 2017a). Adversities that emerge from a child experiencing the impact of trauma cause disruption; this disruption can remain and indeed grow with them, compromising their very sense of self (Bowlby, 1969, 1973, 1980). Bombèr et al. (2020: 67) articulate this simply yet powerfully as a 'shame-based sense of self'. For a child with secure attachments, traditional support mechanisms, and learning and teaching interactions, can invariably be drawn on to facilitate working through challenging behaviour or offering advice for a particular action. In this context constancy is the 'capacity to take it for granted that no matter what part of the self you are currently experiencing, all the other parts of the self, continue to exist' (van Gulden, 2000: 1). Constancy, for these children, is present. However, for the child with resultant trauma, it is inordinately difficult for them to draw on other parts of themselves for resilience, reassurance and soothing purposes if the spotlight is shone on one part of them. For these children, it is fundamental to nurture their self-efficacy. This capacity-building can be approached sensitively and compassionately through creative and playful contexts. Miller and Saxton (2011: 119) encapsulate this perfectly: '[w]ith imagination, we have the ability to dream, to invent, to conjure new possibilities. Its power lies in its ability to take us outside the box of our daily routines and conventions, enabling us to see different horizons.'

Policy documents and discourse in Scotland relating to fostering relationships and attachment guide teachers and school communities towards providing safe places for children. Education Scotland's document, *Applying Nurture as a Whole School Approach* (Education Scotland, 2017a), is one such example. It sets out a framework for educational settings to offer safe environments, championing nurture groups and embedding nurturing approaches in Scottish early learning and childcare centres as well as primary and secondary schools (see Chapter 8). Yet there is another way to foster sense of self, self-worth and a sense of belonging as this can all be nurtured safely in imaginative contexts (Taylor, 2000). Story drama, through its creative, expressive and reflective nature, has the power to build bridges between both the real and the imaginative space. For all children, but most importantly for those who are emotionally vulnerable, safety is paramount. This is especially true when working in drama and many teachers will co-construct with the children a drama contract to establish safe working frameworks (Baldwin, 2008). The agreed contract is values-driven, agentic in nature and is intended ultimately to provide security and respect for all participants. Yet safety does not come simply from agreed rules, norms and expectations; rather, it can and should also be nurtured within the imagined space.

Story Drama

As discussed previously, there is a wide range of understanding of what drama in the classroom encompasses. Story drama is a social encounter, and it is important for teachers to appreciate that drama can be used as a method to make connections between learners, emotion and space (Baldwin, 2024). When a child participates in make-believe play, they are engaged actively in the suspension of disbelief. It is this removing of themselves from reality into a fictitious setting that helps them reflect and make meaning of self and others. Participants subconsciously bring their lived experience to the make-believe narrative they engage with. Indeed, Taylor (2000: 7) contends, '[a]lthough teachers may safely assume that there are conventional readings of the material, they also are aware that people's relationship to content is dependent on their own interpretation of the world'. This imagined role play experience is a safe space when a participant is exploring and interpreting the content through the lens of trauma. When careful thought is given to the dramatic learning material and when children move into pretend worlds, their actions become symbolic. This type of play is symbolic play (Trawick-Smith, 2014). Taking on a role and *pretending to be someone other than themselves* is a natural part of child development and learning about the world through play. Bolton (1979) highlights there is a clear difference educationally, in behavioural terms, 'between what a child is doing when he is "playing" compared with what he is doing when he is using the art form of drama' (Bolton, 1979: 32). It is vital that teachers have knowledge and understanding of this subtle and powerful distinction as drama has the rich capacity to nurture and develop the imagination's ability to 'make believe' (Neelands, 1992: 7). It is more than simply developing a set of drama or acting skills. Rather, what emerges is an increased perception and growth of ideas beyond their developmental stage. Vygotsky (1978: 102) states that '[i]n play a child behaves beyond his age, above his daily behaviour; in play it is as though he were a head taller than himself'. Working within a story allows children to form knowledge and understanding of self, others and the world in which they live. Working within a drama story provides the children with an opportunity for a participative role where they can take action, make decisions and become agents of change. Roles respond to dilemmas or problems, and it may be that these decisions are contrary to the children's personal opinions and/or ideas. The outcome of using role work as a medium for learning is for children to experience 'new ways of seeing and, perhaps, shifts in understanding' (Miller and Saxton, 2011: 122).

The imaginative and creative involvement that evolves from drama can be a powerful catalyst for writing (Booth and Barton, 2000). Role work embodies such creativity and can take many forms. The drama convention *Writing in Role* (Bladwin, 2024) provides purpose and frames perspective thinking within a range of writing strategies and styles. For example, children may be required to pen a letter, prepare a journal article, complete a diary entry, complete, provide a witness statement, compile a questionnaire or prepare a town criers announcement! Whatever genre of writing, the child is engaging – either individually or as part of a group – *in role*. Kitson and Spiby (1997) describe this creative engagement within a fictitious narrative as working from the affective to the cognitive.

Thinking Point 13.3

a. When a teacher enters a different 'space' in role what benefits come from this strategy?
b. In what way does the strategy of Teacher in Role (TiR) provide an opportunity for a transitory and imaginary shift in the teacher-child relationship?
c. In what way can the strategy of TiR be utilized to support safe places for all children?

Teacher in Role: A drama convention to activate dramatic engagement

Central to story drama is the idea that the teacher actively co-constructs the imagined world with the participants. One way in which the teacher can do this is to utilize the drama convention of Teacher in Role (TiR). Baldwin (2024: 12) acknowledges that this way of working 'can be liberating and surprisingly productive, for both the pupils and the teacher'. Baldwin goes on to assert that '[p]upils find their teacher working in role to be highly engaging and are often fascinated by this unusual type of pupil/teacher interaction' (Baldwin, 2024: 40).

The Role of the Teacher

When the teacher is adopting a role, they must consider and be clear about the purpose that role will play in relation to children's learning, engagement and the overarching story drama. A small-scale research project outlines a scenario when working with a primary 7 class (aged 10–11). The children were asked what it was like for them when their teacher went into role. It was the first time the teacher had used this strategy and there were many responses: 'it was exciting'; 'it was a bit strange at first'. One child's response was unexpected and caused the teacher and the researchers to reflect on the power, potential and value of the strategy. 'I don't mean to be disrespectful, but you were different, and it was a relief when you were someone else for a while' (Killen and Cooney, 2017).

For some teachers, working *in role* can be challenging (Baldwin, 2008); however, it is a way of working that allows teachers to be receptive in a different way to the children, whilst engaging in dramatic contexts. This is listening and not just hearing. It is important to highlight that when using the strategy of TiR teachers are not performers, nor is the class an audience (Morgan and Saxton, 1987). Rather, the teacher assumes a role in which they communicate a range of beliefs and attitudes. There are many reasons why TiR is used when working within a story-based drama. Most importantly, it provides the children with an opportunity to direct the fictional pathways with teachers problem-solving collaboratively alongside them. When a teacher enters the fictitious narrative, it allows them to work with the learners. For some children, as highlighted in the narrative above, this way of working can be a *way in* to learning experiences that may not have been achievable before. The convention demands that teachers respond to the ideas of the children. When reflecting on the efficacy of teacher in role as a way of working, Taylor (1998: 106) reflects that it can help 'students find a voice for themselves'. The act of engaging in role invites the children to enter the fictitious space and this reinforces a sense of ensemble: we are in it together! Baldwin (2024) explains that a teacher may use this pedagogical strategy for a range of learning and teaching reasons. TiR, for example, could be utilized to deliver and/or collect information, to present an important message, to pose a problem or difficulty that requires to be collectively resolved or, even, to seek help. These examples offer a unique way of working as the teacher is in role when working through the dilemma and/or problem alongside the children. This alters quite subtly, yet significantly, the traditional teacher-child relationship. To implement effectively, the teacher must also navigate children's learning. Raising both planned and spontaneous questions and exploring possibilities as the story drama unfolds helps to capture and deepen children's learning experiences. Miller and Flint Stipp (2024: 2) assert that within the field of trauma-informed practices there is growing recognition of the need to form 'positive relationships with students, attuning to students' needs, integrating culturally responsive social emotional learning and practising self-care'. When teachers employ the strategy of TiR, they invite children to engage in a way of working that naturally creates opportunities to foster positive relationship building. The power of this way of working lies in the fictitious context; the learning experience becomes a safe place. As a teacher works in role alongside the children, their authentic response emerges through active engagement. It is worthwhile noting that there is no need in this scenario for the teacher to consciously plan for separate trauma-informed learning contexts; these emanate naturally as this inclusive approach evolves. Story drama offers a shift away from the 'deficit-based view of children' that Miller and Flint Stipp (2024: 4) caution against. The safe space permits the children to participate on their own terms rather than the teacher imposing predetermined, preconceived ideas. Cummings et al. (2017, cited in Miller and Flint Stipp, 2024: 4) highlight this beautifully: 'educators should respond to student behaviours with curiosity rather than assumptions about trauma and its impact.'

For teachers and children who are not acquainted with the dramatic convention of TiR, it is advisable to introduce the strategy within a pre-existing learning context for a short period of time; this helps grow familiarity and instil confidence in its dynamics and possibilities. Central to the approach is that it is clear to the children when exactly the teacher is in and or out of role (Baldwin, 2024). This can be achieved by using a visual aid. For example, 'when I am carrying this clipboard, I am taking on the role of the Second World War billeting officer' or 'when I put these gloves on, I am taking on the role of Scot of the Antarctic'. Additionally, the teacher should not overact. It is not about the efficacy of one's performance. The purpose of taking on a role is to communicate an attitude, a belief or to engender feelings and emotions belonging to that role. In so doing the children are invited to engage, interact and connect in and out of role.

Thinking Point 13.4

In what way can drama provide emotional safety?

Distancing provides a safe place

Circle Time is a familiar way of working in the primary classroom. Teachers use this pupil-centred approach to encourage emotional and behavioural awareness as well as promoting positive well-being. Through working within a shared fiction, story drama fulfils this function too. Baldwin (2012) makes an important distinction between drama and circle time:

> ....in drama the child is being asked to work in a distanced way through adopting a role. In Circle Time the children's personal attitudes and opinions are publicly presented and remain personally attached to the child whereas, more flexibly, in drama a character's attitudes and opinions are presented for response. Drama, like dramatic play, provides a powerful and unique, playful yet serious, social forum which is distanced safely from the child through role play.
>
> (Baldwin, 2012: 17)

Over time we have been conditioned in society to divorce ourselves from the reality of our emotional state (Van der Kolk, 2014) and therefore talking about personal feelings, for many children who have experienced trauma, can be an uncomfortable proposition. Van der Kolk (2014: 403) stresses that '[t]raumatised people are afraid to feel deeply'. The construction of creative spaces that are safe for participants to engage is critical. Van der Kolk (2014) recognizes the transformative potential of drama stating that '[a]cting is an experience of using your body to take your place in life' (Van der Kolk, 2014: 398). This physical and cognitive experience provides opportunities for the social emotional domain to be nurtured. Greene (1995: 14), the American educational philosopher, 'thinks of teaching as a way of finding space'. When children step into a role, when they embody the role's attitude, beliefs and perspectives, their personal 'alarm systems' (Van der Kolk, 2014: 424) are temporarily quietened. This transitory shift away from self, it seems, offers children who hurt, the space in which to grow and to *be*. In studies of process drama, distancing is traditionally considered within the theme of estrangement (Eriksson, 2011), a concept that evokes feelings of detachment. Yet there is positivity here too when using this approach in our classrooms as '[t]hrough estrangement, the familiar can be made strange, so that things are seen in a new light, with new awareness' (Eriksson, 2011: 103). Bolton (2006: 58) claims that 'dramatic art does have its own means of protection. We call it "distancing"'. Through engaging in the world of make-believe a sense of detachment is facilitated and this, in turn, 'creates a protective distance between oneself and one's fictive role' (Eriksson, 2011: 104). It is this emotional protection that allows for reflective engagement and active contemplation. The very act of exploring difficult and sensitive issues relating to others within a fictitious context helps to build a safe space for all children. O'Neill (2017) explains this in relation to a folktale story drama activity: '[t]he pre-text – a very brief and simple re-telling of the folk tale, provides an immediate degree of distance in time and location, and in its non-realistic, mythic quality. This distance will allow the participants to engage with powerful and possibly painful themes' (O'Neill, 2017: 27).

Summary

For children who have experienced trauma, 'fear restricts, and safety expands learning and relationships' (Treisman, 2017: 10). Establishing and nurturing a safe space and environment for children lies at the heart of Scottish educational discourse and policy (Education Scotland, 2024b). This chapter has considered ways in which the well-being of all children, particularly those who have a 'fragile sense of self' (Treisman, 2017: 209), can be supported through the curricular discipline of drama. The theoretical perspective of process and story drama was explored, a pedagogical approach that creates imagined experiences where children 'learn to feel what they feel and know what they know' (Van der Kolk, 2014: 411). When children are in role a safe space is established, leading to a climate or culture where 'protection into emotion' can germinate (Bolton, 1984: 128). Furthermore, when teachers become involved in the story drama through the dramatic convention of Teacher in Role, the impact is powerful and transformative. This collaboration decreases the distance between teacher and the children, changing the traditional relational dynamic; the teacher here is 'as much a receiver as a giver of signals when working with a class' (Wagner, 1999: 28). In this way, the teacher can swiftly gauge and respond authentically and naturalistically to the emotional pulse or the social health of the children (Wagner, 1999: 28).

14

In Conversation with ...

Part 1: Hayley Clacy, Headteacher (Retired 2025), Spenvalley High School, England

Christine: Why did you agree to be part of this project?

Hayley: I believe passionately in running a school in a relational, trauma-informed way. I understand the anxieties of leaders to do so, and if we can get more information out there from people who are doing it, being really honest about the challenges, then that's what we want to do.

Christine: What makes a trauma-informed school?

Hayley: I'll tell you what it doesn't mean first of all, because I think there is sometimes a wilful misinterpretation of what it is. The myth is 'there are no rules, and there are no sanctions'. And that is not true. There are rules and sanctions. And, I would argue, the rules in our school are not dissimilar to the rules in most schools. The difference about our sanctions is how we manage them. There isn't a roadmap of automatic consequences. It's a common-sense approach to how you deal with it on a personal level. You look at every case individually. You look at the reasons why someone has behaved in the way they have and then you put in the appropriate sanction. Often, the conversations you have with a young person are more important than a sanction, in terms of educating them.

Being trauma informed is not just about having a specific behaviour policy, it is everything you do; it's your DNA that runs through the school. It's your curriculum, how you teach, how you recruit your teachers, even in a very difficult climate of recruitment you still have to hold firm to that ethos. It's how you speak to each other as adults. It's how you speak to the children, to the families, and that doesn't mean that you dumb down, but you appreciate when somebody is at crisis, and you look at connection before correction. It is, of course, the behaviour systems and the policies. It has to be that. And it's how we manage young people. And I would say we try to manage young people as if we are taking that idea of 'in loco parentis' properly. Being firm but entirely fair, providing equity rather than equality. It's our staff wellbeing programme, which we pride ourselves on. It's how you lead. We believe in developing kind leaders, leading with kindness and respect. It's every element of the school, and it's about challenging yourself as well as having that honesty. And it's the language that you use. It is also, of course, about additional provision that you might put in places relevant to the students you've got in your school, which we've invested quite heavily in now. It's not what we do; it's who we are.

Christine: What brought you to believing in this approach?

Hayley: I've been teaching thirty-four years, and I've taught for the vast majority of my time in socially deprived areas, and my roles, whilst I am a history teacher, have been predominantly pastoral. When I started teaching, there were no behaviour policies and no schemes of learning. You just taught and learned how to teach. You taught knowing the kids, getting to know the kids, developing relationships, with a bit of chalk and some effort and 'botheredness'. And then, of course, about twenty years ago, these behaviourist approaches had come in, and I was never a big fan of 'You do this (then) you get that'. Then there's an escalation. I've never really, as a teacher, implemented those policies. I've not really needed to, and that's not because I'm brilliant, because I teach in a certain way based on my background. You know, to be able to manage dysregulated young people, with all the skills that we have as teachers, a bit of humour sometimes works. And then I became a head teacher about thirteen years ago. In my first headship, I brought in *The Chimp Paradox* by Professor Steve Peters – and it was to help us as leaders manage those very difficult situations, and they worked with us every fortnight for about two years. It was really helpful, learning about the brain. It wasn't about trauma; it was about understanding the science of the brain. And then I came here, and the school had a behaviourist approach, and I knew that something different was needed. We'd already started to try and do restorative approaches, and then we applied to the Alex Timpson programme. We got onto that. And I guess, as they say, the rest is history. And then, all of a sudden, Covid-19 hit, and we were being told that we need to worry about the mental health of young people, as if this was some sort of new thing.

We'd already started that journey. And actually, the approach fitted in really well with how we were supporting the young people during the pandemic. When we came back after Covid-19, there was a directive that was coming from the Department for Education (DfE) about being more robust with behaviour because children have been 'feral' and they had their mobile phones, etc. Well, they had faced trauma. Every child had faced trauma, and I think our approach was better. I think it's been really hard, because we've had to keep going back and saying there have been increased dysregulations, different types of dysregulation from six years ago. Is that because of the approach? Or is it because of what's going on in their lives? And what we've had to say is 'the system' is wrong for our children. We can't change the system at the moment, although I'd love to. We have to change our approach. The other bit, as well, which I didn't realize, my mum died when I was twelve, and I thought, I didn't realize that I was a child of trauma, because we didn't talk about it.

The other thing is, over the years, I've done lots of different things in terms of pastoral work and, we know this from attachment theory, there is an innate need to belong, and if they don't belong to school, and if they don't get a sense of secure belonging in the family, they will gravitate towards somewhere where they do belong. We don't have easily accessible alternative provisions here; if they are kicked out of school, whether it's suspensions or permanent exclusions, they will go somewhere, and there are people who will make those young people feel like they belong, whether they are gangs, extremists of all different factions, using sexual exploitation. Those people, you know, paedophiles and gangs don't appear to be baddies to children to begin with. There are places where children feel they are looked after, they are part of something, and then the badness comes out. And it's not just about improving my school; it's about making sure those vulnerable people are not exploited. But more important than that, I want our young people to develop their own kindness and respect, so that when they are adults, they will be better parents and kinder parents, they'll be kinder partners, kinder brothers and sisters. That's a really ideological thing, but you've got to have ideology to do your job and be in the eye of the storm.

Christine: What would you say has been the impact of your trauma-informed approach?

Hayley: Well, it's not a linear impact. That's for sure. I'll say the impact is three steps forward, two steps backwards. Suspensions are down quite significantly, but we do still suspend more than I would want. But we are seeing, at the moment, a number of very dysregulated children, since Covid-19, actually getting in and staying in the lesson is a problem. But the high level of behaviour that used to happen six years ago isn't happening. It's a different type of behaviour. It's much more manageable. But time consuming. One of the impacts which I hadn't recognized is that we had some interviews for student leaders and one of my governors is an educational psychologist. She interviewed with me. The children talked about regulation, reflection; they talked about things that I thought were normal for them.

She [the educational psychologist] said that she didn't think I understood that the language our children use naturally is something that even psychologists have to learn. And of the nineteen children we interviewed, fourteen of them said they wanted to go into caring professions, and I don't think that's a coincidence. We have a lot of children who want to go work in social care or work as care assistants, that sort of thing. I do think the relationship with staff and kids is good. Visitors come and look around – they say that it is palpable; the relationships are palpable, and it's just little things like you say to a kid, 'How are you doing?' And they say, 'I'm alright, and you, Miss?' Kids will ask us, 'Did you have a nice weekend?' And that for me, that interaction was not there six years ago. So, it's not a key performance indicator. But, oh my God, it feels good.

Christine: What have been the challenges for you to create this?

Hayley: The biggest challenge was winning the hearts and minds of people. We did it gradually, and we did it using really good quality training which the Timpson programme gave us, and we did it over a year. We started off by doing restorative approaches anyway. Using the evidence to show this, we went to places where there was this sort of practice going on. It's also how you treat your staff as well. If they see that you are being benevolent and kind to them, then that almost becomes by default that they understand that. And then there came a bit of a turning point, and I've had some challenging dialogues with staff. We involved staff in writing the relationship policy. We are very open if the behaviour is not good enough. The other one was Covid-19. It's about building relationships, and those children were not there to build the relationships with, instead it was contact through zoom. So, we did home visits when other people didn't. We stood at the end of drives and did it. We didn't focus on their learning as much as perhaps other schools did. We talked about how well they were. We did a lot of videos to make them laugh. We did a lot of very good communication as well about managing anxiety when they came back in. But more importantly, stemming from Covid-19 is that some of our children were locked down in the very place where they were facing trauma. And that's going to make it worse, isn't it?

The curriculum is a barrier, because we have to fit children into something, and I think they should have a broad and balanced curriculum. The performance measures do not suit because schools are competing with schools. And the way to get those levels up is to off-roll those difficult children, and that for me, the barrier of removing those huge support mechanisms outside around sure starts, all the things that help families that are in crisis. We're removing all of those yet we're squeezing those children down, and then we're saying they are misbehaving.

Ofsted is a problem, because we know that it puts leaders under huge pressure and pressure to do things in a certain way. But I think probably one of the biggest barriers is ourselves losing faith when it gets hard and saying, is it the system? We did this the November we came back after lockdown, we got some help, and I brought our educational psychologist in and she was great; it's about having somebody you can trust. If you give children the space to express their emotions in fear, anger and sadness, then you might see some of that, and I say of my school, 'It's not always pretty', and that for me it's about holding the line when things get tough. It's about having people around you to be able to do that. So there have been lots of barriers we keep ploughing through because we can only do what we can do.

Christine: Do you think trauma informed is the term we should be using?

Hayley: I think it's probably suggesting that it's quite a negative thing. I do think language is really important. I'm very careful about the language that I use. What I try to do now is, and you sort of mix and match, sometimes we say we're attachment aware, trauma informed, a relational approach. I think we are sort of evolving into it. But we do still use all three phrases.

What I do is I talk about the phrase 'in loco parentis', and I say, it is like being a parent. Being a parent means sometimes you have to sit down with them and explain things. Sometimes you have to say, 'No! That's enough! That's not up for negotiation'. So, certain things I will negotiate as I work and other I will not. We try not to permanently exclude our own children, and we manage this. And I have a mantra: 'If it's not good enough for my children, it is not good enough for the children that we teach.' **Christine:** What still needs to be done?

Hayley: Loads! Resilience is our biggest focus at the moment, and it's not just children. We've done one parent workshop. We do a lot of parent workshops around helping them support with exams and learning, etc., but we started doing one around helping to develop resilience. Because I think a lot of the parents, for all sorts of very understandable reasons allow their children not to be resilient, and because of their own complexities struggle to help. We know society has become less resilient anyway. During the next term we're going to be working with guiding people to develop a charter in kindness and respect. All of the children will be working on it and some of them will be leading it.

We are facing some quite significant financial issues in the local authority. So, the access to any alternative step-outs is gone. We are developing an on-site step-out placement, which is part of our school. We already have a huge, personalized learning provision in the heart of the school. This is for the children whom we are increasingly getting. They may have been permanently excluded from another school and it's really hard to get them into our way of working, because they're angry and they're resistant, but that provision would keep them on-site.

I was able to talk to a couple of MPs about what we're doing and one of them said to me, 'What about the good children?' And I said, 'They're all good children, first of all, and secondly, every child may experience trauma in their life, and it might be that you get those very, very studious girls who then break down when it comes to exams.' You want a trauma-informed approach, then, or a relational approach, at least. It's for all children.

Part 2 Pupils and Staff from The Bothy, Larbert High School, Scotland

Context: In Scotland a 'bothy' is defined as a small, simple building to shelter in, or one that is used on a farm for workers to live in. In Larbert High, it is a room created in partnership with a Scottish social enterprise (Beinn Unity – https://www.beinnunity.co.uk). The aim is to provide a safe environment for pupils to access interventions, build resilience and develop positive experiences. Kitbag (https://www.iffkitbag.com) is a resource used within The Bothy to help young people discover ways of expressing their feelings and sharing their thoughts. Its elements include a colour card, to express feelings, and a set of animal cards with particular words on them, for example, confidence, trust, celebration, etc., used as prompts for discussion. The following is an extract from a conversation with the founder of The Bothy (Lisa), a member of support staff (Steph) and some pupils (P1, P2, P3, P4) who use it.

Christine: I'm Christine. I used to be a teacher, and now I'm a lecturer, so I work with people that are going to be teachers. Now I'm trying to talk to people about things that are important to young people.

Lisa: I'm just Lisa, you all know me. I'm the one that makes them come here and talk about how they feel and try and help them with their world problems.

Steph: I do a lot of intervention work with Lisa, so I take a group of young people to the local dog behavioural centre we work with. We work on reducing anxiety, reducing stress and also overcoming judgement and feeling like there's stigma attached to being a young person who might be from a particular background or have particular things going on in their life. And Wednesdays we do 'dare to venture' together and I do a lot of Kitbag sessions on my own out with this space.

Christine: And you've got Kitbag in here as well. Do you like Kitbag?

P1: Yeah.

Lisa: Does it feel good to know that you're not the only person that has big feelings sometimes?

P1: Yeah.

Lisa: You've met quite a new, a good group of girls. It's an all-girls group. And it's good. It's a good array of ages. There's maybe six or seven girls in that group, but I think they've all gelled really well. They're like wee friendships that they didn't have before.

Christine: And do you like the animal cards?

P1: I like the animal cards because I feel like it allows you to talk further into it and actually explain how you feel better than just choosing a colour.

Lisa: P2 always keeps me on point because I always forget to do the card of the week. We have it on the wall. She gets the vibe for the group and how we've been feeling and then she says these are the ones we need. You pick up what we feel as a community.

Lisa: What's your favourite bit of Kitbag?

P2: Probably the animal cards. I feel like at the very start, I didn't know what I was meant to do with them. And I got a bit stuck, but I've done it so many times now that I feel like I'm a pro.

Lisa: What about you, P3? What do you think's the best part about Kitbag?

P3: Probably the cards.

Christine: Well, tell me about The Bothy because I've never been anywhere like this.

Lisa: You come in on a Thursday morning first too, because you're part of the young carers group. So, what happens on a Thursday?

P3: Well, we kind of all just come and sit down and then once Lisa registers us we start with Kitbag. We start with the colour card, and we go around and pick a colour for just kind of how you're feeling and then you do the animal cards.

Lisa: And what do we normally do with the animal cards? What's the two questions we focus on most?

P3: Well, you can take two and then keep one for yourself in case you might need it like 'confidence' or you could give one away to someone else who you think might need it. Or someone in your family.

Lisa: And then on a Thursday morning, young carers is one of my biggest groups. It's classed as a drop-in one.

Christine: So why do you think young people like it?

P3: It's just kinda. It's like an easy thing to start with before you go into school. That's what I found. Cos I was really struggling coming into school. I'd been off for ages, but it was quite easy coming in here and just kind of chilling for the first two and then going to your classes rather than just being thrown in and doing work immediately.

Lisa: Yeah well, you've got a lot going on at home. Sometimes it's just harder to get here and focus. Young Carers is a really good group cause it's a massively mixed bag, isn't it? Some people come in and it's a family thing where there are brothers and sisters in the group as well, and then there's ones that it's friends that have got the same kind of things going on at home. It's a community. I see a difference in P3 coming in chatting to people he would never talk to before because there's people in that group you would never even have known their names.

Christine: And what about you, P4? When do you come in here?

P4: After break on a Tuesday and Wednesday.

Lisa: So, on a Tuesday. What do you do?

P4: We go to the care home.

Lisa: What do we do normally? Why do we go to the care home?

P4: We do activities and that like karaoke, gardening, fishing.

Lisa: What were you doing with C the other week? We were doing time in the garden. A lot of them have lost the ability to do the basic things they used to be able to do like tell time or simple maths or reading due to their injuries or whatever has happened to them. So, we sat in the garden, and we did time with them. Like a bit of teaching.

Christine: Ah right. Do you like it?

P4: Aye it's good.

Lisa: He loves it. He's got a favourite, C, who's crazy for him, isn't she? You literally walk in and she's like 'P4 my boy' and then everybody's shoved out the way till P4 gets to give her a hug. What do we do on a Wednesday? It's called 'dare to venture'. When I started here, I wanted to do outdoors stuff as well and it just grew arms and legs. We literally steal the minibus every Wednesday and fill it full of young people and go. It's timetabled, obviously, but there's fourteen young people that can be on it. We basically try to do a mix between museums and cultural things and outdoor walks. This year, we booked on Stirling Castle; we went tubing and skiing. And we did a big reservoir walk. We went to the stables last week. We went to a fire station. We've got partnerships with all those people that take us in and show us their job and their role and why it's important that we just understand it and some of them are inspired by it.

Christine: It sounds like a good part of the week.

P4: Yeah, it is.

Christine: Do you think every school should have a Bothy?

P3: Yeah, because it's just a kind of calm place or a place to kind of have a chat.

Lisa: Yeah, this isn't meant to be a strict environment, it's good to know that you actually appreciate having some down time. Schools don't always appreciate that; they don't understand that sometimes young people need a bit to themselves, because they don't get it at home, especially being a young carer, you don't get as many moments to yourself, don't you not?

P3: No, not really. It's every ten minutes, I'm being shouted on for something or to go do something.

Lisa: Do you think other schools should have what we've got?

P3: Yeah, for people who don't go to classes, I guess they can come here instead.

Lisa: They don't wander. I think that it's really good if people are feeling overwhelmed that they've got a place they can come to. Relationships are key, that's the whole reason you guys are part of small groups and not individual things like counselling. It's for you guys to build relationships with one another and me and the school. It's kind of a three-tiered thing like you come in, you trust me cause walking in my door the very first time is not the easiest thing. They can have that kind of panic when we're talking about our brains and you're right down the bottom part of your brain thinking like, no, I'm not going. And there's people in there I don't know. And then eventually you just realize I'm not a scary person.

P3: I feel like I had it quite lucky coming in because I came in with N for the fun of it and now, I'm actually, I like it. Now I'm here every week.

Christine: And what do you think makes you keep coming back?

P3: Lisa obviously. You're just really easy to talk to; even if you don't think you have something to talk about, you always end up talking about something. And sometimes it makes you feel better, but sometimes it makes you like, feel sad, which is also kind of what you need sometimes.

Lisa: Yeah, you're just allowed to feel your feelings.

Christine: And I can see your pictures of the brain up there [on the wall]. So, have you learned about your brains?

Lisa: Some groups have. If they're part of the mental health groups we kind of touch on stress, anxiety. Where do we find it in our bodies? But also, if you can understand the layers of your brain are like a cake, we've got how many layers?

P2: Three.

Lisa: And you can't go from one layer to the other without going through the bottom one first. If they understand that, it just gives them that wee peace of mind that this is normal. Everybody's got a brain like this. Every single person goes through these motions. I just have to get better at recognizing them before they set off. I mean the brain is something we talk about every second week. I'll bring it back up and I can see them being like, 'here she goes again with the brain'. We had play dough out last week, didn't we? And we were making them out of plasticine, our brains. And we were just chatting about what's the bottom bit called again? They remember little things like it's the survival brain. 'That's where you run away or you freeze.' And I'm like, 'yeah sort of.' It's just seeing what they remember. And we talk about motivation. Sometimes we'll talk about how we get ourselves motivated and goal setting. We were doing aromatherapy last week.

Christine: Why were you doing that?

P1: To calm you down.

Lisa: We were talking about our senses and how if we smell something, it reminds us of somebody. It can bring back a memory and a feeling.

Christine: I spend my time talking to people who are studying to be teachers. What would you tell me to tell them to do?

P3: Don't just immediately get angry at a pupil if they start to kick off a little bit because there's a lot of teachers that have like zero patience, and if a kid's not in a good mood or something, they immediately just kind of get held back or get at them or they get a negative or something. They don't wait to think if they're just maybe having a bad day or anything like that.

P4: Just don't be crabbit*. [*Bad tempered]

Christine: How does it make you feel when they're crabbit?

P4: Brilliant. I love arguing with them. I'm up for an argument all the time, though.

Christine: So, what happens if you argue with them and they don't argue back?

P4: It's just pointless, then, isn't it?

Lisa: So, you don't start then, do you? Anything else you would tell them?

P2: To look less scary.

Lisa: Okay what does that look like?

P2: I don't know. Just more casual.

Lisa: They're too scary in what way? Like not as smiley and chirpy.

P2: Yeah.

Lisa: Okay, their face rather than what they're wearing? So be more approachable. I think that if you ask, 'what's your favourite subject in school?' They'll pick a subject where they like the teacher. What's your favourite subject?

P3: Drama.

Christine: So, what makes her the best then?

P3: She's just great. She was literally the only teacher I had, that didn't baby me while I was being off where they were just 'take it at your own pace'. That wasn't what I needed. She kind of just said to me, 'It's just if you're not gonna come in, you're gonna fail. I'm gonna help you, I'm going to do everything I can to help you, but if you're not here, I can't.' So, I started coming in again.

Lisa: She gave you the hard truth, but in a kind way.

P3: But I liked that. She can be really scary though sometimes but never to me.

Christine: So, she gave you some really clear boundaries then, didn't she? And that worked for you?

P3: Yeah. She also said even if you don't want to go to class, you can just sit in here. So, I would do that.

Lisa: I think that you have all kind of proven my point there. When it comes to people, your favourite subject is heavily influenced by your teacher.

Christine: So, that's something I can go back and tell our students.

Lisa: I think a lot of them don't get treated as young adults. I think that's the biggest problem.

P3: That's why I like it.

Lisa: You just need to be heard. Teachers don't get time to do it, though, which is really hard. It's that balance, if you've only got them for fifty minutes or whatever, how are they meant to fit that in? But also, if you don't know your young people, you don't know how to get the best out of them.

Christine: So, what would you tell head teachers?

P3: Don't be a ****.

Lisa: So, we've got teachers to be not so scary, be more patient not to be a ****. What else?

P1: I think most teachers are really nice. And I think sometimes people are just not very nice to teachers. Then the teachers aren't nice back, but they are actually nice people.

P3: If a teacher has an understanding why you've not got your homework or why you've turned up late they're less likely to be, 'Nah, they're at it.' They'll be, 'you know what, I get that, that's fine do you need any help?' Because I don't think anyone gets into teaching to be a ****.

Section IV

Building Systemic Responses

15

Building a Trauma-Informed Education Community

Lorna Aitken and Sandra Ferguson

Key ideas

This chapter will:

- examine a model that reflects the spectrum of trauma-informed and responsive practice to meet the needs of children and young people,
- explore the need for a consistent multi-disciplinary and multi-agency approach,
- explore the importance of culture and leadership to implement and sustain change, and
- outline the process underway in Scotland.

Introduction

We write as leaders in different settings who are supporting the ambition of the paradigm shift towards trauma-informed and responsive public services in Scotland. This chapter will look at the foundations which were laid or are already in place to enable the building of a trauma-informed and responsive workforce, with a focus particularly on education. But we will also explore how education fits into the *bigger picture* of a trauma-informed workforce, society and community premised on the idea that 'trauma is everyone's business' (NHS Education for Scotland, 2017: 33). There is also recognition that this needs to be balanced with the reality that not everyone needs to be a trauma expert to support these changes to happen. We will consider how individuals, organizations and wider society being *trauma informed* are necessary but not sufficient for real transformational change that will meet the diverse needs of children, young people and adults where they are adversely affected by trauma. This helps to outline how to enable sustainable change to happen, informed by implementation science.

Thinking Point 15.1

Why do you think trauma is everyone's business?

For children and young people and their families and carers, although many or most will recover well, the scientific evidence indicates that experience of psychological trauma (see Chapter 2) is linked with both the risk of poorer outcomes but also risks poorer engagement with the services that paradoxically are available to mitigate these outcomes of which we know education is key. Overall, we know that trauma does not stand alone as a risk factor and that there is a multiplicative effect on the risk of poor outcomes; that is, the more trauma you experience the higher the risk (Fellitti et al., 1998). This is further complicated with the intersectionality of gender, age, minority ethnic group, sexuality and poverty. However, poor outcomes are not inevitable and the recent upsurge in interest in trauma-informed and responsive services is one response which is gathering evidence and momentum in education and beyond.

We start from the premise as outlined in the previous chapters (see Chapters 2 and 3) that the evidence about the prevalence and impact of trauma is robust, replicated and relatively uncontroversial (Linden and LeMoult, 2022). There is an increasing evidence based on the effectiveness of a range of psychotherapeutic ways to respond to the mental health consequences of trauma including post-traumatic stress disorder (PTSD) (NICE, 2018; NES, 2024). The challenge has been how we translate this narrower clinical approach and developing scientific evidence base into supporting a paradigm shift across policy, systems, societal attitudes and beliefs. Critically, we need practice to change much earlier and upstream of developing entrenched difficulties in order to improve outcomes for children and young people.

A trauma-informed approach should recognize the invisible barriers that are often experienced by people affected by trauma (see Figure 15.1). SAMSHA (2014: 12) state that 'it is recognised that not all public institutions and service sectors attend to trauma as an aspect of how they conduct business, understanding the role of trauma and a trauma informed approach may help them meet their goals and objective'. A trauma-informed and responsive approach is fundamentally a relational approach. We know '[r]ecovery can only take place in the context of relationships; it cannot occur in isolation' (Herman 1992: 133).

There is a growing literature that trauma-informed practice and organizations can improve outcomes for those who are served by the system but also those who deliver critical services (Hales et al., 2019; Schmid et al., 2020). Supporting sustained and effective change in practice is challenging. To enable planning for this approach in Scotland, implementation science was an important guiding approach. This

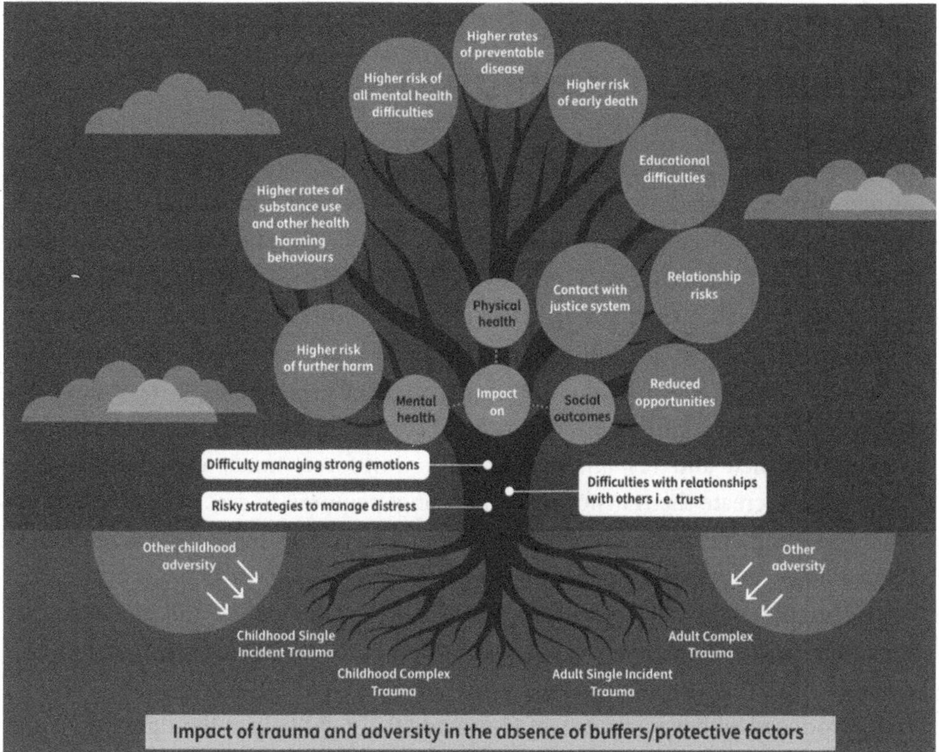

Figure 15.1 Impact of trauma.

From NHS Education for Scotland/Scottish Government Transforming Trauma website. Reproduced with permission.

highlights the factors that are found to influence uptake, scale and sustainability of programmes that evidence suggests are likely to lead to better outcomes, including policy drivers, leadership and culture (Metz et al., 2020).

Thinking Point 15.2

a. What would you as a leader need to consider in order to develop a trauma-informed and responsive approach across your education community?
b. What do you need to look for to support your practice as a practitioner?

Wider Policy Context in Scotland's Educational Communities

In an education setting in Scotland, the ambition of a trauma-informed and responsive workforce is set in a specific policy context for children and young people which has been developed and nurtured over a generation through legislation (e.g. Children and Young People (Scotland) Act 2014 (Scottish Parliament, 2014)) and policy initiatives (e.g. *Getting it right for every child (GIRFEC)* (Scottish Government, 2022a)). This context provides a foundation of readiness for introducing these approaches in the Scottish educational setting. However, although there has been considerable time, effort and investment to date to support the development of a trauma-informed and responsive education workforce, much more needs to be happening to create the transformational change required to reach the aspiration of having safe and effective trauma-informed education communities and being able to fully evaluate and evidence that.

During the early 2000s, Scotland saw a shift towards policy and guidance that supported children and young people's safety and well-being in Scotland. An ambitious multi-agency approach called Getting it right for every child (GIRFEC) was introduced with a commitment to provide the 'right help at the right time' from the right people (Scottish Government, 2022a: 12). This provided Scotland with a consistent framework and shared language to safeguard and support children and young people.

The Getting it right for every child (GIRFEC) approach focused on children's well-being linked with the launch of Scotland's curriculum, *Curriculum for Excellence* (Scottish Government, online), providing staff in schools with a framework which included a specific focus on health and well-being (Education Scotland, 2014), called Responsibility of All. This suggests everyone in a learning community shares the responsibility to consider the mental, emotional, social and physical well-being of every child to create a positive ethos and climate of respect and trust. This context, carefully developed over time, laid the foundation to put the child at the centre and this was further embedded with the drive towards enshrining children's rights into legislation (Scottish Parliament, 2024). In Scotland, another key strategic priority has been to improve outcomes for care-experienced babies, children and young people. This is encapsulated in the national focus of *The Promise* (Scottish Government, 2020b). This innovative and user-led policy development highlights the key role of a trauma-informed workforce as part of the solution of improving outcomes and became an important, specific policy driver.

Alongside this shift in education towards supporting the well-being of children and young people, the Scottish Parliament (then Scottish Executive) came into existence in 1999, as part of the process of the devolution of powers to the nations that constitute the UK. From the outset, driven by campaigning from people with lived experience of trauma and particularly those who had lived experience or advocated for people who had experienced childhood sexual abuse, there was a policy focus on the needs of survivors. Over the intervening years, this was widened to reflect the awareness of the potential, and potentially avoidable, negative impact of Adverse Childhood Experiences (ACEs) (Felitti et al., 1998) (see Chapter 3). This culminated in Scottish Government's commitment to develop a trauma-informed workforce, building on work commissioned from NHS Education for Scotland (NES) towards the development of a national approach to education and training (Scottish Government, 2018). This has ultimately led to the National Trauma Transformation Programme (NTTP) with a remit which extended to the whole Scottish public sector (Scottish Government, 2024d).

National Approach to Trauma-Informed and Responsive Workforce

The NTTP reflects a joint commitment from Scottish Government and local government represented through the Convention of Scottish Local Authorities (COSLA). Other key partners include NHS Education for Scotland (NES) and Improvement Service and Resilience Learning Partnership (RLP), the latter bringing the crucial lived experience perspective. This national ambition reflects the huge range of services that everyone will intersect with across their lives and the potential for each of them to transform lives, particularly if barriers to access, potentially caused by experience of trauma, were removed or reduced.

Trauma-informed practice was initially conceptualized through the work of Harris and Fallot (2001), explicitly using the lens of trauma theory to consider the design of service systems. This has been further operationalized by SAMSHA (2014) (see Chapter 2). Although this is not a formal international agreement on definition, it has been pivotal in providing considerable consensus on key components. In Scotland, this definition was developed to reflect the particular national context, and the model underpinning the trauma-informed element of the work is illustrated in Figure 15.2. Although there are some adaptations to the national context, the model is closely aligned with SAMSHA (2014). This is predicated on the 4 R's:

- **realizing** the prevalence of trauma and understanding potential paths for recovery,
- **recognizing** the impact of trauma,
- **responding** effectively to difficulties arising due to trauma, and
- **resisting** retraumatization.

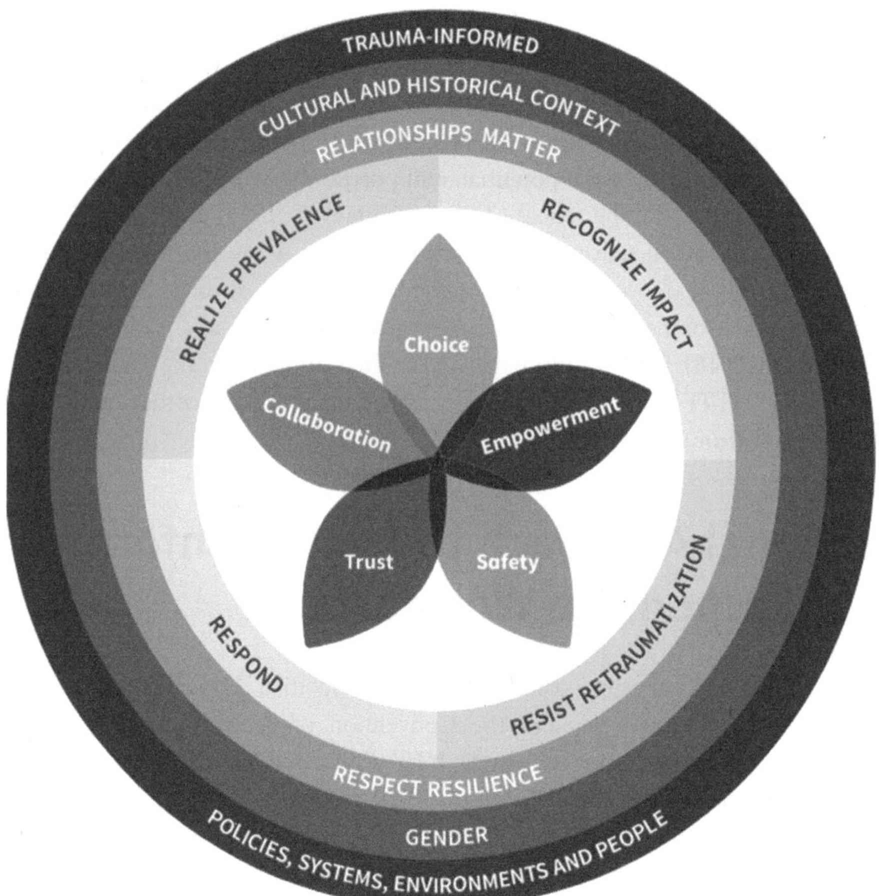

Figure 15.2 National Trauma Transformation Programme (NTTP) elements of developing a trauma-informed system.

From NHS Education for Scotland/Scottish Government Transforming Trauma website. Reproduced with permission.

This can be achieved using the relational principles of safety, choice, empowerment, collaboration and trust. These principles represent the antithesis of the experience of trauma in a relationship, which would create for instance disempowerment and lack of safety.

The NTTP seeks to provide a consistent framework and shared language, to be able to produce core and key resources that support organizations in the task of the implementation of trauma-informed and responsive practice while recognizing that individual organizations or sectors would need to adapt to their specific circumstances. Trauma-informed and responsive approaches will feel different in prisons, in early learning and childcare, in courts, in cancer screening and sports clubs. However, there will be core elements which should be evident in how we experience the workforce that serves the community and how the workforce experience each other and the organizations that employ them. It is an insufficient response for trauma-informed and responsive practice to be evident in individual practice, as it should be embedded within all elements of organizations, in this case education settings, supporting children and young people.

What Does This Mean for Scottish Education Establishments?

We argue that a trauma-informed approach is entirely consistent with and builds upon a nurturing or relational approach embodied in *Getting it right for every child (GIRFEC)* (Scottish Government, 2022a), *Applying Nurture as a Whole School Approach* (Education Scotland, 2017a) and the 'Responsibility of All' aspect within the Health and Wellbeing area of Curriculum for Excellence (Education Scotland, 2017b). Being trauma informed and responsive should encompass a whole-community approach and be complementary to other relational practice approaches including how we support the workforce (Education Scotland, 2018).

The NTTP programme was built on the implementation of science principles that reflect the need not just to *let things happen* through the passion and dedication of individual staff who recognize and rise to the challenge but to *make it happen* by identifying and supporting the factors that the literature and evidence show are required (Metz et al., 2020; NES, 2023a). These factors are outlined in Figure 15.3, which reflects a synthesis of the international literature and local learning across implementation in Scotland. It illustrates the key factors that require attention in the creation of a trauma-informed system and published as part of the Scottish Government's (2023b) Roadmap for Creating Trauma-Informed Change.

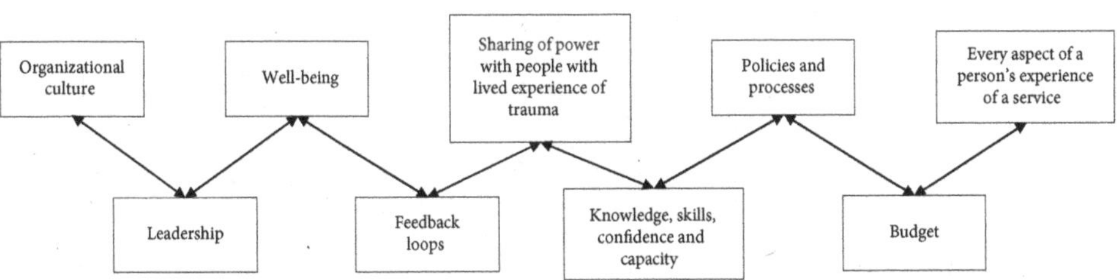

Figure 15.3 Key elements for creating trauma-informed and responsive change (Scottish Government, 2023b).

From NHS Education for Scotland/Scottish Government Transforming Trauma website. Reproduced with permission.

Table 15.1 NTTP practice types in an education setting – this would require support and scaffolding from a trauma-informed system (NES, 2017)

Practice type	Who is this relevant to?	Examples in education setting	What would you expect to see?
Informed	All members of the workforce.	Janitors, reception and admin staff, parents/carers.	Use of the core trauma-informed principles to ensure the entire school community is safe, inclusive and relationship based. Compassionate and non-stigmatizing views of children and young people (CYP).
Skilled	Staff with direct and frequent contact with CYP (and their parents/carers) who may be affected by trauma.	Teachers, classroom assistants.	Teachers being able to make sense, for example, of distress using a trauma lens and give basic normalizing, developmentally appropriate psychoeducational messages. Kind, clear boundaries.
Enhanced	Staff with regular and intense contact with people affected by trauma and who have a specific remit to respond by providing support and advocacy.	Nurture teachers, guidance teachers, social workers, educational psychologists.	Development and implementation of individual trauma-enhanced support plans depending on needs. Provision of guidance and support to colleagues.
Specialist	Staff who have a remit to provide evidence-based psychological therapies and interventions and treatment for those affected by trauma and complex needs.	Educational psychologist, wider mental/health services.	Delivery of psychological therapies, differential diagnostic assessments. Provision of supervision and training to colleagues.

In settings such as schools and education establishments where educators will need sophisticated interpersonal and relational skills to support learners, opportunities to learn and listen along with intrapersonal skills to self-manage make it clear that being trauma informed is necessary, but not sufficient. Recognizing the range of needs arising from trauma, Fondren et al.'s (2020) systematic review examines the effectiveness of a tiered approach (where levels of support varied depending on students' needs) in education settings and concludes that there is strong, recent evidence to support the implementation of this approach (see Chapter 10). This means universal, informed practice aligned with the principles in Figure 15.2 and building on this with an evidence based and incremental set of skills, competences and interventions that match increasing needs and complexity.

Focusing on the knowledge and skills of the whole workforce, the NTTP developed four practice types to reflect the differing needs of all workforces in public services. The practice types are outlined in Figure 15.4. This creates a common language between different areas of the workforce. For children and young people this includes General Practitioners (GPs), health visitors, library staff, dentists, social workers, police officers and sports leaders to name a few. For those working with children and young people in education settings, given the direct and frequent contact with children and young people who may be affected by trauma, we propose educational practitioners should meet the skilled practice type as a minimum with recognition that specific roles and tasks may require additional knowledge and skills (see Table 15.1).

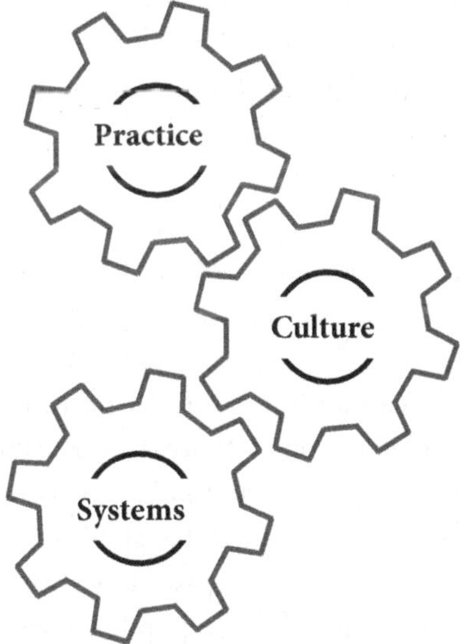

Figure 15.4 Systems, culture and practice in creating change.

Trauma-Informed and Responsive Practice in Scottish Educational Establishments

The education setting offers a long-term opportunity to create safe, empowering, collaborative, relational experiences at a critical point in lives. However, in line with the ambition of the NTTP, responding to children and young people should not be the responsibility of education settings alone but a shared societal endeavour where everyone who impacts on a child or their parent/carers' lives embodies the principles that allow people impacted by trauma to thrive. This is highly aspirational; it will require a lengthy journey of organizational change and one which will require long-term commitment. Given the early and explicit policy focus on education, Education Scotland led the development of professional learning and implementation for the education workforce. Working alongside colleagues at NES and in collaboration with key stakeholders in education authorities, Education Scotland developed a train the trainer programme called Compassionate Connected Communities, which aspired to provide education practitioners with a trauma-aware knowledge, skills and understanding (Education Scotland, 2019). At its core was an enquiry-based element to support evidence-based, small steps of change in practice. However, Covid-19 impacted on the rollout of this model and education authorities and practitioners were seeking more practical supports and strategies that could be understood and implemented in classrooms and settings (Education Scotland, 2019). As such, the programme shifted to online modules, still keeping the core evidence base and shared language from the NTTP but removing the inquiry-based element. This updated version became *Keeping Trauma in Mind* (see https://education.gov.scot/resources/keeping-trauma-in-mind/).

At the time of writing, the Keeping Trauma in Mind programme has been delivered to over 3,000 practitioners across Scotland with bespoke delivery in a number of education authorities. In some locations, delivery has been in collaboration with NHS Education for Scotland (NES), trauma champions and educational psychologists, exemplifying the commitment to working together to ensure the workforce has a consistent approach to developing their trauma-informed and trauma-responsive knowledge, skills and understanding. There is early emerging evidence of the impact of this, including a recent *Behaviour in Scottish Schools Report 2023* (Scottish Government, 2023a: 11) which highlighted that staff 'described improvements to the way that behaviour is described and understood, particularly the understanding of the impact of trauma and neurodiversity on pupil behaviour and the use of trauma-informed language and approaches'. This report highlights education and training focused on trauma has been very much welcomed by school staff, but some expressed the view that it could be tokenistic, with little time to reflect and integrate training into teaching practice. In some cases, a small number of staff are trained and are then expected to cascade the learning to their colleagues, though this approach is not always viewed as being successful. This illustrates the need for opportunities for further embedding trauma-informed and responsive approaches across an education community. Coaching, supervision and ongoing learning are likely to be key to the level of individual practice change, and we continue to look at options to further embed these.

Building a Trauma-Informed and Responsive Education Community

Having staff who are trained – and supported – in understanding and implementing an approach informed by the science of how trauma affects children and young people does not mean they will always use this learning. As outlined in Figure 15.4 it also requires the other key elements of systems, culture and practice to be in place for success to be embedded. This means that appropriate systems are required to be in place and made clear for all staff working across the setting. Best practice would suggest everyone across the school community should be involved in the development of these systems to ensure ownership across the school community. The third wheel on the cog (see Figure 15.4) is ensuring a positive culture across the school or setting is embedded, emphasizing to all in the community that they are valued and will be supported.

Fundamentally, the drive and the vision of creating relational, trauma-informed approaches in an education setting comes from highly effective leadership. School or setting leaders have a critical role in creating the conditions for supporting a whole-community approach to being trauma informed. Having positive leadership, a clear vision and a clear implementation plan, backed up by a robust policy framework is central to the success of creating a trauma responsive education system. The *How Good Is Our School* (HGIOS4) self-evaluation framework supports staff in all sectors to look inwards, to scrutinize their work and evaluate what is working well for learners and what could be better (Education Scotland, 2015). Specifically, section 2.1 focuses on the leadership within the school. Closer detail of those schools achieving very good or excellent often highlights the prioritization of high-quality relationships along with effective learning and teaching embedded within a culture where the school community feel empowered to be active and collaborative leaders of change. Additionally, supporting, motivating and empowering staff to have ownership of the change they want to see is vital. In the same way we would encourage the children to learn from their mistakes, we need to provide that safe space for reflective practice to take place and allow education staff to improve their practice through discussing how situations were handled or dealt with. Within the NTTP, educators and leaders are able to join the Scottish Trauma Informed Leaders (STILT) training programme, where they have the opportunity to learn with others about the elements of successful implementation (Scottish Government, 2021b).

Another critical element of the factors which support implementation of a trauma-informed and responsive approach is the need to consider the well-being of staff within a school or setting. The *Behaviour in Scottish Schools Report 2023* (Scottish Government, 2023a) highlighted the negative impact on staff well-being and morale of both serious and low-level disruptive behaviour. Frustration as a result of managing consistent low-level disruptive behaviour had a particular impact on staff morale and mental health including greater burnout and persistent stress. Education authorities have a duty of care to support the well-being of their staff. Chapter 17 will take a closer look at the need for reflective practice in supporting staff with safe spaces to discuss responding to distressed behaviours as a result of the impact of trauma. However, it is vital that we all recognize that 'you can't pour from an empty cup', and in order to ensure we look after children and young people's well-being, we need to look after ourselves first. Recognizing that for children and young people to regulate, they require emotionally regulated adults around them. It is important to be aware that when we, or our colleagues, are outside our own window of tolerance (Siegel, 1999) as well as how to respond effectively to support our own or others' mental health and well-being.

The National Action Plan on relationships and behaviour in schools: 2024–7 states that '[i]f we are to create the safe and consistent environments in our schools that will enable everyone to thrive, there needs to be a strengthening of relationships across our whole school community' (Scottish Government, 2024c: 2). And suggests that we '[e]mpower schools and staff to apply relational approaches based upon high warmth and high expectations, whilst providing further guidance to support interventions in situations where children and young people are not responsive to such approaches and where assessment would dictate that a more individualised plan will more likely lead to change over time' (Scottish Government, 2024c: 5).

Another vital aspect is consideration of the totality of the curriculum itself placing the well-being of the child at its centre. Curricular approaches should ensure children have meaningful opportunities to contribute and promote their own understanding of their development, including how to build their own resilience and develop their own strategies to support themselves and others. Learning from lived and living experience is a core element of trauma-informed practice and this should not be different in educational settings. Another area of consideration when looking at the development of a whole-education community approach, and being trauma responsive is to have clear and robust arrangements in place to identify need, respond to and monitor the impact of any specific therapeutic interventions whilst acknowledging that often the most effective and upstream way of intervening is via quality relationships, by being attuned to young people and by being present for them.

Trauma-Informed and Responsive Communities

The triangle of a family-school-community partnership through working closely with parents, carers and the wider community is critical in supporting the development of a trauma-informed and responsive education community. Involving parents and carers in discussions and developments along with effective partnership working with local groups and agencies and the third sector can reinforce the consistency in language and approach, therefore strengthening the trauma-responsive community. The workforce, trained to provide trauma-informed and responsive services, are also members of the community and this should ultimately support the wider paradigm shift. Where the prison officers, police officers, judges and sheriffs understand, for instance, that the route to criminal behaviour is often or usually seeded in traumatic childhoods, this changes attitudes and offers a different starting place. For example, 91 per cent of women in Scottish prisons have experienced both childhood and adult trauma (Karatzias et al., 2017). Where general practitioners, nurses and support workers can view substance use and addictions through the lens of self-soothing the effects of trauma, we start to create a more compassionate, relational approach to those most vulnerable in society. This can reflect the needs of our parents, their children and members of our communities. Trauma is everyone's business, and we all have a part to play through trauma-informed and responsive practice and systems.

Summary

In summary, a trauma-informed, and responsive education community should be underpinned by a focus on relationships including nurturing and restorative approaches alongside a shared commitment to understanding the rights of the child (UN, 1989: Scottish Parliament, 2024). The vision, values and aims of the education setting to have relationships at its core should be embedded throughout the ethos and life of the education community. We finish with some extracts from a Scottish Government (2024e) commissioned report which identified a number of impacts being reported in education settings. Following five years of local implementation, these start to illustrate the impact of this ambition:

It seems to have had a really positive impact on staff wellbeing, and it seems to be being embedded into practice, which is really positive (page 44).

I can hear people have had training or are trying to understand it more than just the behaviour, you know, they're trying to think what's gone on for somebody. So that heartens me a lot (page 32).

I think there's a real wider understanding now in that kind of non-judgmental culture, understanding processes of shame, where does responsibility lie, the kind of behavioural consequences model. There's a real understanding within, certainly within education, I presume across other teams of the real importance of looking compassionately at where a child's coming from and thinking with them about next steps (page 32).

These highlight that following a process of implementation and embedding of trauma-informed and responsive practice within a supportive organizational structure that we can see evidence emerging of improved life chances for children and young people through compassionate connections. This may be coupled with better well-being for staff, so ultimately a 'win-win' scenario for everyone in an educational setting.

16

Education Workers as Part of a Bigger Picture

Elizabeth Black and Marie McQuade

Key ideas

This chapter will:

- explore the challenges to embedding trauma-informed practice, including competing pressures and the influence of neoliberal ideologies,
- outline three C's for refocusing the narrative and supporting trauma-informed approaches, and
- introduce case study examples illustrating community connections, contexts for changing practices and resistance through prioritizing care.

Introduction

Given the growing awareness of the prevalence of trauma due to such factors as family instability, community violence, poverty and global crises, trauma-informed practice (TIP) is increasingly recognized as essential rather than simply another passing trend for the education workforce. However, practitioners can feel subject to prevailing winds of political and educational change. Schools often adopt competing frameworks simultaneously (e.g. restorative practice at the same time as a nurturing approach) and these can create a feeling of fragmentation rather than a coherent, integrated way of working. Without sufficient training, support or supervision for effective implementation, educators can become overwhelmed by new programmes (Thomas et al., 2019). Schools lacking these supports due to funding and staffing constraints can mean initiatives are only adopted at surface level rather than the deep, sustained integration necessary for embedding changes in practice. Also, while TIP is an established approach, the long-term impacts on outcomes are still being uncovered, and therefore, some educators may be sceptical about adopting another new model that might be perceived as simply the current political fad (Langley et al., 2013).

It is necessary to work from a position that TIP represents a fundamental shift in education. It also potentially redefines what it means to be an education worker. Within this chapter we will explore some of the systemic challenges to implementing TIP, looking particularly at the barriers created by policy narratives based on neoliberal economic priorities. Tassone (2025: 423) defines neoliberalism 'as a political ideology that focuses on competition and free markets and is associated with globalisation'. We will identify educators as an extended workforce inclusive of practitioners across such varied settings as early learning and school-aged childcare, community development projects, prisons, further and higher education, as well as teachers and other individuals working in schools. Previous chapters situate these workers in relation to other sectors; here we will consider the competing pressures experienced by all educators. We will examine the bigger picture surrounding educational practices, from macro-level narratives of *quality* and *best practice* to institutional cultures and entrenched pedagogical principles, and the way in which they shape the responses of individual educators, settings and governments. In the second part of the chapter, we will then identify some potential solutions to these challenges, with illustrative examples from across the education sector. We will argue that meaningfully embedding TIP requires substantial refocusing of policy aims at all levels, from *quality* to *well-being.*

Thinking Point 16.1

Considering the groups outlined above:

a. How do you define yourself within the education workforce?
b. How does your role as an educator impact on children, families and others?

Challenges to Trauma-Informed Practice

This first half of the chapter outlines key challenges facing those seeking to embed TIP within the education sector, identifying these as coming from external, macro-level policies, but also found within entrenched personal beliefs and local cultures. The pervasive influence of neoliberal practices of monitoring and individual accountability will be highlighted as particularly problematic across all levels of practice.

Policy Drivers

At the macro level, it is possible to trace the influence of international organizations on national policy directions. Here, the guiding presence of neoliberal ideology is evident, defined by Roberts-Holmes and Moss (2021: 6) as based on three C's: competition, choice and calculation. We will show how attempting to integrate trauma-informed or child-centred frameworks into national policy agendas built on neoliberal objectives leads to competing and conflicting messages for practitioners (Langley et al., 2010; Thomas et al., 2019).

The Influence of the OECD

When looking at policy drivers in education, the influence of the Organisation for Economic Co-operation and Development (OECD) must always be recognized, and in doing so, using the full organizational title is a helpful reminder that this body has an explicitly economic focus (OECD, online-a). Seeking to identify the most efficient ways of building strong national workforces, to benefit the global economy, has led the OECD to expend significant resources on research into effective educational practices, with investment in education – from before compulsory schooling age – a key priority (OECD, 2021). Among other benefits, investment in education is associated with personal development and well-being, competitiveness in international markets, democratic participation and improved health outcomes (World Bank, 2011; UNESCO, 2013).

The OECD education agenda focuses on equipping school pupils with the skills and knowledge required to thrive in a rapidly changing world, highlighting the need to make education systems more adaptive, inclusive and effective at preparing children and young people for the complexities and demands of the twenty-first century. Key themes highlighted include the development of future-ready skills and competencies, for example, critical thinking, creativity and socioeconomic skills (OECD, 2019). These parallel the themes which underpin many national curricula, for example, the four capacities of the Scottish *Curriculum for Excellence* (successful learners, confident individuals, effective contributors, responsible citizens) (Scottish Government, online). The OECD *Learning Compass 2030* (OECD, 2019) is an evolving framework outlining the skills, attitudes and values students need to succeed in the future, including adaptability, global awareness and responsible citizenship. Within this agenda, *quality provision* is an important target, with definitions reaching beyond academic performance to incorporate factors such as equitable access, inclusivity and the development of a broad set of competencies considered essential for personal and societal well-being and growth (OECD, 2019; 2021). These outcomes are built onto neoliberal assumptions about the value of market-oriented reform, individualism, requirements for surveillance, accountability measures and international benchmarking. The term 'high quality' then becomes shorthand for this raft of expectations (Moss, 2016; Hunkin, 2019).

The Programme for International Student Assessment (PISA) exemplifies the neoliberal influence of the OECD. By ranking countries based on standardized test scores, PISA pushes educational systems and governments to concentrate on metrics that align with global economic performance targets (Roberts-Holmes and Moss, 2021). The accompanying focus on lifelong learning, skills development and employability belies the organization's primary drive to prepare students to meet labour market demands, evidencing how, in this world view, education is closely linked to economic productivity and global competition (Sims, 2017). The often-discussed *best practice* agenda is strengthened by an OECD approach which promotes measurable data and rankings (OECD, online-b). Countries are driven towards policy convergence as politicians and policy makers make decisions based on those models and approaches found to be most successful in competitive rankings (Roberts-Holmes and Moss, 2021). The globalization agenda can reduce education to a product needing to be optimized, thereby negating alternative educational goals such as critical thinking, emotional well-being or civic engagement (Roberts-Holmes and Moss, 2021; Delahunty, 2024). Embedding TIP across education requires both recognizing the neoliberal thinking underpinning international and national policy and finding ways to resist, work around or work through these existing structures (Tett and Hamilton, 2019).

Competing National Policy Agendas

Supranational messages about the nature of quality educational provision (such as those described above) directly influence national policy agendas, combining with local and national political priorities to shape guidance and directives provided to educational practitioners (Roberts-Holmes and Moss, 2021). Across the UK, and beyond, a pervasive neoliberal emphasis on organizational and personal accountability has infused successive policy initiatives, leading to an emphasis on inspection of establishments, ranking through league tables and publication of graded inspection outcomes, combined with performance tracking of individual educators and regular assessment of children's academic prowess (Tassone, 2025). This volume of assessment and monitoring has led some critics to use the term 'datafication of education' and of childhood (Roberts-Homes and Bradbury, 2016), with ratings scales developed to enable all aspects of care and education to be turned into numerical data for evaluation and comparison. Genuine TIP, however, requires deep engagement with theory and research, understanding of students' emotional needs, flexibility in teaching and family engagement, and reflective practice, all of which can be constrained by a focus on metrics and meeting externally set targets (Langley et al., 2013).

The tension between assessment and measurement versus child-centred TIP stems from conflicting priorities, quantifiable outcomes versus individualized and holistic support (Moss, 2019). Trauma-informed practices are grounded in understanding and responding to the unique emotional needs of each individual child or young person (NHS Education for Scotland, 2017). This expects educators to view children holistically, considering factors such as trauma history, emotional regulation, and child and family mental health. It is an approach requiring flexibility, patience and the prioritization of relational trust (National Trauma Transformation Programme (NTTP), 2023). Conversely, traditional assessment and measurement focuses on standardized outcomes and professional metrics, and can create rigid, inflexible learning environments, driven by top-down curricula, potentially disregarding the learning needs of individual children. This can be particularly difficult for children with a history of trauma, the added pressure to perform exacerbating day-to-day challenges with positive engagement and creating barriers to learning (Brunzell et al., 2016; Tassone, 2025). The dichotomy between TIP and established expectations for assessing academic performance may also create a tension for teachers who want to support all children to meet assessment standards while adhering to personal values and meeting the needs of children utilizing a trauma-informed approach (Behrent, 2016).

Similar tensions can be found in competing messages about professional autonomy and performance measurement. The argument that neoliberalism encourages demonstrative performance to meet targets and undermines genuine professional autonomy is well-rehearsed (Osgood, 2006; Ball, 2016). Where effective performance of educators, and viability of schools, and other educational settings, is measured through targeted inspections of classroom practice or standardized test results, a clear message is sent to educators that these aspects matter most, and that failure to perform can have serious consequences (Behrent, 2016). As already outlined, TIP is an approach built on responsive engagement with individual children and recognition of the interconnected nature of experiences inside and outside formal learning environments. This can be time-consuming and difficult to measure meaningfully and, in a context of strict performance measurement, may seem too risky for individual educators or establishments to prioritize if not a requirement (Langley et al., 2010; Thomas et al., 2019). Even where TIP has become central to policy, continued demands for measurement risk pressurizing educators into seeking shortcuts to the required numbers, rather than meaningful connections. Balancing these competing priorities could, in the longer term, involve redefining success for children and young people, particularly in school or higher education environments, potentially incorporating learner-centred indicators of emotional well-being to assess progress in learning and development, but also reviewing the impact of conflicting policy imperatives on educators' practices (Thorburn, 2014).

Accountability and the Surveillance of Practice

In addition to the bigger picture created by the macro-level drivers identified above, there are also potential barriers to effective implementation of trauma-informed approaches at the micro – local and personal – levels. Across the sector, educational establishments are highly regulated, with external inspection just the starting point for hosts of quality-assurance measures that can be internalized by educators in anticipation of these requirements. Assessment and ratings scales have been developed to support evaluation of practice, for example, the Early Childhood Environment Rating Scale (ECERS) or Leuven scales for early years settings (Laevers, 2000; Sylva et al., 2006) and self-evaluation at both group and individual level, through reflective practice, is promoted. Leaders are expected to have oversight, being held accountable for the actions of their teams, and practices such as learning walks (Steiny, 2009) are encouraged in order to evidence that leaders know what is happening throughout the establishment.

While it can be argued that many of these tools were initially developed with supportive aims – to identify strengths in practice and highlight areas where educators might enhance children's educational experiences – once built, their continued positive benefit depends significantly on the way in which they are used (Hunkin, 2019). Where educational policy focuses on results such as school readiness, test performance or *outstanding* or *excellent* inspection gradings, individuals and establishments can become conditioned to demonstrate the expected performance defined by *best practice* exemplars. In this educational climate, evaluative tools need careful deployment if they are to enhance well-being and support the reflective, nuanced practice required of trauma-informed educators seeking opportunities for change.

As has previously been noted, TIP requires flexibility to respond and adapt to children's needs, both long and short term. Written plans, recorded learning observations and tracking documents are further examples of tools that can potentially support learning but might also constrain the ability of educators to be responsive to specific needs (Shin and Partyka, 2017). Genuine engagement with children and families requires time that can be hard to find in contemporary educational settings where the processes of accountability dominate. Improved relationships and engagement with learning can be slow to fruition and hard to measure using such blunt tools as attendance rates or test scores (Thomas et al., 2019). For individual educators, confidence to exercise professional judgement and autonomy in the face of external targets can be facilitated by a supportive organizational culture, including a collaborative, rather than confrontational, approach to inspections (Hunkin, 2019; McIlroy, 2022; NTTP, 2023). In turn, leaders need to have confidence that TIP meets children's learning and development needs as well as trust in their team to implement responsive approaches appropriately. This is likely to require collective learning and exploration of the underpinning research base at the establishment level, as well as clear guidance from policy makers (Record-Lemon and Buchanan, 2017; Thomas et al., 2019).

Individual Concepts of Effective Education

A final barrier to embedding TIP that will be outlined in this chapter lies in individual understandings of the purpose of education. Within the wider field of education, there are many different pedagogical traditions and historically established approaches to learning. Debates about what counts as learning and how educators should spend their time are both entrenched and evolving (Biesta, 2015; Murray, 2023). As thinking evolves over time, educators are influenced by different key messages in their formative stages, with these shaping lifelong beliefs about effective learning and teaching practice (Nespor, 1987). For both new and experienced practitioners to take trauma-informed approaches forward, it requires each educator to work on building personal understanding of how these can be enacted in their own practice, combined with shared definitions to facilitate effective local working methods (Langley et al., 2013; Thomas et al., 2019).

In the UK and elsewhere, different branches of the education sector have traditionally had separate training routes, professional guidance and professional identities, often linked to particular pedagogical approaches (Smith and Grace, 2011; Nutbrown, 2021; Richardson, 2022). In the face of challenges to professional autonomy from the pressures already outlined, one line of defence is to define specific professional practices and ideologies more tightly, using professional standards or qualifications to determine unique characteristics and make an assertion of worth (Richardson, 2022). Neoliberal thinking encourages development of a mindset that requires value to be identified and articulated in this way (Biesta, 2015; Behrent, 2016) feeding competition rather than collaboration between professionals and potentially reinforcing existing silos, meaning that different educators working with the same children, families or communities might have minimal contact with each other.

Embedding trauma-informed practices requires not only a holistic understanding of individual children but a more holistic approach to education. Seeing education within the bigger picture of the child's life, and the different elements of education is part of a more holistic approach to education (NHS Education for Scotland, 2017; Thomas et al., 2019). This might diverge from an educator's sense of where learning should happen, or whose perspective should count; to an extent, this might demand redefinition of what it means to be an educator. Such a challenge to established, and sometimes hard-won professional, identities might be overwhelming at a time when educators are struggling with the requirements placed on them (Howard, 2019). Expectations that educators and establishments will step outside the silo to build networks and work collaboratively with other agencies, or branches of education, need to be supported with the means to achieve this, both in terms of practicalities, such as time to be released from establishments, and in terms of stated policy priorities to avoid the conflicting messages already discussed (Hymans, 2008; Langley et al., 2013; Thomas et al., 2019).

Thinking Point 16.2

a. What policy and practice drivers are you aware of and how are these influencing your sector?
b. What challenges and debates described here resonate with your own experience?

Potential Solutions

In the first half of this chapter, we explored some key challenges to embedding trauma-informed approaches across the education sector. Common to all these was the underlying narrative of neoliberalism that can be seen to shape policies and practices at all levels, from global initiatives to personal responses. Roberts-Holmes and Moss (2021: 6) suggest that there are three core premises of neoliberal ideology: competition, the primacy of market forces; choice, for the consumer; and calculation, the resulting focus on evaluating the worth of everything. Our argument here is that trauma-informed approaches are fundamentally inconsistent with the pursuit of these neoliberal goals, representing a paradigmatic shift in understandings of effective educational practices and requiring practitioners to resist, work around or work through the available political and organizational structures. For education workers to truly understand themselves as part of a bigger picture, we suggest focusing on an alternative three C's – community, context and care (see Figure 16.1) – that draw from alternative sociopolitical contexts and world views including culturally

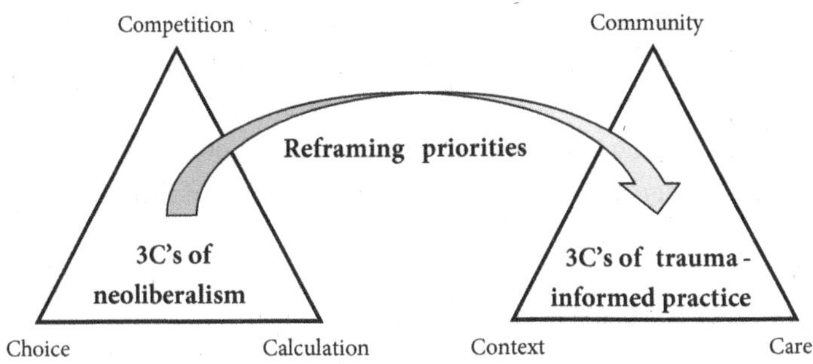

Figure 16.1 Refocusing the narrative.

responsive practice and relational pedagogy (Papatheodorou, 2009; Price and Steed, 2016; Gravett et al., 2021).

Competition between providers needs to be replaced by community, with a focus on identifying the networks within which we work, to establish collaborative approaches (Watson and Astor, 2025). Individual choice needs to become less important than locating ourselves in context, recognizing the interconnected nature of our actions and existence, and that any individual choice has implications elsewhere (Moss, 2019). Finally, rather than calculating the potential value of everything, trauma-informed approaches need to be built on an attitude of care, looking outside our own interests to focus on the concerns of others (Price and Steed, 2016).

This second half of the chapter now provides three short case studies illustrating organizations where these principles are being enacted by policy makers and practitioners, illustrating ways in which TIPs might become part of a new narrative for education.

Building Networks: Working Together to Support Well-Being

As noted above, inter-agency or collaborative working has been a feature of educators' practice for some time but may focus mainly on those children deemed most at risk. Educators from different branches of the sector do not always have equal standing within these partnerships, particularly when health and social care professionals are also present, and degrees of authority and professional recognition can vary substantially (Richardson, 2022).

Outside of case conferences, high levels of contact time and other demands can leave educators lacking in opportunities to meet and build supportive cross-sector or interdisciplinary relationships (Thomas et al., 2019). While the challenge to professional identities created by taking a *big picture* view of education might be problematic for some individuals, it can also be understood as the current phase in an ongoing evolution and an opportunity for resisting neoliberal imperatives. Osgood (2006) identifies potential for *resisting the regulatory gaze* by constructing practitioner identities as shifting and negotiated, not predicated on codified disciplinary knowledge and skills, but open to new ways of thinking and being.

Case study 1: Community

St Mirin's Out-of-School Club (OSC) made use of their involvement in the Scottish Government-funded Access to Childcare pilot project (Children in Scotland, 2022; Scottish Government, 2023c), to enhance their integrated working with the school in which the OSC is based. In addition to working with school pupils to develop the school grounds as a play and learning space, the OSC created an in-school specialist service to support children who were struggling at school, and a crisis intervention service to support families. Trauma-informed approaches underpinned all aspects of the service, based on an understanding that support for children requires close partnerships both with families and with other educators. Evaluation of the 'school specialism' programme indicated success in supporting children with trauma, adverse childhood experiences, anxiety and distressed behaviours to develop coping skills and strategies, and in some cases, this meant that they no longer required support from the local child and adolescent mental health service. Project leaders highlighted the immense value of having both regular set meeting times for school and OSC leaders to meet, and an 'open-door policy' for facilitating open dialogue as required (Children in Scotland, 2022: 42).

Awareness of Context: Challenging Definitions to Build Momentum and Change the Narrative

Understanding ourselves as part of a bigger picture can be difficult when policy drivers guide us towards working in certain ways. Making TIP a core part of system-wide education agendas represents one way to work through the structures that currently exist to effect change, while recognizing the interconnectedness of contemporary issues (Thomas et al., 2019; Watson and Astor, 2025). Many countries face rising mental health challenges due to factors including socioeconomic inequalities, the climate crisis, increasing migration, and the societal and educational repercussions from the Covid-19 pandemic, all of which are leading to increased levels of individual and collective trauma (Kałwak et al., 2024). An OECD agenda prioritizing TIP permits services, systems and governments to acknowledge the pervasive impact of this trauma across countries and communities (Tanyu et al., 2020) but does not address the role of neoliberal processes in creating this situation. Overall, trauma-informed services can better support individuals facing poverty, or discrimination, enhancing their social and economic integration, where these are applied in a manner responsive to the needs, features and strengths of local contexts (Thomas et al., 2019).

Case study 2: Context

Trauma-Informed Oregon (TIO) is a statewide initiative in Oregon, the United States, focused on promoting trauma-informed care across various sectors including healthcare, education, child welfare services, criminal justice system and community outreach programmes (Trauma-Informed Oregon, online). Founded in 2014 and based at Portland University Hospital, TIO works to create environments that recognize and respond to the impact of trauma on individuals and communities, with a primary goal being the reduction of re-traumatization, which can occur when individuals and families experience systems or services that reinforce the effects of trauma. This has been achieved by educating practitioners at all levels and across systems in recognizing signs of trauma and adopting responsive and individualized practice, as well as by providing resources, training and guidance on TIPs to support organizations at all levels to implement policies supportive of the needs of individuals with a history of trauma. TIO's framework is underpinned by the principles of safety, empowerment and trust. Similarly to Scotland's Getting It right for every child (GIRFEC) approach (Scottish Government, 2022a), TIO seeks to promote collaboration across agencies to address trauma's complex impact on community health.

The organization has been internationally notable in its establishment of a culture of trauma awareness within Oregon, influencing state policy and serving as a model for TIPs worldwide. Partnership working has been enabled by a range of key initiatives, including:

- creation of a shared language and understanding of trauma to reduce miscommunication and build trust;
- development of cross-sectoral training;
- focus on culturally responsive and inclusive practices; and
- advocacy for policy change at state and system level.

A Focus on Care: Using Monitoring to Direct Attention to the Well-Being of Others

For TIP to become fully embedded, it could be argued that this narrative needs to become as omnipresent as neoliberal ideology is currently (NTTP, 2023). Another way of working through existing structures can be to redirect the focus of surveillance so that it reinforces different practices. Castelao-Huerta (2025) identifies caring behaviours as potentially showing resistance to narratives of neoliberalism. If national monitoring organizations, such as the Office for Standards in Education (OFSTED), build an understanding of trauma into their frameworks for evaluating provision, or centralize this knowledge within expectations for professionals, the same mechanisms that currently lead to rigid professional identities and concern for self-protection might be put to work in promoting effective collaborations and furthering the interests of others (Hymans, 2008).

Case study 3: Care

The General Teaching Council for Scotland's (GTCS) professional standards support and promote professionalism, leadership, professional learning and partnership (GTCS, 2021b). Standards such as those for teaching and leadership emphasize that teachers should be aware of how a pupil's family and home circumstances – including trauma – may affect their learning (GTCS, 2021b). Teachers are encouraged to engage in professional learning around TIPs, understand the impact of adverse childhood experiences (ACEs) and apply this understanding to foster supportive and empathetic classrooms (Education Scotland, 2025).

In Scotland, the regulator of the early learning and childcare sector, Scottish Social Services Council (SSSC), has published a continuous lifelong-learning framework with a mandatory requirement relating to trauma and protection of children (SSSC, 2024). This places a requirement on practitioners to reach the level of training and learning appropriate to their job role from a spectrum of options ranging from trauma informed, trauma skilled, trauma enhanced and trauma specialist (NHS Education for Scotland, 2017). In this way, the SSSC acts to embed trauma-informed approaches, ensuring that educators of the youngest children are able to recognize where children and families are affected by trauma and guiding them towards a caring focus on responses that reduce risks of re-traumatization while helping support recovery and reflection.

Thinking Point 16.3

a. How might you build your networks to develop a community in support of trauma-informed practice?
b. What contexts can you connect within to support yourself and others?
c. What opportunities do you currently have for avoiding performativity in favour of genuinely caring actions?

Summary

In this chapter we set out to explore key systemic challenges to embedding TIP within the practices of education workers across a range of roles and settings and to provide case study examples of ways in which educators are overcoming these to advance the well-being agenda. We have argued that neoliberal systems and narratives of education can create barriers to effective trauma-informed working practices. Recognizing these competing drivers of practice and developing a clear sense of education workers as part of a bigger picture (Thomas et al., 2019) has potential to allow educators to move beyond traditional professional divisions, and challenge non-trauma-informed approaches. While it is important to recognize the significant personal impact that such changes might create, professional identities are not static, and replacing the neoliberal narrative of competition, choice and calculation (Roberts-Holmes and Moss, 2021) with an alternative narrative of community, context and care offers a way to reframe education policy and practice in response to interconnected and disruptive contemporary global challenges (Kałwak et al., 2024), bringing the well-being agenda to the forefront of policy recommendations for trauma-informed times.

17

Professional Supervision for Education Staff

Alison Macdonald and Claire Slocombe

Key ideas

This chapter will:

- examine the key role of relationships in delivery of education and children's services,
- outline the importance of staff well-being in effective service delivery and as an end in itself,
- discuss supervision as good practice in children's service delivery,
- outline limitations on access to opportunities for reflection on practice for education staff, and
- examine the outcomes and impact of Scottish Attachment in Action's Wee Breathers project.

Introduction

There is emerging interest in the potential role of supervision within an educational context. This is in light of increasing emphasis on the importance of fostering positive relationships and on the need to address the well-being of children, young people and education staff (Barnardo's Scotland, 2020; Scottish Government (SG), 2020c). The impact of the Covid-19 pandemic has intensified this, resulting in a growing concern about the emotional well-being of children and young people, together with the impact of stress on school staff, which is experienced across all four nations of the UK. The main focus of this chapter will be the educational landscape of Scotland, whose approach and policies comprise some significant differences from those of its nearest neighbours. The Wee BREATHERS project (see https://scottishattachmentinaction.

org/wee-breathers-2/), which will be described later in this chapter, is taking place within Scotland and is clearly rooted within a Scottish educational context; the principles upon which it is built will be useful to consider by those working in other policy settings. The chapter will also examine supervision, which is a well-established practice across a range of healthcare, social care and psychological disciplines. The Health and Care Professions Council (HCPC) describes supervision as

> an essential aspect to continuing professional development and plays a key role in ensuring good practice and high-quality care. At its core, supervision is a process of professional learning and development that enables individuals to reflect on and develop their knowledge, skills and competence through agreed and regular support with another professional.
>
> (HCPC, 2024: online)

Policy Context

Scottish Education is distinctive in that it has long had a key focus on well-being. Curriculum for Excellence (CfE) indicates that it is important to 'develop the knowledge and understanding, skills, capabilities and attributes which they need for mental, emotional, social and physical wellbeing now and in the future' (Education Scotland, 2017b: 1). In addition, *Getting it right for every child (GIRFEC)* (SG, 2022a) places entitlement to all aspects of well-being as expressed by the SHANARRI (Safe, Healthy, Achieving, Nurtured, Active, Respected, Responsible, Included) indicators as the basis of planning for children and young people and is the overarching practice model for children's services. Scottish Education policy has at its heart the right of all children and young people to grow up safe, protected and with opportunities to thrive. As mentioned in previous chapters, it places nurture, relationships and connectedness at the centre of policy and practice and emphasizes the responsibility of all to ensure that Scotland is the best place in the world to grow up and learn. A key national outcome, that our children are *loved, safe and respected* so they realize their full potential, is supported by a raft of education policy and legislation which has been evolving over two decades and is most recently captured by the Promise Scotland (SG, 2022b). This is responsible for driving the work of change in wider children's services brought about by the findings of the *Independent Care Review* (Independent Care Review, 2020). The Getting it right for every child (GIRFEC) policy statement 2022 (SG, 2022a) draws together the elements of policy to support the well-being of children and young people and highlights the priorities for achieving its ambition:

> GIRFEC, the Promise and children's rights are the indivisible components in our delivery of Scotland's vision for all children, young people and families … Those foundations of Voice, Family, Care, People and Scaffolding of the Promise carry over

> into the first of three Plans: The Plan 21–24 with priorities in A Good Childhood, Whole Family Support, **Supporting the Workforce**, Planning and Building Capacity.
> (SG, 2022a: 13, our emphasis)

An understanding of how early experiences affect children and young people and the importance of relationships in shaping later outcomes are the foundations which underpin much of the Scottish policy landscape and curriculum. The shift from a focus on specialist services to meet the needs of the most vulnerable to a universal approach based on ecological systems thinking (Bronfenbrenner, 1981) has also contributed to this changing context. Health and Wellbeing is a key driver of the *National Improvement Framework (NIF)* (SG, 2023d), which is designed to deliver the twin aims of equity and excellence for all children and young people. Rights-based and relational approaches engendering safe and nurturing environments underpin the Scottish Education policy context and form a key element of Education Scotland's self-evaluation and inspection framework *How good is our school 4* (HGIOS4) (Education Scotland, 2015), whose Quality Indicators emphasize the central importance of relationships in promoting wellbeing and learning.

Also underpinning the current educational context within Scottish education is the promotion of the Common Core of Skills, Knowledge and Understanding (SG, 2012), which sets out the expectations for children's services staff based on the articles of the United Nations Convention on the Rights of the Child (UNCRC) (UN, 1989). The Common Core clearly emphasizes the centrality of relationships and the importance of being 'self-aware, empathetic, non-judgemental and having a grasp of non-verbal communication (e.g., body language)' (SG, 2012: 10). This is further developed in the General Teaching Council for Scotland's (GTCS) refreshed and revised Professional Standards (GTCS, 2021b), which reinforce the commitment of Scottish Education to support the development of children and young people's wellbeing. It includes a new section called 'Being a Teacher in Scotland', which highlights the professional values of social justice, trust and respect, and integrity as central to what it means to be a teacher in Scotland.

The Scottish Government promotes nurture as a key approach to supporting behaviour, well-being, attainment and achievement in Scottish Schools. The principles of nurture were originally developed by Bennathan and Boxall (2000), based on attachment theory (Bretherton, 1992). The nurture principles were developed to meet the needs of children requiring additional support in a small group setting. More recently the concept has been widened to develop whole-school approaches (Education Scotland, 2017a). Along with the focus on well-being and the centrality of relationships there has been a growing awareness of the importance of trauma-responsive practice. This may be partly linked to the findings of the Independent Care Review (Independent Care Review 2020) and the body of evidence which draws attention to the impact of early experience on brain development (Centre on the Developing Child, 2007) as well as a recent upsurge in interest in the Adverse Childhood Experiences Study (Felitti et al., 1998). The *National Trauma Transformation Programme* (NHS Education for Scotland, 2023b) aims to create a trauma-informed Scottish workforce and recognizes the importance of staff wellbeing.

The Case for Supervision

There is evidence that not all education staff feel well prepared to address the mental health needs of children and young people, particularly of those who present with issues associated with developmental trauma (Scottish Association for Mental Health (SAMH), 2017; Scottish Attachment in Action (SAIA), 2022). Indications from surveys across the UK show that levels of stress and compromised health and well-being amongst education staff are increasing (Educational Institute of Scotland, 2023; Department for Education, 2024b).

Christian-Brandt et al. (2020) point out that teachers are often on the front line with regard to childhood trauma, responding to emotional and behavioural crises in schools as well as hearing about student traumas. They refer to the *cost to caring* and the phenomenon of secondary traumatic stress which mirrors post-traumatic stress disorder and may be experienced by teachers and others who hear the stories of others affected by trauma. Another aspect of occupational stress is burnout, which refers to job-related exhaustion, depersonalization or cynicism and low self-efficacy. Unlike secondary traumatic stress, burnout does not imply exposure to trauma but rather is the result of work-related factors such as long hours and workload. They highlight that researchers have found high rates of occupational stress, including burnout and secondary traumatic stress amongst teachers.

Dr Adam Burley, Consultant Clinical Psychologist, in his foreword to Barnardo's *Trauma Informed Schools Discussion* (Bernardo's Scotland, 2019: 2) describes a staff group (teachers) 'who are experiencing high levels of stress with little or no opportunity to have it recognised or cared for'. He further states that teachers are supremely placed to make a difference to children and young people who have experienced trauma and adversity but that 'to do so effectively and over time, their own care simply must come first' (Bernardo's Scotland, 2019: 2). He cites the example of the Child Protection Case Conference, where 'it is the person with the highest level of contact with the child – the teacher – that typically receives the lowest level of clinical supervision' (Bernardo's Scotland, 2019: 2). The calls on teachers' emotional engagement cannot be underestimated. Unlike some other approaches, the involvement of self is key in relational work. Inevitably this can touch vulnerability and at the very least will often invoke a stress response as a natural result of challenge. The skill involved in containing and managing this and responding empathically and effectively to a child or young person in distress is a high-level one. Education practitioners must model positive interpersonal relationships at work. They must always maintain a professional demeanour, despite the unpredictable and complex nature of the classroom, resolving challenges and difficulties on a daily basis.

Teachers and support staff act as emotional containers for the children in their care. They support those who are overwhelmed, distressed and sometimes abusive and are expected to soothe, listen and contain. In order to do this with any degree of effectiveness, staff need to manage their own anxieties, frustrations, anger and stresses without feelings *leaking out*. They often do so with limited support as the classroom can be a lonely and isolating place. The consequence of maintaining this and consistently regulating one's own stress response can result in the deterioration of both mental and physical health over time. The potential for teachers to reach burnout, taking extended sick leave, leaving the profession early or taking premature retirement due to poor mental or physical health is a recognized threat to our education system. The General Teaching Council for Scotland reported recently that more than 1,300 teachers have left the profession within the first five years of their career since 2018 (McEnaney, 2024). New figures obtained by TES Scotland show almost one in five probationer teachers on the 2023–4 induction scheme, which starts at the beginning of each school year in August, had opted out by the January (Seith, 2024b). Teacher absence in Scotland hit its highest level in over a decade with teachers in Scotland taking an average of 6.8 sick days in 2022–3, the highest level of absence since councils started tracking the data in 2010–11 (Seith, 2024a). For children and young people to have better outcomes teachers need to be healthy. Although challenging relationships are the cause of many of these stressors, the most effective way to reduce their impact is by developing and deepening the connection with others.

'I define connection as the energy that exists between people when they feel seen, heard, and valued; when they can give and receive without judgment; and when they derive sustenance and strength from the relationship' (Brown, 2018: 182). This means making sure that we extend the well-being imperative to staff as well as pupils: '[t]he more healthy relationships a child has, the more likely he will be to recover from trauma and thrive. Relationships are the agents of change, and the most powerful therapy is human love' (Perry and Szalavitz, 2017: 230).

Practitioners need at least one supportive-containing relationship in which stressful experiences can be explored, reflected upon and learned from. Without access to this type of support, teachers are at risk of feeling isolated in trying to help pupils with extreme levels of distress without access to appropriate opportunities for emotional regulation themselves.

> [T]eachers need more support, supervision, and meaningful coaching, and if there isn't time and space for teachers to reflect then we won't make progress. The system must allow for teachers to give their all to children but when you have had chairs thrown at you from across the room, displays ripped off the walls, by day 3 or 4 they are

> exhausted and how do they cope? We need to think about support, create therapeutic webs and for that to happen we need it on a national basis (SAIA, 2022: 36).

The updated *National Guidance for Child Protection in Scotland 2021* (SG, 2023e) has recognized and begun to address the role of supervision within education. The Promise (Independent Care Review, 2020) also makes clear its commitment to the provision of space and time for support for education staff. 'Supervision and reflective practice are essential for all practitioners, regardless of their professional discipline or role, who are working with children' (Independent Care Review, 2020: 100). Education Scotland, in partnership with Barnardo's, has also set up a programme of supervision sessions for school leaders (Barnardo's Scotland, 2024).

Thinking Point 17.1

Relational approaches uniquely involve the self. Consider how opportunities for reflection enhance professional skill, staff well-being and job satisfaction.

Supervision

Supervision has been defined in a number of ways depending on the context in which it takes place, theoretical orientation and intended outcomes. The British Psychological Society guidelines describe supervision as 'having a space where it is possible to open up thinking to the mind of another with a view to extending knowledge about the self' (British Psychological Society, 2017: 12). Hawkins and McMahon (2020) define supervision as follows:

> [s]upervision is a joint endeavour in which a practitioner, with the help of a supervisor, attends to their clients, themselves as part of their client-practitioner relationships and the wider systemic and ecological contexts, and by so doing improves the quality of their work, transforms their client relationships, continuously develops themselves, their practice and the wider profession.
>
> (Hawkins and McMahon, 2020: 66)

Kennedy et al., (2018) point to increasing empirical evidence for supervision because of its role in:

- promoting skill acquisition, transfer and application of learning across contexts;
- enhancing client outcomes through supporting adherence to high-quality practices; and

- reducing worker burnout through fostering professional and personal engagement (Kennedy et al., 2018: 282).

While these outcomes align well with the needs of school staff tasked with developing and implementing relational and trauma-responsive approaches, there is ongoing discussion both about the term 'supervision' and the applicability of clinical models to education. The term 'supervision' is familiar in health care and social care settings but is not so readily understood in an education context as its meaning might imply managerial or evaluative functions. Furthermore, clinical supervision models may not be wholly applicable to education settings.

Implementing Approaches to Supervision in Scottish Schools

A number of organizations across Scotland are exploring the application of supervision in education and looking at relevant models. Highland Educational Psychology Service (Highland Council, 2024) and Barnardo's (Barnardo's Scotland, 2020) are examples of organizations looking to develop models of supervision. The Scottish Attachment in Action (SAIA), a small Scottish Charity (see https://scottishattachmentinaction.org/), is amongst those organizations piloting approaches to supervision in education. Their work is described in detail below.

Case study

Scottish Attachment in Action's project Wee BREATHERS – Supporting the education workforce through relationships (see https://scottishattachmentinaction.org/wee-breathers-supporting-the-education-workforce-through-relationships/) – is designed for change, offering reflective spaces to education practitioners with the aim of supporting supervision to become embedded in their practice. This innovative and timely work is funded by the Promise Partnership, Corra Foundation on behalf of Scottish Government.

Wee BREATHERS Context

Making Scotland the best place in the world to grow up and learn is one of the many commitments which have provided the policy and legislative context for life in Scotland over the past decade. Scotland also made The Promise (Scottish Government, 2022b) to care-experienced children and young people that they will grow up loved, safe and respected. 'Schools in Scotland must provide space and opportunity for all members of school staff to develop kind, supportive relationships with care experienced children' (Independent Care Review, 2020: 71).

SAIA's research *Mapping Attachment-Informed and Trauma-Sensitive Practice in Scottish Education* (SAIA, 2022) echoes *The Promise* (Independent Care Review, 2020), in highlighting that an attachment and trauma-informed workforce built upon supportive relationships will enable Scotland to keep the Promise. SAIA's research highlighted that in terms of ongoing Career-Long Professional Learning (CLPL) (GTCS, 2021c) there is a growing need for opportunities for support and reflective practice. As already described, despite the commitment within Scottish Education to promote attachment-informed, trauma-sensitive approaches in schools and early years settings, education staff have had little formal support, unlike professions which have built in opportunity for reflection (e.g. social work supervision structures). There is currently no consistent structure in place to provide staff with safe and confidential spaces to gain insight into the needs of pupils in their classrooms who have experienced disrupted attachment and/or trauma. The Scottish Attachment in Action Wee BREATHERS project aims to provide such opportunities while supporting staff well-being. The aspiration is to support practitioners to address their own distress/well-being and provide them with strategies that allow them to support pupils who become dysregulated in class as a result of their unmet emotional needs.

Wee BREATHERS Model of Supervision

In developing its model, SAIA researched supervision models used in other professions, as well as models that have been tried previously within education to determine how best supervision could be delivered in an education setting. The following models were considered as having particular relevance to the needs of education staff.

Reflective supervision

The Learning Cycle, developed by Kolb (1984), comprises four different stages of learning from experience. The learning cycle suggests that it is not sufficient to have an experience in order to learn. It is necessary to reflect on the experience to make generalizations and formulate concepts which can then be applied to new situations. This learning must then be tested out in new situations. The learner must make the link between the theory and action by planning, acting out, reflecting and relating it back to the theory. Morrison's (2005) application of the Kolb learning cycle to promoting critical reflection and learning from experience forms the bedrock of the concept of reflective supervision most widely used in social work settings. Morrison (2005) advocated using the cycle both in supervision and in practice to help practitioners understand a child or parent's perspective through considering their experiences, the meanings given to those experiences and how families see their own future as a result (Gibbs et al., 2014).

Restorative supervision

Safeguarding Restorative Supervision (SRS) was initially developed by Wallbank and Wonnacott (2015) for use in health organizations but is held to have relevance to all safeguarding settings. The underlying premise of SRS is that developing the practitioner's resilience is a fundamental aspect of the supervisory relationship and that to achieve this the supervisor needs to provide a safe and emotionally contained space. This enables the practitioner to slow down their thinking so that critical reflection on a family's experiences can occur.

Containment and Parallel Process

Containment is a significant element in relationship-based practice and is particularly important as a means to manage anxiety, which is the most common obstacle to reflection (Ruch, 2002). Containment allows supervisees to reflect upon:

- the emotional experiences of children, young people, parents, carers and the actions they (the supervisee) take to *contain them*; and
- their own emotional responses and the actions taken by managers and the organizations to help *contain them* in the course of their work.

The latter should be a form of parallel process, enabling a practitioner to experience the relationship-building skills and learning processes they need to use with children and families. In addition to these underpinning models, collaboration with practitioners and young people informed the development of an education-specific framework based on attachment theory. The Wee BREATHERS model has connection at its heart and provided new opportunities to support and educate teachers to successfully mitigate the negative impacts of exposure to childhood adversity while simultaneously assisting teachers to nurture their own workplace wellbeing. It did this by:

- providing opportunities for reflective supervision that is valued by the education workforce;
- deepening learning and understanding about the impact of disrupted attachment and developmental trauma;

- building capacity in staff to better understand and respond to distressed behaviour and pupil needs, particularly those who have experienced disrupted attachment and trauma;
- supporting staff to reach a greater understanding about their practice and how their own emotions and behaviour can become engaged;
- promoting staff wellbeing; and
- encouraging positive and supportive adult-pupil relationships.

Wee BREATHERS offered education colleagues protected time to connect, reflect and learn within a safe and confidential space. It is based on key principles of an attachment-informed, trauma-sensitive approach. These principles form the core components of the relationship between the supervisor and practitioner/s as well as mirroring what it is hoped would be promoted within attachment-informed, trauma-sensitive learning environments. This is represented in the Wee BREATHERS Model (see Figure 17.1).
The key principles of Wee Breathers model are outlined below:

[B] **Belonging:** One of the fundamental needs that motivate human behaviour; defined as that feeling of connectedness to a group or community. Wee BREATHERS' aim is for practitioners to feel attached and accepted.

[R] **Reflecting:** Stepping back from immediate, intense experience and taking the time to reflect on meaning. Wee BREATHERS offers an opportunity for practitioners to examine their thoughts, feelings and areas for growth and development.

[E] **Empathizing:** Being open to the experience and feelings of others. Empathy is important both between supervisor and practitioner and between practitioner and pupils within the classroom.

[A] **Acceptance:** Important for wellbeing and can enable us to show compassion to ourselves and others. Accepting painful emotions is important for healing and moving forward. Wee BREATHERS offers a non-judgemental stance where thoughts, feelings and wishes are accepted, not evaluated.

[T] **Thinking:** Thinking critically is important for bridging the gap between theory and practice. Wee BREATHERS aims to support practitioners to reflect on their practice through an attachment-informed, trauma-sensitive lens.

[H] **Hearing:** The feeling of being properly heard and understood can be transforming. Wee BREATHERS aims to offer a safe environment where practitioners can be heard and accepted without being judged.

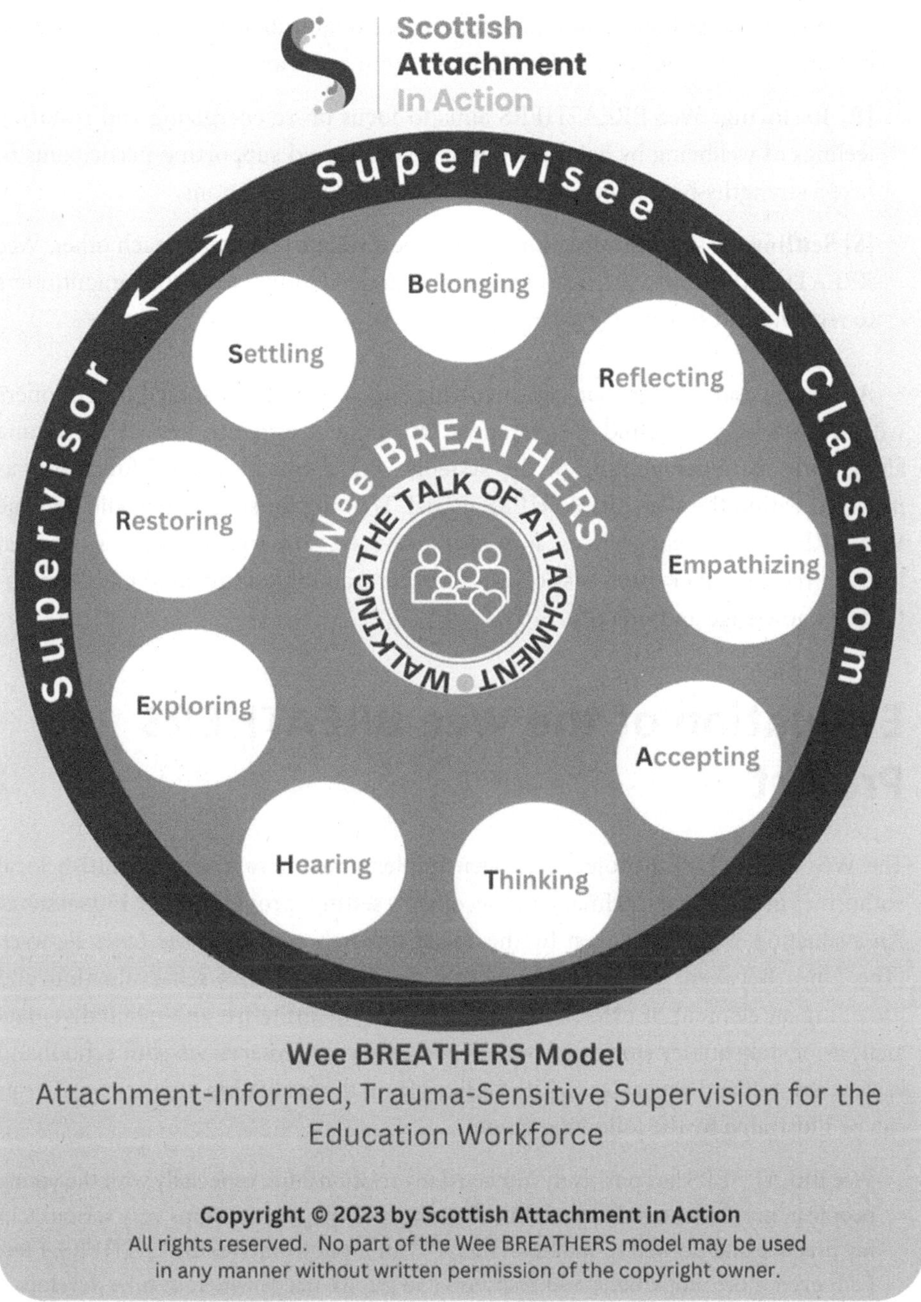

Figure 17.1 The Wee Breathers Model.

Reproduced with permission from Scottish Attachment in Action.

> **[E] Exploring:** Wee BREATHERS aims to take a 'not knowing' stance that seeks to understand without making assumptions. We aim to support practitioners to explore thoughts, feelings and behaviour within a safe and supportive space.
>
> **[R] Restoring:** Wee BREATHERS aims to focus on re-energizing and restoring feelings of wellbeing by acknowledging successes and supporting participants to take a strengths-based approach to managing difficult situations.
>
> **[S] Settling:** In stressful situations we can be a source of calm for each other. Wee BREATHERS aims to provide comfort and understanding to enable practitioners to regulate and sit with *big feelings*.

A training and support package involving supervision from skilled practitioners with a knowledge of child development, attachment and the impact of trauma along with an understanding of the systems within which schools' function was provided within the Wee BREATHERS model. Training for staff who would become Wee BREATHERS supervisors was also provided. Supervisors were supported through regular supervision sessions and further training was given to maintain up-to-date knowledge and practice.

Evaluation of the Wee BREATHERS Project

The Wee BREATHERS project has been implemented across seven Scottish local authorities in early years, primary and secondary settings providing over 150 sessions. An evaluation was undertaken by the social research company *The Lines Between* (The Lines Between, 2025). This involved supporting SAIA's self-evaluation and providing an element of external evaluation using quantitative and qualitative data analysis of stakeholder survey responses and case study interviews with school and early years staff and supervisors. The findings from the evaluation are very positive as can be illustrated by the following quote:

> Wee BREATHERS has positively impacted my relationships, especially with the young people in my classroom. I already take building positive relationships very seriously in my practice and do well to maintain them. With input from Wee BREATHERS, I feel I am even more empathetic and responsive to pupils' needs which in turn develops a stronger sense of trust and connection.
>
> (The Lines Between, 2025: 12)

Participants commonly reported changing their perspective on children and young people's behaviour resulting from the new knowledge gained. As one stated, 'I am now able to distance myself from behaviours and not take them so personally' (The

Lines Between, 2025: 12). Newly qualified teachers were among the participants who described how their skills, knowledge and understanding improved as a result of the sessions. This is particularly important in view of some of the recruitment and retention issues already highlighted. It was common for staff to report feeling reassured and encouraged. They noted the value of discussing interactions with young people and colleagues. The interconnectedness of staff wellbeing and responsiveness to children and young people was also highlighted: '[h]aving the time, space and support to reflect on my practice has helped to improve my confidence by helping me to see the positives and improvements in relationships with specific children' (The Lines Between, 2025: 10). All case study interviewees across early years, primary and secondary were highly positive about the usefulness of the sessions. Improved relationships at work were also highlighted, 'I have found that as I begin to understand behaviours and reactions, I am better able to adjust my emotional reactions in conversation, making it easier to interact with everyone in my workplace' (The Lines Between, 2025: 13). Such was the success that all case study interviewees wanted others to experience the benefits they had felt. As one stated, '[m]ake it available to everyone! I think it is the single most important support mechanism for teachers to process experiences with a compassionate, non-judgemental individual who sits totally separate from the school body and allows for real meaningful reflection, behaviour change and mental health improvement. THANK YOU!' (The Lines Between, 2025: xx).

Thinking Point 17.2

In what ways might current practice need to alter to allow access to reflective space for education staff?

Summary

This chapter has explored the potential role of supervision models in supporting staff well-being in schools. This is presented as integral to the professional development of the relational approaches which underpin Scottish Government policy. There is early evidence from a small-scale attachment-informed, trauma-sensitive project – Wee BREATHERS – of the effectiveness of opportunities for reflection in attaining positive outcomes for school and establishment staff and children and young people.

18

In Conversation with ...

Part 1: Dr Elizabeth N. King, MBE. Chartered Psychologist and Former Principal Educational Psychologist

Christine: Why did you agree to be part of this project?

Elizabeth: It's forty years of a vision (I've held) where society understands attachment theory and the learning from it. I've always been aware that children who've had developmental trauma are inevitably going to have an insecure attachment profile. So, the fact that you're looking at attachment and practice in schools will then inform practice. I would do anything I could to contribute to that debate but more so to the understanding that comes from attachment theory, from being trauma sensitive and having trauma-informed models, especially given developments in neuroscience over the past decade to fifteen years.

Christine: What do you think about the use of the term 'trauma informed?

Elizabeth: I think it's perfect, and I think the phrase 'trauma sensitive' is really good. In South Lanarkshire, the work that I initiated, they called it the Attachment Strategy, and they use the terminology trauma sensitive. I like trauma informed, and I like attachment informed. It's not simply what we do but how are we going to be with this young person? I think trauma sensitive is almost a part of that continuum to ensure your practice is attachment informed. You've got to be sensitive to it, but I think the power is in the action. Just to repeat again, 'What is it we do?' And how are we informed about young people who've experienced developmental trauma? It's about action and informed thought.

Christine: Why did you start down this route in South Lanarkshire?

Elizabeth: That's a good question, because there was a route to it. It wasn't random. Part of it is personal. Part of it came from being a young person with a particular family dynamic. There was a young person closely related to me with issues. I was only eighteen and asked to a family meeting and discussion. In the meeting, the therapist, who was a trained psychologist, talked about attachment theory. We had all reached crisis, and that's the first time I'd ever heard of attachment theory. And I was blessed that, because of the interest I then developed, somebody funded a visit to London, where John Bowlby, as a very old man, was speaking about attachment theory, about the understanding that was necessary to help families. Very quickly, as a young person in my late teens–early twenties, I formed a vision of how I could get into a job that I could use to help others. I have got to give credit to that therapist who spent time with me to help me understand. She was ahead of the game because at that time to use attachment theory to understand disrupted family relationships was not the predominant paradigm. The inspiration of hearing Bowlby talk about the impact of early 'disruption', 'separation'. If I hadn't had that I wouldn't have developed that vision. And then, within educational psychology, the dominant paradigm when I was a young psychologist was that there was no room for attachment theory, no room for understanding it. My drive is as old as that.

When I was young you had to have taught for at least two years in order to apply for educational psychology. That's not the case now, but I'm totally thankful for that, because I taught for those two years and loved it but got so much insight into the drive in teachers to do the very best for children who were struggling. I saw passionate people, but they didn't have the information, the training. The understanding on what I thought was missing was the pivotal part, which was understanding attachment theory. When I was successful in applying for educational psychology, right from day one it was always there, and it was a long, hard road to use every opportunity to explain the theory. I can remember an era, probably thirty years ago, when I mentioned 'attachment' in one multi-agency group, they honestly thought it was about a physical link. It was either about, you know, mother and baby or it was something about a group dynamic where you ensured a really troubled child was attached, physically. So, I've seen wonderful change for the good. But that's where it started, and it has been a long journey but being embedded within a local authority, being part of children services gave me a voice. I was at the table when there was intense challenge because of poor outcomes, in particular for looked-after children, now care experienced. I had a particular interest in the reasons for the poor outcomes and what we were going to do about it. I was blessed to see the attachment strategy written.

Christine: South Lanarkshire Council is doing work on attachment. How did you convince the others?

Elizabeth: I think that for anyone who has passion and belief there's a set of understandings that could really help the whole improvement agenda, and I don't mean improvement in education, I mean in society, then it is important to be at the key planning meetings. But it's also important that you ensure what you say is tapping into current dominant agendas. So, the importance of describing what the understanding from attachment theory could bring to finding solutions and leading to improvement is so important. And then you get a listening ear. And I think that was a pivotal process; I made sure that I didn't go to a meeting without having thought out beforehand. What's the agenda here? What's the challenge for this children services group? And in particular education? And how is it I can help explain that actually the learning from attachment theory could actually address finding solutions?

Christine: What kind of things did you implement as a local authority?

Elizabeth: That did take time. There are competing theories, so it was important that I was also very aware of some of the other theories that were being put forward in making a difference. My argument was always that attachment theory is like the foundations you're walking on. You're trying to build a society, build the capacity in society, build it in children's services, and I always had a passion for schools, and a great belief in them. It's not that everything else then becomes irrelevant or models aren't relevant; it's that all those models or those other processes, or procedures, they should be built on the understanding of attachment theory. I think that's what made the big difference: the acknowledgement that that's got to be fundamental.

One of the very first things I was given agreement to do was being able to have a key role in the probation programme for the newly qualified teachers in South Lanarkshire and include attachment theory and attachment-informed practice. But, even better, was that I was invited to do the same with newly qualified social workers. Now that was wonderful, because looking back over the decades, the vision that we had, I would say, was the Scottish Government's Getting it right for every child (GIRFEC) agenda and, obviously, it's policy now. That drove and gave encouragement to me. That was probably one of the first things that happened and then, alongside that, was an agreement from the Director and the Heads of Service, that I could set up and establish a multi-agency Attachment Strategy group. Within a year, there was agreement in that multi-agency group that to get a strategy written that would be meaningful, focused and for education, there needed to be resources dedicated to an Attachment Strategy Steering group. There was a wonderful social work manager from what was in those days called 'corporate parenting' who was passionate about improving what we do to support young people who are accommodated, but very, very committed to how we help parents and carers. She was an absolute inspiration on that steering group, and we also had somebody from *Child and Adolescent Mental Health Services (CAMHS).*

We had people from a broad spectrum of education, including catering and facilities managers. It was a real joy to have them bringing their creativity and curiosity. They brought a curiosity because they didn't know a lot about attachment theory but were convinced by what I and other colleagues had explained. That year was a very important year for the attachment strategy that was eventually written. But thereafter, it was an Education Resources Attachment Strategy steering group which still sits.

Christine: Your multi-agency approach almost embodied that holistic view of attachment that's now coming through South Lanarkshire.

Elizabeth: That is a good point. It helped the beginnings of a common language. I would say there was a lot of agreement between education and social work. I'm talking about the corporate parenting manager, the terminology we used was very similar, but sometimes in the health service slightly different terminology was used. The importance of language guided me in my earlier research within education. That can be part of the challenge. I go back to GIRFEC when it was launched; the dream of a lot of the early proponents of GIRFEC was that the multi-agency group that you're talking about would have a more common, agreed language. I think we've still got a long way to go.

Christine: Do you think that in Scotland we have a national policy that facilitates an attachment-aware system?

Elizabeth: I do think there's been great progress. Decades ago, if you tried to sit down with a young person in a multi-agency case conference and say, 'Do you know there's insecure attachment?' 'How does that knowledge inform our long-term planning?', the majority of people would not have understood what you were saying. I think there is huge progress. I think GIRFEC, despite all of its challenges, has forged significant progress and I've got huge admiration for the commitment to make Scotland a trauma-informed and responsive society. I think that's great, but if I were in government, I would constantly be putting attachment informed and trauma informed, or trauma sensitive closely together. It was not like that in NHS education programmes, even ten to fifteen years ago. I can't help but think of Scottish Attachment in Action (SAIA) and the power of a group like SAIA to be ambassadors and champions, and to do more than that, it's about action making a difference, intervening and providing training. I think that's needed. I think there's been great progress but there's a lot more to be done.

Christine: What barriers do you think remain for us in Scotland?

Elizabeth: A general point I'd make, whether it's a barrier or a challenge, is to take the learning from ongoing research and make it meaningful and let it influence. Take the work of, say, Eamon McCrory and his colleagues on latent vulnerability (e.g. McCrory et al. (2017)). It is powerful research that's highlighting the importance of early intervention and preventative work and not waiting for the crisis. I do think there's great work going on in exploring epigenetics. All of that research though and the different categories, the neuro-cognitive category, the epigenetics category, it's still all saying the same thing and that is that whatever you actually do, it's got to be grounded in relationships.

I think that could be called a challenge rather than a barrier, an ongoing challenge to take the wonderful learning from researchers, who are totally committed to finding out what we can do to prevent embedded mental health problems and translate what they are saying so that it can inform policy and procedure. Organizations like SAIA could make a difference there in bringing together academic research and applied practice.

Christine: What impact do you think Covid-19 will have had on education, on children?

Elizabeth: I lived through it with my Pathfinder research (from South Lanarkshire Council Youth Family and Community Learning Service) (King, 2022). The research started off in three secondary schools and ended up in seven. In each of the schools there were two community learning and development officers, and through our relational approach, they became very quickly embedded. The word 'collaboration' is coming into my head all the time in speaking to you. The importance of collaboration, the importance of schools having the opportunity to collaborate with partners who are within the school setting as opposed to external, so-called specialists who are helicoptered in. What that research showed me was the impact, the strength, the power of people who are based in the school, who are part of the staff. They've got their own professional standards. They're a different profession, but they're working within the school. What a difference they made during the Covid-19 pandemic, compared to other schools. At that point, there were just a small number of schools involved. The community learning and development officers were called Pathfinder Officers; the initiative was called Pathfinder. When you asked me that question, I couldn't help but think of what they did in those schools, because in some ways the research showed, or I would argue, that my research showed that the fact that they could maintain relationships in a way that was harder for school staff.

Christine: It's pupils meeting with a mentor who's not a member of staff, who is from outside of the school. It takes away that teacher-pupil focus.

Elizabeth: I think you're hitting a very important point, because in life often we have 'either/or', either you've got an external specialist counselling service, or you train your teachers, and some pupil support staff can offer counselling. It's not an either/or. With my four years of research, I could see the rich interchange between teaching and Community Learning and Development (CLD) staff and Pathfinders based in the community. I could see the difference in the fact that Pathfinder officers were mentoring and coaching and the fact that they were based in the school and were like a member of school staff and valued as a professional that people got to know. Myths held by CLD and teaching staff about each other, were dispelled. I'm not saying that an external organization can't help. I'm just saying that it works where it's seen as a partnership within the school organization.

Christine: What's your vision for the future?

Elizabeth: I think there's wonderful training and consultation on attachment-informed and trauma-informed practice. I think as much of that should be done as possibly can be done. One of the Pathfinder research case studies was a young person who had been adopted when she was young. She had terrible behaviour problems. She was miserable and unhappy. The school were struggling with her. Her mum and dad were at the end of their tether and Pathfinder became involved. I was trying to work out during the research, what was it they did? But then I spoke to the mum, and it was so powerful because she was explaining that it was the first person that she felt really understood her challenges, really understood her stress, her strain, her worry, and just having someone that didn't pity her. She said she saw both. She saw pity that wasn't informed by, or followed up by any action, and then she also saw what she called ignorance, you know, just tell her she needs to get up in the morning and get in here. She said she saw both, and what Pathfinder did was take time to get to know her. Take time to get to know her child, her daughter, and intervened, because, again, they were not external, they were in the school and intervened.

Part 2 Dr Richard Parker, Trustee of Attachment Research Community and Visiting Research Fellow, Bath Spa University

Christine: Why did you agree to be part of this project?

Richard: It's simply because we all know that attachment matters, or, as we now say, relational understanding or relational approaches. It's just so key to what is going on in education in every society. One of the interesting things is the contrast between the English approach and the Scottish approach. We really need to get some understanding. There's understanding of it from the point of view of practitioners, understanding it from the point of view of children and young people, and also from parents and families and, of course, carers.

Christine: I'm using term trauma informed the right terminology?

Richard: I take the view that there isn't a wrong terminology. I mean, when we started off back in 2012, attachment aware was the only game in town. Then the notion of trauma informed came along on the back of that. There's a whole range of things that you can actually talk about, which, if you boil it down, are to do with relational approaches, developing a sense of belonging for children and actually challenging some of the ridiculous behaviour stuff that goes on.

Christine: Do you think that the behaviourist approach in England is dominating at the moment?

Richard: Yes. The trouble is, it's so deeply embedded into what is certainly 'conservative with a capital C' educational thinking. Unfortunately, New Labour don't get off easily on this either. In my book (Parker, 2024), I trek back and look at it in terms of neoliberal approaches to education, because that's where I think it sits. What you have is a curious mixture. You've got some philanthropic Conservatives like John Timpson or Edward Timpson, who, as a family and as a company, are overtly promoting attachment and relational approaches with their staff, as well as with children. And yet, if you look at what went on under New Labour a huge amount was actually hugely performative. It was to do with keeping kids in place, keeping these naughty kids under control and moving them from school to school if they got too much for anyone, instead of actually going for the really deeper issues.

Christine: Where do you think we are now in England?

Richard: Well, I think it's been very much dependent on individual Secretaries of State. You can track that through the neoliberal agenda, the importance of teaching; nothing to do with the importance of children or the importance of learning, but the importance of controlling the children. What you get in the English education context, just around 2022, as we're coming out of Covid-19, is some really interesting stuff, particularly about attendance and suddenly we're saying we've got to look at this in order to help the kids and the families, and it's no good just being punitive but that was short lived. And now, we're back on the performative focus.

Christine: There is concern about behaviour in schools, and how it's declining.

Richard: There's a complete misunderstanding, in my view, of where behaviour sits in terms of relational approaches. The critique is that it's all this hippie liberal stuff. And actually, we all know that doesn't work. Those of us who taught in schools know darn well that doesn't work. If you let the kids cause mayhem, they'll cause mayhem. So, that's the one thing, is this total misunderstanding, and it's very wilful.

It's absolutely wilful because it challenges the neoliberal rhetoric that soft, progressive stuff is namby-pamby and doesn't work for children. So, we're continuing with an either-or approach but that is quite interesting in terms of those right-wing views, which are determined to say that progressivism doesn't work. Unless you go back to Skinner's experiments with rats in the sixties, there is no hard evidence for behaviourism other than with laboratory rats.

Christine: We start getting to fundamental questions about what the role of education is? What is the role of the teacher? What does success look like?

Richard: I've got a quotation that I use when I do presentations on attachment awareness. It's from a pupil. It says, basically, 'you didn't give up on me and all the time I was giving you hell as a student you didn't give up on me; you pushed me'. This was someone who spent most of her year 11 sitting with the Headteacher's Personal Assistant (PA), who didn't go to any of the school events because she couldn't trust herself not to have a fight with someone. And yet this is someone who fresh-started herself, got herself into college, got quite good GCSE results. But the school understood that and initially telling her to sit with the HT's PA was punitive, but the HT's PA became her mentor and was chasing her up when she didn't turn up, and they had a really good relationship. The other point I take from that story is that it is to do with management attitudes. That HT had said, well, we do this for these children. We know we will take a hit on results, but we think it's worth it.

Christine: How would you define a trauma-informed school?

Richard: I think it's to do with an attitude towards the children that actually says, 'this is child centred'. It's also to do with an attitude within the staff that we're in this together. It's teamwork across the staff and also teamwork between staff, students and parents. I think it's also an attitude of collaborating with other agencies and recognizing that teachers are not social workers, but they can work with others and it's also about taking responsibility. It then becomes a management approach, which has to be owned from the top down across the whole school. That then relates back to some sort of relational approach, but it doesn't have to be dogmatic. It's a matter of saying let's have a relational approach. In my own research I had three schools that had totally different approaches. One was a very traditional down-the-line attachment awareness using emotion coaching. Another was very much on brain science, and being trauma informed. The third was a school that started off with restorative approaches and for them, this then began to develop into an understanding of it in terms of attachment awareness. So, there are different ways.

Christine: Tell me about the roles that you've had.

Richard: I was a local authority officer for twenty-five years as we went through, we started to understand integrated work, integration across the council, and then, of course, along came *Every Child Matters* (HM Treasury, 2003). We started an integrated children's services much sooner than everybody else. I'm not saying we got it right at all; we set up a children's trust under the [*Children Act*] 2004 Act, which had everybody in it from voluntary services to police, health and even army welfare, because there were lots of army families. We decided we'd put together *Connections, Youth Service and Youth Offending* and I'd do a feasibility report. These guys, and they were all guys, all had their territory and different ways of working. It wasn't an attachment aware narrative. No, I was very ignorant on that sort of thing, but this notion of having a single service for all vulnerable young people; that's where it came from. My journey to attachment awareness has come very much from working with vulnerable young people rather than through any sort of theoretical model. That's what we did. And it was great, we had some real go-ahead people, particularly in Youth Service, who had really creative ideas and the great turnaround came with that. After about another six months we'd have conferences. We did big cross-service conferences, and we had some of the junior people saying we weren't moving fast enough. We really got to integrate this, and that was where we knew. Bang! We've done it, and that became the basis of my work at Bath Spa.

Janet [*Rose*] had started at the same time as one of the early years' practitioners. She and I cobbled together this stuff on *Emotion Coaching* which Janet was just starting to work on; we started a project with the focus on a deprived area. And from this we did develop this programme, which we then called 'In Care, In School', which was to enable them [*care-experienced children*] to explain to teachers and their peers just how it felt to be in care and at school. That kind of spiralled out and that's where the attachment awareness came from. We knew we had to have a more universal approach, and it was a blessing. It was the early years people in Bath, Northeast Somerset whom we suddenly came across and they had brought in Kate Cairns and her team, they'd been bought in to target reception classes where they were getting pulled in as early year specialists and told, 'This child has a terrible behaviour problem.' They said, 'No. The child has attachment issues.' It's one of those things that happened by osmosis almost, that we were all singing from the same song sheet, and by pulling together these different strands, that this could be used as a support mechanism for developing what we were doing in schools. That's where my involvement in attachment awareness came from. Janet's initial input was very much around emotion coaching, John Gottman's model (Gus et al., 2015).What we did was persuade. Some of the early work we did, a school came to us. It was actually RAF Lyman, which was about to close and so there were all sorts of issues. They said to us, 'Look, these kids have got issues. Obviously, because of all the uncertainties we want to train all of our year six in emotion coaching so they can support the rest of the school.' So, Janet said to the rest of the early years' team, 'Okay, guys, roll your sleeves up. On Thursday afternoons for the next four weeks, we're going to do emotion coaching', and they just did it. No grants, no nothing. They just did it. Amazing stuff.

Christine: What do you think of the barriers to us embedding this across the system?

Richard: I'll come back to that. One thing I did want to say was about the impact of Covid-19. I do think that Covid-19 has had a real severe impact. The view of the then Secretary of State was that we just get things back to normal, what we actually needed to do was get pupils back into school and learning. That was a real wake up call to a lot of teachers. I think this notion that we've actually got to understand children's mental health is still there. The danger of the mental health perspective is that we then get into these orthodoxies, mental health is only for mental health practitioners. It's for the CAMHS team, it's not for the classroom teacher. We've always argued that we don't want teachers to become mental health practitioners. We don't want them to become social workers, etc. But, if you've got a working knowledge of relational approaches, then you're going to have a better time in the classroom. They're going to have a better time in the classroom, and you might actually have a better and more sophisticated understanding of whether you've got to bring in the expert practitioners, whether it's someone on your pastoral side or your SEN side within your school, or whether it's someone from CAMHS or the external agencies.

Let's talk about the barriers. I think the key barrier to me is the neoliberal attitude to education. Education is about sitting in rows, having facts pumped into you, and while that is being pushed around, whether it's from government ministers or heads of year, that is the biggest single barrier, because if we turn that around then we look at education as about developing the person. Another barrier is defensiveness from other professions. It's quite easy for social workers to say they're very attachment aware; in fact, they think developing a child's attachment is more important than the child going to school. No, it's not, because if they don't go to school and get some sort of exam results and be challenged to do their best, then they're not going to cope in later life.

The third thing related to that is people imposing definitions on children, there's a lot in neuroscience. There's a lot in attachment. But if you have this crude view that attachment theory explains everything, then you actually miss other crucial things. I think the understanding of parents is another of the barriers. We had a meeting with a former primary head teacher who was an adoptive parent, she was just so frustrated. She was saying, 'If I go into a school as a professional, I'm listened to. If I go into school talking about the needs of my daughter, I get dismissed as a silly, over-anxious, middle-class parent'.

Christine: So, what's your vision for the future?

Richard: My vision for the future – I want politicians to be more aware, somehow, we've got to turn this around and make this a priority. What we're trying to do as ARC [Attachment Research Community – //the-arc.org.uk] is to build alliances and partnerships across the board in England, with Scottish Attachment in Action, with anyone who will partner with us. We're not a dogmatic organization promoting one particular approach to attachment; we've really pushed on the restorative side. We've got a lot of other organizations who are willing to work with us, and more mainstream groups like the Association of School and College Leaders. That is us getting influence at those different levels. We need to influence the politicians. The trouble is politicians are hugely busy, and you have got to say the right things at the right time.

In my research, three very different approaches were used in three different schools. But what was significant was that each of the management teams in the schools had handled it really well. In the primary school, which had a relatively new head teacher, three to four years in, a young head teacher. What I thought the head teacher did well, was he didn't force things, but led from the front and took people with him. There was no antagonism. Whereas the secondary school, a very large secondary school, had all the issues and tensions you get in a secondary school but (everyone was) really positive about the head teacher, who ran what was an empowerment model. The third one was a PRU [*Pupil Referral Unit*] which had been through trials and tribulations. It had been closed by Ofsted at one point and had management team after management team. What was quite interesting was that within eighteen months, the new head teacher had brought the staff along to her way of thinking. The staff were well inclined; they cared about the kids rather than their performance, but they also understood about the need to get performance (results) for the kids. This head teacher led from the front. She used the management team, reconstituted the leadership team and said, 'We are going to model this'. It's a bit like the kids, you know, if you challenge them on their own terms, they will respond. Instead of looking at what would be done to punish a pupil, they were discussing what was going on for the pupil in the situation, and how they could support the pupil.

References

Ainsworth, M.S. (1979). Infant-Mother Attachment. *The American Psychologist*, 34(10): 932–7.

American Academy of Pediatrics (AAP) (2012). Early Childhood Adversity, Toxic Stress, and the Role of the Pediatrician: Translating Developmental Science into Lifelong Health. *Pediatrics*, 129(1): e224–31.

Andersson, S.-O., Annerback, E.-M., Sondergaard, H.P., Hallqvist, J. and Kristiansson, P. (2021). Adverse Childhood Experiences Are Associated with Choice of Partner, Both Partners' Relationship and Psychosocial Health as Reported One Year After Birth of a Common Child. A Cross-sectional Study. *PLoSONE*, 16(1): 1–19.

Aranda, K. and Hart, A. (2015). Resilient Moves: Tinkering with Practice Theory to Generate New Ways of Thinking About Using Resilience. *Health*, 19(4): 355–71.

Asmussen, K., McBride, T. and Stephanie Waddell, S. (2019). The Potential of Early Intervention for Preventing and Reducing ACE-Related Trauma. *Social Policy and Society*, 18(3): 425–34.

Aspelin, J. (2021). Teaching as a Way of Bonding: A Contribution to the Relational Theory of Teaching. *Educational Philosophy and Theory*, 53(6): 588–96.

Aumann, K. and Hart, A. (2009). *Helping Children with Complex Needs Bounce Back: Resilient Therapy (TM) for Parents and Professionals*. London: Jessica Kingsley.

Avery, J., Deppeler, J., Galvin, E., Skouteris, H., Crain de Galarce, P. and Morris, H. (2022). Changing Educational Paradigms: Trauma-Responsive Relational Practice, Learnings from the USA for Australian Schools. *Children and Youth Services Review*, 138(106506): 1–11.

Avery-Overduin, B.L. and Poed, S. (2023). Breaking the Culture of School Suspension: Alternatives to External Suspension and Exclusion for P-6 Students. *Emotional and Behavioural Difficulties*, 28(4): 249–62.

Ayers, H., Clarke, D. and Murray, A. (2015). *Perspectives on Behaviour: A Practical Guide to Effective Interventions for Teachers* (Second edition). London: Routledge Taylor Group.

Aytur, S.A., Carlino, S., Bernard, F., West, K., Dobrzycki, V. and Malik, R. (2022). Social-Ecological Theory, Substance Misuse, Adverse Childhood Experiences, and Adolescent Suicidal Ideation: Applications for Community–Academic Partnerships. *Journal of Community Psychology*, 50(1): 265–84.

Backett-Milburn, K., Wilson, S., Bancroft, A. and Cunningham-Burley, S. (2008). Challenging Childhoods: Young People's Accounts of 'Getting By' in Families with Substance Use Problems. *Childhood*, 15(4): 461–79.

Baker, S. and Simpson, M. (2020). *A School Without Sanctions: A New Approach to Behaviour Management*. London: Bloomsbury.

Baker, C.N., Brown, S.M., Wilcox, P.D., Overstreet, S. and Arora, P. (2016). Development and Psychometric Evaluation of the Attitudes Related to Trauma-Informed Care (ARTIC) Scale. *School Mental Health*, 8(1): 61–76.

Baldwin, P. (2008). *With Drama in Mind*. London: Continuum International Publishing Group.

Baldwin, P. (2012). *With Drama in Mind: Real Learning in Imagined Worlds* (Second edition). London: Continuum International Publishing Group.

Baldwin, P. (2024). *40+ Drama' Strategies to Deepen Whole Class Learning: A Toolbox for All Teachers*. London: Routledge.

Ball, S.J. (2016). Neoliberal Education? Confronting the Slouching Beast. *Policy Futures in Education*, 14(8): 1046–59.

Bancroft, A., Wilson, S., Cunningham-Burley, S., Backett-Milburn, K. and Masters, H. (2004). *Parental Drug and Alcohol Misuse: Resilience and Transition Among Young People*. York: Joseph Rowntree Foundation.

Bandura, A. (1977). Self-Efficacy: Toward a Unifying Theory of Behavioral Change. *Psychological Review*, 84(2): 191–215.

Bandura, A. (1986). *Social Foundations of Thought and Action: A Social Cognitive Theory*. Englewood Cliffs, NJ: Prentice-Hall.

Bandura, A. (1997). *Self-efficacy: The Exercise of Control*. New York: Academic Press.

Barnardo's (2020). *Using The PATHS® Programme and Social Emotional Learning to Mitigate the Effects of Adverse Childhood Experiences*. Belfast: Barnardo's.

Barnardo's Scotland (2018a). *Education and Skills Committee: Inquiry into the Attainment and Achievement of School Aged Children Experiencing Poverty*. Edinburgh: Barnardo's Scotland.

Barnardo's Scotland (2018b). *Briefing for Members Debate on Adverse Childhood Experiences*. Edinburgh: Barnardo's Scotland.

Barnardo's Scotland (2019). Supporting the Mental Health and Wellbeing of Education Staff Through Professional Supervision Structures: Trauma Informed Schools (Discussion Paper 1). Ilford: Barnardo's.

Barnardo's Scotland (2020). Supervision in Education – Healthier Schools for All Barnardo's Scotland Report on the Use of Professional or Reflective Supervision in Education. Trauma-Informed Schools (Paper Number 2). Ilford: Barnardo's.

Barnardo's Scotland (2024). *Taking Care of People You Lead*. Ilford: Barnardo's.

Barnardo's Wales (2022). *Adverse Childhood Experiences (ACEs): Briefing Paper*. Cardiff: Barnardo's Wales.

Barrett, S., Muir, C., Burns, S., Adjei, N., Forman, J., Hackett, S., Hirve, R., Kaner, E., Lynch, R., Taylor-Robinson, D., Wolfe, I. and McGovern, R. (2024). Interventions to Reduce Parental Substance Use, Domestic Violence and Mental Health Problems, and Their Impacts upon Children's Well-Being: A Systematic Review of Reviews and Evidence Mapping. *Trauma, Violence & Abuse*, 25(1): 393–412.

Barton, E.R., Newbury, A. and Roberts, D.J. (2018). *An Evaluation of the Adverse Childhood Experience (ACE)-Informed Whole School Approach*. Cardiff: Public Health Wales.

Behrent, M. (2016). More than a Score: Neoliberalism, Testing and Teacher Evaluations. *Workplace*, 26: 50–62.

Bennathan, M. and Boxall, M. (2000). *Effective Intervention in Primary Schools: Nurture Groups* (Second edition). London: David Fulton.

Berger, E. and Martin, K. (2021). Embedding Trauma-Informed Practice Within the Education Sector. *Journal of Community and Applied Social Psychology*, 31(2): 223–7.

Berger, E., Bearsley, A. and Lever, M. (2021). Qualitative Evaluation of Teacher Trauma Knowledge and Response in Schools. *Journal of Aggression, Maltreatment and Trauma*, 30(8): 1041–57.

Bergin, C. and Bergin, D. (2009). Attachment in the Classroom. *Educational Psychology Review*, 21(2): 141–70.

Berridge, D. (2017). The Education of Children in Care: Agency and Resilience. *Children and Youth Services Review*, 77: 86–93.

Bethell, C., Jones, J., Gombojav, N., Linkenbach, J. and Sege, R. (2019). Positive Childhood Experiences and Adult Mental and Relational Health in a Statewide Sample Associations Across Adverse Childhood Experiences Levels. *JAMA Pediatrics*, 173(11): 1–10.

Biesta, G. (2015). What Is Education for? On Good Education, Teacher Judgement, and Educational Professionalism. *European Journal of Education*, 50(1): 75–87.

Black, P.J. and Wiliam, D. (2018). Classroom Assessment and Pedagogy. *Assessment in Education Principles Policy and Practice*, 25(1): 1–25.

Bland, K.D. and Gershwin, T. (2023). Understanding Trauma: A Primer for Developing a Trauma-Focused Lens in Schools. *Beyond Behavior*, 32(3): 141–51.

Bodenheimer, G. and Shuster, S.M. (2019). Emotional Labour, Teaching and Burnout: Investigating Complex Relationships. *Educational Research*, 62(1): 63–76.

Bolton, G. (1979). *Towards a Theory of Drama in Education*. London: Longman.

Bolton, G. (1984). *Drama as Education. An Argument for Placing Drama at the Centre of the Curriculum*. London: Longman.

Bolton, G. (2006). 'A History of Drama Education: A Search for Substance', in L. Bresler (ed.), *International Handbook of Research in Arts Education*. Dordrecht: Springer, pp. 45–66.

Bolton, G. and Heathcote, D. (1999). *So You Want to Use Role-play? A New Approach in How to Plan*. Stoke-on-Trent: Trentham Books.

Bombèr, L.M. (2020). *Know Me to Teach Me: Differentiated Discipline for Those Recovering from Adverse Childhood Experiences: The Latest Neuroscience Applied and Made Practical!* Broadway: Worth Publishing Ltd.

Bombèr, L.M., Golding, K.S., Hughes, D. and Phillips, S. (2020). *Working with Relational Trauma in Schools: An Educator's Guide to Using Dyadic Developmental Practice*. London: Jessica Kingsley Publisher.

Booth, D. (2005). *Story Drama: Creating Stories Through Role Playing, Improvising, and Reading Aloud*. Markham: Pembroke Publishers.

Booth, D. and Barton, B. (2000). *Story Works: How Teachers Can Use Shared Stories in the New Curriculum*. Markham: Pembroke Publishers.

Bottrell, D. (2009). Understanding 'Marginal' Perspectives: Towards a Social Theory of Resilience. *Qualitative Social Work*, 8(3): 321–39.

Bowlby, J. (1960). Grief and Mourning in Infancy and Early Childhood. *Psychoanalytical Study of the Child*, 15(1): 9–52.

Bowlby, J. (1969). *Attachment and Loss Volume 1: Attachment*. London: Penguin Education.

Bowlby, J. (1973). *Attachment and Loss: Separation Anxiety and Anger*. London: Hogarth Press.

Bowlby, J. (1978). *Attachment and Loss Volumes 1–3*. London: Penguin Education.

Bowlby, J. (1980). *Attachment and Loss: Loss, Sadness and Depression*. London: Hogarth Press.

Bowlby, J. (1982). Attachment and Loss: Retrospect and Prospect. *American Journal of Orthopsychiatry*, 52(4): 664–78.

Bowlby, J. (1988). *A Secure Base: Parent-Child Attachment and Healthy Human Development*. London: Basic Books.

Bowlby, J. and Parkes, C.M. (1970). 'Separation and Loss Within the Family', in E.J. Anthony and C. Koupernik (eds), *The Child in His Family: International Yearbook of Child Psychiatry and Allied Professions*. New York: Wiley, pp. 197–216.

Boxall, M. (2002). *Nurture Groups in School: Principles and Practice*. London: SAGE Publications.

Boyce, W.T. (2014). The Lifelong Effects of Early Childhood Adversity and Toxic Stress. *Pediatric Dentistry*, 36(2): 102–8.

Bretherton, I. (1992). The Origins of Attachment Theory: John Bowlby and Mary Ainsworth. *Developmental Psychology*, 28(5): 759–75.

Briggs, E.C., Amaya-Jackson, L., Putnam, K.T. and Putnam, F.W. (2021). All Adverse Childhood Experiences Are Not Equal: The Contribution of Synergy to Adverse Childhood Experience Scores. *American Psychologist*, 76(2): 243–52.

British Psychological Society. (2017). *Practice Guidelines* (Third edition). Leicester: British Psychological Society.

Bronfenbrenner, U. (1979). *Ecology of Human Development*. Cambridge, MA: Harvard University Press.

Bronfenbrenner, U. (1981). *The Ecology of Human Development: Experiments by Nature and Design*. Cambridge, MA: Harvard University Press.

Bronfenbrenner, U. (1992). 'Ecological Systems Theory', in R. Vasta (ed.), *Six Theories of Child Development*. London: Jessica Kingsley, pp. 187–249.

Bronfenbrenner, U. (1995). 'Developmental Ecology Through Space and Time: A Future Perspective', in P. Moen, G.H. Elder and K. Luscher (eds), *Examining Lives in Context: Perspectives on the Ecology of Human Development*. Washington, DC: American Psychological Association, pp. 619–47.

Brown, B. (2018). *Rising Strong: How the Ability to Reset Transforms the Way We Live, Love, Parent, and Lead*. New York: Spiegel & Grau.

Brummer, J. and Thorsborne, M. (2024). *Becoming a Trauma-Informed Restorative Educator*. London: Jessica Kingsley Publishers.

Brunzell, T. (2021). 'Trauma-Aware Practice and Positive Education', in M.L. Kern and M.L. Wehmeyer (eds), *The Palgrave Handbook of Positive Education*. Cham: Palgrave Macmillan, pp. 205–22.

Brunzell, T. and Norrish, J. (2021). *Creating Trauma-Informed, Strengths-Based Classrooms*. London: Jessica Kingsley Publishers.

Brunzell, T., Stokes, H. and Waters, L. (2016). Trauma-Informed Flexible Learning: Classrooms That Strengthen Regulatory Abilities. *International Journal of Child, Youth and Family Studies*, 7(2): 218–39.

Brunzell, T., Waters, L. and Stokes, H. (2015). Teaching with Strengths in Trauma-Affected Students: A New Approach to Healing and Growth in the Classroom. *American Journal of Orthopsychiatry*, 85(1): 3–9.

Brunzell, T., Waters, L. and Stokes, H. (2022). Teacher Perspectives When Learning Trauma-Informed Practice Pedagogies: Stories of Meaning Making at Work. *Frontiers in Education*, 7: 1–10.

Bryk, A. and Schneider, B. (2002). *Trust in Schools: A Core Resource for Improvement*. New York: Russell Sage.

Burns, E.C., Martin, A.J. and Evans, P.A. (2019). The Role of Teacher Feedback–Feedforward and Personal Best Goal Setting in Students' Mathematics Achievement: A Goal Setting Theory Perspective. *Educational Psychology*, 41(7): 825–43.

Callaghan, J.E.M. (2023). 'Children's Experiences of Domestic Violence and Abuse: Resistances and Paradoxical Resiliencies', in J.C. Taylor and E.A. Bates (eds), *Children and Adolescent's Experiences of Violence and Abuse at Home*. London: Routledge, pp. 9–21.

Callaghan, J.E.M. and Alexander, J.H. (2015). *Understanding Agency and Resistance Strategies (UNARS): Children's Experiences of Domestic Violence*. Northampton: University of Northampton.

Campbell, J.A., Walker, R.J. and Egede, L.E. (2016). Associations Between Adverse Childhood Experiences, High-Risk Behaviors, and Morbidity in Adulthood. *American Journal of Preventive Medicine*, 50(3): 344–52.

Carroll, M. (2023). 'Theories of Child Development', in M. Carroll and M. Wingrave (eds), *Childhood Practice: A Reflective and Evidence-Based Approach*. London: SAGE Publications, pp. 55–67.

Carter, P. and Blanch, A. (2019). A Trauma Lens for Systems Change. *Stanford Social Innovation Review*, 17(3): 49–54.

Castelao-Heurta, L. (2025). 'Fostering Care Within Neoliberalised Doctoral Education'. *Supervising PhDs*, 2 April 2025 (Blog). Available at: https://supervisingphds.wordpress.com/2025/04/02/fostering-care-within-neoliberalised-doctoral-education/ [Last accessed 4 April 2025].

Centre on the Developing Child (2007). InBrief: The Science of Early Childhood Development. Available at: https://developingchild.harvard.edu/resources/inbrief-science-of-ecd/ [Last accessed 28 October 2024].

Chafouleas, S.M., Pickens, I. and Gherardi, S.A. (2021). Adverse Childhood Experiences (ACEs): Translation into Action in K12 Education Settings. *School Mental Health*, 13: 213–24.

Chafouleas, S.M., Johnson, A.H., Overstreet, S. and Santos, N.M. (2016). Toward a Blueprint for Trauma-Informed Service Delivery in Schools. *School Mental Health*, 8(1): 144–62.

Champine, R.B., Hoffman, E.E., Matlin, S.L., Strambler, M.J. and Tebes, J.K. (2022). 'What Does It Mean to Be Trauma-Informed?': A Mixed-Methods Study of a Trauma-Informed Community Initiative. *Journal of Child and Family Studies*, 31: 459–72.

Chang, M. (2013). Toward a Theoretical Model to Understand Teacher Emotions and Teacher Burnout in the Context of Student Misbehavior: Appraisal, Regulation and Coping. *Motivation and Emotion*, 37(4): 799–817.

Chang, M.-L. and Davis, H.A. (2009). 'Understanding the Role of Teacher Appraisals in Shaping the Dynamics of Their Relationships with Students: Deconstructing Teachers' Judgments of Disruptive Behavior/Students', in P.A. Schutz and M. Zembylasb (eds), *Advances in Teacher Emotions Research: The Impact on Teachers Lives*. New York: Springer, pp. 95–127.

Chang, M.-L. and Taxer, J. (2020). Teacher Emotion Regulation Strategies in Response to Classroom Misbehavior. *Teachers and Teaching*, 27(5): 353–69.

Children in Scotland (2022). *Access to Childcare Fund 2020–2022 Final Evaluation Report*. Edinburgh: Children in Scotland.

Choate, P.W. (2020). Where Do We Go from Here? Ongoing Colonialism from Attachment Theory. *Aotearoa New Zealand Social Work*, 32(1): 32–44.

Christian-Brandt, A.S., Santacrose, D.E. and Barnett, M.L. (2020). In the Trauma-Informed Trenches: Teacher Compassion Satisfaction, Secondary Traumatic Stress, Burnout and Intent to Leave Education with Underserved Elementary Schools. *Child Abuse and Neglect*, 110(3): 1–8.

Chudzik, M., Corr, C. and Santos, R.M. (2025). Trauma-Informed Care in Early Childhood Education Settings: A Scoping Literature Review. *Early Childhood Education Journal*, 53(2): 477–88.

Cleaver, H., Unell, I. and Aldgate, J. (2011). *Children's Needs – Parenting Capacity Child Abuse: Parental Mental Illness, Learning Disability, Substance Misuse and Domestic Violence*. London: The Stationery Office.

Conkbayir, M. (2023). *The Neuroscience of the Developing Child: Self-regulation for Wellbeing and a Sustainable Future*. New York: Routledge.

Conners Edge, N.A., Holmes, K., Wilburn, E.H. and Melissa Sutton, M. (2024). Fostering Informed and Responsive Systems for Trauma in Early Care and Education (FIRST:ECE): A Preliminary Evaluation. *Early Childhood Education Journal*, 52: 1–11.

Cowie, H. and Myers, C. (2021). The Impact of the COVID-19 Pandemic on the Mental Health and Well-Being of Children and Young People. *Children and Society*, 35(1): 62–74.

Cozolino, L.J. (2013). *The Social Neuroscience of Education: Optimizing Attachment and Learning in the Classroom* (First edition). New York: W.W. Norton & Company.

Cozolino, L.J. and Siegel, D.J. (2013). *The Social Neuroscience of Education: Optimizing Attachment and Learning in the Classroom*. New York: W.W. Norton & Company.

Cronholm, P.F., Forke, C.M., Wade, R., Bair-Merritt, M.H., Davis, M., Harkins-Schwarz, M., Pachter, L.M. and Fein, J.A. (2015). Adverse Childhood Experiences: Expanding the Concept of Adversity. *American Journal of Preventive Medicine*, 49(3): 354–61.

Crosby, S.D. (2015). An Ecological Perspective on Emerging Trauma-Informed Teaching Practices. *Children and Schools*, 37(4): 223–30.

Crosby, S.D., Howell, P.B. and Thomas, S. (2020). Teaching Through Collective Trauma in the Era of COVID-19: Trauma-Informed Practices for Middle Level Learners. *Middle Grades Review*, 6(2): 1–6.

Crouch, E., Radcliff, E., Bennett, K., Brown, M.J. and Hung, P. (2023). Child and Adolescent Health in the United States: The Role of Adverse and Positive Childhood Experiences. *Journal of Child and Adolescent Trauma*, 17(2): 1–9.

Curran, A. (2008). *The Little Book of Big Stuff About the Brain*. Carmarthen: Crown House Publishing.

Dana, D. (2023). A Beginner's Guide to Polyvagal Theory. Available at: https://www.rhythmofregulation.com/polyvagal-theory [Last accessed 2 April 2025].

Daniel, B. and Wassell, S. (2002). *Assessing and Promoting Resilience in Vulnerable Children* (Vols. 1, 2 & 3). London: Jessica Kingsley Publishers Ltd.

Danielson, R. and Saxen, D. (2019). Connecting Adverse Childhood Experiences and Community Health to Promote Health Equity. *Social and Personality Psychology Compass*, 13(7): 1–13.

Davidson, E. and Carlin, E. (2019). 'Steeling' Young People: Resilience and Youth Policy in Scotland. *Social Policy and Society*, 18(3): 479–89.

Dawes, M., Sterrett, B.I., Brooks, D.S., Lee, D.L., Hamm, J.V. and Farmer, T.W. (2024). Enhancing Teachers' Capacity to Manage Classroom Behavior as a Means to Reduce Burnout: Directed Consultation, Supported Professionalism, and the BASE Model. *Journal of Emotional and Behavioral Disorders*, 32(2): 110–23.

DeCandia, C.J., Guarino, K. and Clervil, R. (2014). *Trauma-Informed Care and Trauma-Specific Services: A Comprehensive Approach to Trauma Intervention*. Washington, DC: American Institutes for Research.

Delahooke, M. (2020). *Beyond Behaviours: Using Brain Science and Compassion to Understand and Solve Children's Behavioural Challenges*. London: Hachette UK.

Delahunty, T. (2024). The Convergence of Late Neoliberalism and Post-Pandemic Scientific Optimism in the Configuration of Scientistic Learnification. *Educational Review*, 1–23. Available at: https://doi.org/10.1080/00131911.2024.2307509 [Last accessed 20 April 2025].

Department for Education (DfE) (2024a). *Behaviour in Schools; Advice for headteachers and school staff*. London: Department for Education.

Department for Education (DfE) (2024b). *Working Lives of Teachers and Leaders–Wave 2*. London: DfE.

de Ruiter, J.A., Poorthuis, A.M.G., Aldrup, K. and Koomen, H.M.Y. (2020). Teachers' Emotional Experiences in Response to Daily Events with Individual Students Varying in Perceived Past Disruptive Behavior. *Journal of School Psychology*, 82: 85–102.

Desautels, L. (2023). *Intentional Neuroplasticity*. Deadwood, OR: Wyatt-MacKenzie Publishing.

de Thierry, B. (2021). *The Simple Guide to Collective Trauma*. London: Jessica Kingsley Publishers.

Dix, P. (2017). *When the Adults Changes, Everything Changes: Seismic Shifts in School Behaviour*. Bancyfelin: Independent Thinking Press.

Dolezal, L. and Gibson, M. (2022). Beyond a Trauma-Informed Approach and Towards Shame-Sensitive Practice. *Humanities and Social Sciences Communications*, 9(1): 1–10.

Donker, M.H., Scheepers, D., van Gog, T., van den Hove, M., McIntyre, N. and Mainhard, T. (2025). Handling Demanding Situations: Associations Between Teachers' Interpersonal Behavior, Physiological Responses, and Emotions. *The Journal of Experimental Education*, 93(1): 91–109.

Dowdney, L. (1999). Annotation: Childhood Bereavement Following Parental Death. *Journal of Child Psychology and Psychiatry*, 41(7): 819–30.

Downey, J. and Greco, J. (2023). Trauma Sensitive Schools: A Comprehensive Guide for the Assessment Planning and Implementation of Trauma Informed Frameworks. *Children and Youth Services Review*, 149(106930): 1–13.

Drygrov, A. (2008). *Grief in Children: A Handbook for Adults*. London: Jessica Kingsley Publishers.

Duschinsky, R. (2015). The Emergence of the Disorganized/Disoriented (D) Attachment Classification. *History of Psychology*, 18(1): 32–46.

Education Scotland (2014). *Health and Wellbeing: Responsibility of All*. Livingston: Education Scotland.

Education Scotland (2015). *How Good Is Our School?* (Fourth edition). Livingston: Education Scotland.

Education Scotland (2017a). *Applying Nurture as a Whole School Approach*. Livingston: Education Scotland.

Education Scotland (2017b). *Curriculum for Excellence: Health and Wellbeing – Principles and Practice*. Livingston: Education Scotland.

Education Scotland (2018). *Nurture, Adverse Childhood Experiences and Trauma Informed Practice: Making the Links Between These Approaches*. Livingston: Education Scotland.

Education Scotland (2019). *The Compassionate and Connected Classroom: Curricular Resource*. Livingston: Education Scotland.

Education Scotland (2024a). *Promoting Positive Relationships and Behaviour in Educational Settings*. Livingston: Education Scotland.

Education Scotland (2025). *Keeping Trauma in Mind*. Livingston: Education Scotland.

Education Scotland (online). Scotland's Curriculum for Excellence. Available at: https://scotlandscurriculum.scot/ [Last accessed 14 August 2024b].

Educational Institute of Scotland (EIS) (2023). *EIS Member Survey: Workload, Health and Wellbeing, and the Cost-of-Living Crisis*. Edinburgh: EIS.

Edwards, R., Gillies, V. and White, S. (2019). Introduction: Adverse Childhood Experiences (ACES) – Implications and Challenges. *Social Policy and Society*, 18(3): 411–14.

Eriksson, S.A. (2011). Distancing at Close Range: Making Strange Devices in Dorothy Heathcote's Process Drama Teaching Political Awareness Through Drama. *Research in Drama Education: The Journal of Applied Theatre and Performance*, 16(1): 101–23.

Esteban-Guitart, M. and Moll, L.C. (2014). Funds of Identity: A New Concept Based on the Funds of Knowledge Approach. *Culture & Psychology*, 20(1): 31–48.

Fazel, M., Hoagwood, K., Stephan, S. and Ford, T. (2014). Mental Health Interventions in Schools in High-Income Countries. *The Lancet Psychiatry*, 1(5): 377–87.

Felitti, V.J., Anda, R.F., Nordenberg, D., Williamson, D.F., Spitz, A.M., Edwards, V., Koss, M.P. and Marks, J.S. (1998). Relationship of Childhood Abuse and Household Dysfunction to Many of the Leading Causes of Death in Adults: The Adverse Childhood Experiences (ACE) Study. *American Journal of Preventive Medicine*, 14(4): 245–58.

Fisher, J. and Jones, E. (2024). The Problem with Resilience. *International Journal of Mental Health Nursing*, 33(1): 185–8.

Fondren, K., Lawson, M., Speidel, R., McDonnell, C.G. and Valentino, K. (2020). Buffering the Effects of Childhood Trauma with the School Setting: A Systematic Review of Trauma Informed and Trauma Responsive Interventions Among Trauma Affected Youth. *Children and Youth Services Review*, 109(104691): 1–18.

Frenzel, A.C., Daniels, L. and Burić, I. (2021). Teacher Emotions in the Classroom and Their Implications for Students. *Educational Psychologist*, 56(4): 250–64.

Freud, S. (2009). 'Mourning and Melacholia' (1917), in L.G. Fiorini, T. Bokanowski and S. Lewkowicz (eds), *On Freud's Mourning and Melacholia*. London: Karnac Books, pp. 19–36.

Freud, S. and Freud, A. (1991). *The Essentials of Psycho-analysis*. London: Penguin Books.

Garcia, A., Sprang, G. and Clemans, T. (2023). The Role of School Leaders in Cultivating a Trauma-Informed School Climate. *Children and Youth Services Review*, 146: 1–11.

García-Rodríguez, L., Iriarte Redín, C. and Reparaz Abaitua, C. (2023). Teacher-Student Attachment Relationship, Variables Associated, and Measurement: A Systematic Review. *Educational Research Review*, 38(100488): 1–26.

Garner, A.S. and Shonkoff, J.P. (2012). Early Childhood Adversity, Toxic Stress, and the Role of the Pediatrician: Translating Developmental Science into Lifelong Health. *American Academy of Pediatrics*, 129(1): 224–31.

Gaskill, R. and Perry, B. (2012). 'Child Sexual Abuse, Traumatic Experiences, and Their Impact on the Developing Brain', in P. Goodyear-Brown (ed.), *Handbook of Child Sexual Abuse: Identification, Assessment, and Treatment*. Hoboken, NJ: John Wiley & Sons, pp. 29–48.

Geddes, H. (2017). 'Attachment Behaviour and Learning', in D. Colley and P. Cooper (eds), *Attachment and Emotional Development in the Classroom*. London: Jessica Kingsley Publishers, pp. 37–48.

Geddes, H., Nash, P., Cahill, J., Satchwell-Hirst, M., Thierry, B.D., Wilson, P., Rose, J., Colley, D., Cooper, P. and Carpenter, B. (2017). *Attachment and Emotional Development in the Classroom: Theory and Practice*. London: Jessica Kingsley Publishers.

General Teaching Council for Scotland (GTCS) (2021a). *The Standard for Full Registration*. Edinburgh: GTCS.

General Teaching Council for Scotland (GTCS) (2021b). *A Guide to the Professional Standards*. Edinburgh: GTCS.

General Teaching Council for Scotland (GTCS) (2021c). *The Standard for Career-Long Professional Learning*. Edinburgh: GTCS.

Gerrard, B. (2006). City of Glasgow Nurture Group Pilot Scheme Evaluation. *Emotional and Behavioural Difficulties*, 10(4): 245–53.

Gibbs, J., Dwyer, J. and Vivekananda, K. (2014). *Leading Practice: A Resource Guide for Child Protection Leaders* (Second edition). Melbourne: Victoria Government Department of Human Services.

Giboney Wall, C.R. (2021). Relationship over Reproach: Fostering Resilience by Embracing a Trauma-Informed Approach to Elementary Education. *Journal of Aggression. Maltreatment and Trauma*, 30(1): 118–37.

Gill, M.E., Zhan, L., Rosenberg, J. and Breckenridge, L.A. (2019). Integration of Adverse Childhood Experiences Across Nursing Curriculum. *Journal of Professional Nursing*, 35(2): 105–11.

Giovanelli, A., Mondi, C.F., Reynolds, A.J. and Ou, S.-R. (2023). Evaluation of Midlife Educational Attainment Among Attendees of a Comprehensive Early Childhood Education Program in the Context of Early Adverse Childhood Experiences. *JAMA Network Open*, 6(6): 1–13.

Golding, K.S. (2020). Understanding and Helping Children Who Have Experienced Maltreatment. *Paediatrics and Child Health*, 30(11): 371–7.

Golding, K.S. and Hughes, D. (2012). *Creating Loving Attachments: Parenting with PACE to Nurture Confidence and Security in the Troubled Child*. London: Jessica Kingsley Publishers.

Golding, K.S., Phillips, S. and Bombèr, L.M. (2021). *Working with Relational Trauma in Schools: An Educator's Guide to Using Dyadic Developmental Practice*. London: Jessica Kingsley Publishers.

Gorin, S. (2004). *Understanding What Children Say: Children's Experiences of Domestic Violence, Parental Substance Misuse and Parental Health Problems*. London: Jessica Kingsley Publishers.

Gose, R. (2025). Dancing Within Windows of Tolerance: Considerations for a Trauma Informed Pedagogy for Dance Education. *Journal of Dance Education*, 25(4): 402-12.

Grady, M.D., O'Toole, R. and Schneider, D.A. (2022). Growing Up in the Age of COVID-19 Through the Lens of Psychodynamic Theory. *Psychoanalytic Social Work*, 29(1): 44–73.

Gravett, K., Taylor, C.A. and Fairchild, N. (2021). Pedagogies of Mattering: Reconceptualising Relational Pedagogies in Higher Education. *Teaching in Higher Education*, 29(2): 388–403.

Greene, M. (1995). *Releasing the Imagination: Essays on Education, the Arts, and Social Change*. San Francisco: Jossey-Bass.

Greer, J.A. (2023). Introducing Trauma-Informed Care Principles in the Workplace. *Discover Psychology*, 3(1): 31–6.

Gus, L., Rose, J. and Gilbert, L. (2015). Emotion Coaching: A Universal Strategy for Supporting and Promoting Sustainable Emotional and Behavioural Well-Being. *Educational and Child Psychology*, 32(1): 31–41.

Haine, R.A., Ayers, T.S., Sandler, I.N. and Wolchik, S.A. (2008). Evidence Based Practice for Parentally Bereaved Children and Their Families. *Professional Psychology: Research and Practice*, 39(2): 113–21.

Hales, T.W., Green, S.A., Bissonette, S., Warden, A., Diebold, J., Koury, S.P. and Nochajski, T.H. (2019). Trauma-Informed Care Outcome Study. *Research on Social Work Practice*, 29(5): 529–39.

Hall, R. (2024). '"Bittersweet": Covid Report Does Not Go Far Enough, Say Bereaved Families', *The Guardian*, 18 July. Available at: https://www.theguardian.com/uk-news/article/2024/jul/18/bereaved-families-hail-uk-report-noting-damning-analysis-of-an-unprepared-britain [Last accessed: 3 August 2024].

Hanna, F., Oostdam, R., Severiens, S.E. and Zijlstra, B.J.H. (2019). Domains of Teacher Identity: A Review of Quantitative Measurement Instruments. *Educational Research Review*, 27: 15–27.

Harlow, E. (2021). Attachment Theory: Developments, Debates and Recent Applications in Social Work, Social Care and Education. *Journal of Social Work Practice*, 35(1): 79–91.

Harris, M. and Fallot, R.D. (2001). *Using Trauma Theory to Design Service Systems*. San Francisco, CA: Jossey-Bass/Wiley.

Harris, N.B. (2020). Screening for Adverse Childhood Experiences. *Journal of American Medical Association*, 324(17): 1788.

Harrison, E. (2013). Bouncing Back? Recession, Resilience, and Everyday Lives. *Critical Social Policy*, 33(1): 97–113.

Harrison, N. (2022). *Attachment and Trauma Awareness Training: Headteachers' Perspectives on the Impact on Vulnerable Children, Staff and the School*. Oxford: Rees Centre.

Hart, A., Blincow, D. and Thomas, H. (2007). *Resilient Therapy: Working with Children and Families*. Hove: Routledge.

Hart, A., Gagnon, E., Eryigit-Madzwamuse, S., Cameron, J., Aranda, K., Rathbone, A. and Heaver, B. (2016). Uniting Resilience Research and Practice with an Inequalities Approach. *SAGE Open*, 6(4): 1–13.

Hart, S., Dixon, A., Drummond, M.J. and McIntyre, D. (2004). *Learning Without Limits*. Maidenhead: Open University Press.

Hartas, D. (2019). Assessing the Foundational Studies on Adverse Childhood Experiences. *Social Policy and Society*, 18(3): 435–43.

Hawkins, P. and McMahon, A. (2020). *Supervision in the Helping Professions* (Fifth edition). Maidenhead: Open University Press.

Head, G. (2007). *Better Learning, Better Behaviour*. Edinburgh: Dunedin Academic Press.

Health and Care Professions Council (HCPC) (2024). What Is Supervision? Available at: https://prod.hcpc-uk.org/standards/meeting-our-standards/supervision-leadership-and-culture/supervision/what-is-supervision/ [Last accessed 24 April 2025].

Herman, J.L. (1992). *Trauma and Recovery: From Domestic Abuse to Political Terror*. New York: Basic Books.

Hewson, H., Galbraith, N., Jones, C. and Heath, G. (2023). The Impact of Continuing Bonds Following Bereavement: A Systematic Review. *Death Studies*, 48(10): 1001–14.

Higgins, A., Kilkku, N. and Kristofersson, G.K. (eds) (2022). *Advanced Practice in Mental Health Nursing: A European Perspective*. Cham: Springer.

Highland Council (2024). 'Professional Reflective Supervision for Highland Head Teachers', Highland Council Psychological Service [Blog], 4 March 2024. Available at: https://highlandcouncilpsychologicalservice.store/ [Last accessed 28 October 2024].

Hirschberger, G. (2018). Collective Trauma and the Social Construction of Meaning. *Frontiers in Psychology*, 9: 1441.

H.M. Treasury (2003). *Every Child Matters*. Norwich: The Stationery Office.

hooks, b. (2010). *Teaching Critical Thinking: Practical Wisdom*. New York: Routledge.

Houghton, S., Kyron, M., Hunter, S.C., Lawrence, D., Hattie, J., Carroll, A. and Zadow, C. (2022). Adolescents' Longitudinal Trajectories of Mental Health and Loneliness: The Impact of COVID-19 School Closures. *Journal of Adolescence*, 94(2): 191–205.

Howard, J.A. (2019). A Systemic Framework for Trauma-Informed Schooling: Complex but Necessary! *Journal of Aggression, Maltreatment and Trauma*, 28(5): 545–65.

Howard, J.A. (2021). *National Guidelines for Trauma-Aware Education*. Brisbane: QUT and Australian Childhood Foundation.

Howard, J.A. (2022). *Trauma-Aware Education: Essential Information and Guidance for Educators, Education Sites and Education Systems*. Samford Valley: Australian Academic Press.

Howard, J.A., L'Estrange, L. and Brown, M. (2022). National Guidelines for Trauma-Aware Education in Australia. *Frontiers in Education*, 7: 1–11.

Hunkin, E. (2019). If Not Quality, then What? The Discursive Risks in Early Childhood Quality Reform. *Discourse: Studies in the Cultural Politics of Education*, 40(6): 917–29.

Hymans, M. (2008). How Personal Constructs About 'Professional Identity' Might Act as a Barrier to Multi-agency Working. *Educational Psychology in Practice*, 24(4): 279–88.

Independent Care Review (2020). *The Promise*. Edinburgh: Independent Care Review.

Jacobson, M.R. (2021). An Exploratory Analysis of the Necessity and Utility of Trauma-informed Practices in Education. *Preventing School Failure*, 65(2): 124–34.

Jarvis, P. (2022). Attachment Theory, Cortisol and Care for the Under-Threes in the Twenty-First Century: Constructing Evidence-Informed Policy. *Early Years* (London, England), 42(4–5): 450–64.

Jones, E.-L. and Harding, E. (2023). Exploring Perspectives of Whole-School Attachment and Trauma Aware Approaches in a Specialist Provision. *British Journal of Special Education*, 50(2): 293–313.

Joseph, J. (2013). Resilience as Embedded Neoliberalism: A Governmentality Approach. *Resilience*, 1(1): 38–52.

Joyce, T., McKenzie, M., Lindsay, A. and Asi, D. (2023). Don't Call It a Workforce, Call It a Profession! Perceptions on Their Roles from Past to Future. *Education*, 3(13): 1–14.

Kałwak, W., Weziak-Bialowolska, D., Wendołowska, A., Bonarska, K., Sitnik-Warchulska, K., Bańbura, A., Czyżowska, D., Gruszka, A., Opoczyńska-Morasiewicz, M. and Izydorczyk, B. (2024). Young Adults from Disadvantaged Groups Experience More Stress and Deterioration in Mental Health Associated with Polycrisis. *Scientific Reports*, 14(8757): 1–12.

Karatzias, T., Power, K., Woolston, C., Purva, P., Begley, A., Mirza, K., Conway, L., Quinn, C., Jowett, S., Howard, R. and Purdie, A. (2017). Multiple Traumatic Experiences, Post-Traumatic Stress Disorder and Offending Behaviour in Female Prisoners. *Criminal Behaviour and Mental Health*, 28(1): 72–84.

Kariou, A., Koutsimani, P., Montgomery, A. and Lainidi, O. (2021). Emotional Labor and Burnout Among Teachers: A Systematic Review. *International Journal of Environmental Research and Public Health*, 18(23): 1–15.

Kearney, M. (2004). Nurturing Confidence: The Impact of Nurture Groups on Self-Esteem. *Educational Psychology in Scotland*, 7(1): 2–5.

Kearns, S. and Hart, N. (2017). Narratives of 'Doing, Knowing, Being and Becoming': Examining the Impact of an Attachment-Informed Approach Within Initial Teacher Education. *Teacher Development*, 21(4): 511–27.

Kelly, P., Watt, L. and Giddens, S. (2020). An Attachment Aware Schools Programme: A Safe Space, a Nurturing Learning Community. *Pastoral Care in Education*, 38(4): 335–54.

Kelly-Irving, M. and Delpierre, C. (2019). A Critique of the Adverse Childhood Experiences Framework in Epidemiology and Public Health: Uses and Misuses. *Social Policy and Society*, 18(3): 445–56.

Kennedy, B.L. (2008). Educating Students with Insecure Attachment Histories: Toward an Interdisciplinary Theoretical Framework. *Pastoral Care in Education*, 26(4): 211–30.

Kennedy, E.-K., Keaney, C., Shaldon, C. and Canagaratnam, M. (2018). A Relational Model of Supervision for Applied Psychology Practice: Professional Growth Through Relating and Reflecting. *Educational Psychology in Practice*, 34(3): 282–99.

Kennedy, J.H. and Kennedy, C.E. (2004). Attachment Theory: Implications for School Psychology. *Psychology in the Schools*, 41(2): 247–59.

Keyes, C.L.M. (2002). The Mental Health Continuum: From Languishing to Flourishing in Life. *Journal of Health and Social Behavior*, 43(2): 207–22.

Killen, A. and Cooney, P. (2017). Discovering the Value of 'Not Knowing': Using Drama for a Deeper Understanding of Pedagogy and Learning. *Drama Research*, 8(1): 1–21.

King, E.N. (2022). A Mixed-Methods Investigation of the Application and Impact of Attachment Theory on the Policy and Practice Within Early Years and Primary Education in a Scottish Local Authority. PhD Thesis, University of Strathclyde.

Kitson, N. and Spiby, I. (1997). *Drama 7-11: Developing Primary Teaching Skills.* London: Routledge.

Klass, D., Silverman, P.R. and Nickman, S.L. (2014). *Continuing Bonds: New Understandings of Grief.* London: Taylor & Francis.

Klass, D. and Walter, T. (2001). 'Processes of Grieving: How Bonds Are Continued', in M.S. Stroebe, R.O. Hansson, W. Stroebe and H. Schut (eds), *Handbook of Bereavement Research: Consequence, Coping and Care.* Washington, DC: American Psychological Association, pp. 431–48.

Kohn, A. (2018). *Punished by Rewards: The Trouble with Gold Stars, Incentive Plans, A's Praise and Other Bribes.* New York: Houghton Mifflin.

Kolb, D.A. (1984). *Experiential Learning: Experience as the Source of Learning and Development.* Englewood Cliffs, NJ: Prentice-Hall.

Kübler-Ross, E. (1969). *On Death and Dying.* London: Routledge.

Kukla, K. (1987). David Booth: Drama as a Way of Knowing. *Language Arts*, 64(1): 73–8.

Kural, A.I. and Kovacs, M. (2021). Attachment Anxiety and Resilience: The Mediating Role of Coping. *Acta Psychologica*, 221(103447): 1–8. Available at: https://www.sciencedirect.com/science/article/pii/S0001691821001979 [Last accessed 16 April 2024].

Lacey, R.E. and Minnis, H. (2020). Practitioner Review: Twenty Years of Research with Adverse Childhood Experience Scores – Advantages, Disadvantages and Applications to Practice. *Journal of Child Psychology and Psychiatry*, 61(2): 116–30.

Laevers, F. (2000). Forward to Basics! Deep-Level Learning and the Experiential Approach. *Early Years*, 20(2): 20–9.

Langley, A.K., Nadeem, E., Kataoka, S.H., Stein, B.D. and Jaycox, L.H. (2010). Evidence-Based Mental Health Programs in Schools: Barriers and Facilitators of Successful Implementation. *School Mental Health*, 2(3): 105–13.

Langley, A.K., Santiago, C.D., Rodríguez, A. and Zelaya, J. (2013). Improving Implementation of Mental Health Services for Trauma in Multicultural Elementary Schools: Stakeholder Perspectives on Parent and Educator Engagement. *Journal of Behavioral Health Services and Research*, 40(3): 247–62.

Lawrence, M. (2023). The Theory of Educational Attachment. *Journal of Organizational and Educational Leadership*, 8(3): 1–25.

L'Estrange, L. and Howard, J. (2022). Trauma-Informed Initial Teacher Education Training: A Necessary Step in a System-Wide Response to Addressing Childhood Trauma. *Frontiers in Education*, 7(929582): 1–12.

Linden, W. and Le Moult, J. (2022). Editorial Perspective: Adverse Childhood Events Causally Contribute to Mental Illness – We Must Act now and Intervene Early. *Journal of Child Psychology and Psychiatry*, 63(6): 715–19.

Lipscomb, S.T., Swander, W. and Mason, E. (2024). Building Cultures of Care in Schools: Centering Relationships at the Intersection of Trauma-Informed Education and Restorative Practices. *Contemporary School Psychology*, 28(4): 653–69.

Loveday, S., Hall, T., Constable, L., Paton, K., Sanci, L., Goldfeld, S. and Hiscock, H. (2022). Screening for Adverse Childhood Experiences in Children: A Systematic Review. *Pediatrics*, 149(2): 1–12.

Lowthian, E. (2022). The Secondary Harms of Parental Substance Use on Children's Educational Outcomes: A Review. *Journal of Child and Adolescent Trauma*, 15(3): 511–22.

MacKay, T., Reynolds, S. and Kearney, M. (2010). From Attachment to Attainment: The Impact of Nurture Groups on Academic Achievement. *Educational and Child Psychology*, 27(3): 100–10.

MacLochlainn, J., Kirby, K., McFadden, P. and Mallett, J. (2022). An Evaluation of Whole-School Trauma-Informed Training Intervention Among Post-Primary School Personnel: A Mixed Methods Study. *Journal of Child and Adolescent Trauma*, 15(3): 925–41.

Macvarish, J. and Lee, E. (2019). Constructions of Parents in Adverse Childhood Experiences Discourse. *Social Policy and Society*, 18(3): 467–77.

Mahdiani, H. and Ungar, M. (2021). The Dark Side of Resilience. *Adversity and Resilience Science*, 2(3): 147–55.

Main, M. and Solomon, J. (1986). 'Discovery of an Insecure-Disorganised/Disoriented Attachment Pattern', in T.B. Brazelton and M.W. Yogman (eds), *Affective Development in Infancy*. New York: Ablex Publishing, pp. 95–124.

Mannarini, T., Rizzo, M., Brodsky, A., Buckingham, S., Zhao, J., Rochira, A. and Fedi, A. (2022). The Potential of Psychological Connectedness: Mitigating the Impacts of COVID-19 Through Sense of Community and Community Resilience. *Journal of Community Psychology*, 50(5): 2273–89.

Manning, V., Best, D.W., Faulkner, N. and Titherington, E. (2009). New Estimates of the Prevalence of Children Living with Substance Using Parents: Results from the National UK Households Surveys. *BMC Public Health*, 9(1): 1–12.

March, S. and Healy, N. (2007). What Is the Parental Perception of Progress Made by Nurture Group Children? *Educational Psychology in Scotland*, 9(1): 2–7.

March, S. and Kearney, M. (2017). A Psychological Service Contribution to Nurture: Glasgow's Nurturing City. *Emotional and Behavioural Difficulties*, 22(3): 237–47.

Marryat, L. and Frank, J. (2019). Factors Associated with Adverse Childhood Experiences in Scottish Children: A Prospective Cohort Study. *BMJ Paediatrics Open*, 3(1): 1–7.

Masten, A. (2001). Ordinary Magic: Resilience Processes in Development. *American Psychologist*, 56(3): 227–38.

Mate, G. (2022). *The Myth of Normal: Trauma, Illness and Healing in a Toxic Culture*. London: Penguin Random House.

Matlin, S.L., Champine, R.B., Strambler, M.J., O'Brien, C., Hoffman, E., Whitson, M., Kolka, L. and Tebes, J.K. (2019). A Community's Response to Adverse Childhood Experiences: Building a Resilient, Trauma-Informed Community. *American Journal of Community Psychology*, 64(3–4): 451–66.

Maynard, B.R., Farina, A., Dell, N.A. and Kelly, M.S. (2019). Effects of Trauma-Informed Approaches in Schools: A Systematic Review. *Campbell Systematic Review*, 15(1–2): 1–18.

McCluskey, G., Fry, D., Hamilton, S., King, A., Laurie, M., McAra, L. and Stewart, T.M. (2021). School Closures, Exam Cancellations and Isolation: The Impact of Covid-19 on Young People's Mental Health. *Emotional and Behavioural Difficulties*, 26(1): 46–59.

McCrory, E.J., Gerin, M.I. and Viding, E. (2017). Annual Research Review: Childhood Maltreatment, Latent Vulnerability and the Shift to Preventative Psychiatry – The Contribution of Functional Brain Imaging. *Journal of Child Psychology and Psychiatry*, 58(4): 338–57.

McCulloch, M. (2018). 'Social and Emotional Contexts for Learning', in M. Carroll and M. McCulloch (eds), *Understanding Teaching and Learning in Primary Education* (Second edition). London: SAGE Publications, pp. 83–100.

McCulloch, M. and Stewart, T. (2023). 'Diversity, Equity and Inclusion in Early Years', in M. Carroll and M. Wingrave (eds), *Childhood Practice: A Reflective and Evidence-based Approach*. London: SAGE Publications, pp. 29–40.

McEnaney, J. (2024). 'Scottish Education: Serious Trouble as New Teachers Walk away', *The Herald*, 5 January. n.p.

McIlroy, C. (2022). Learning Together – A Radical Approach to Inspections. Available at: https://improvingcareand.education/2022/02/04/learning-together-a-radical-approach-to-inspections-strong/ [Last accessed 4 April 2025].

McKay, C. and Macomber, G (2021). The Importance of Relationships in Education: Reflections of Current Educators. *Journal of Education*, 203(4): 751–8.

McKee, C. and Breslin, M. (2023). 'Attachment-Focused and Trauma-Aware Early Childhood Practice', in M. Carroll and M. Wingrave (eds), *Childhood Practice: A Reflective and Evidence-Based Approach*. London: SAGE Publications, pp. 95–106.

McKinney, S.J., Graham, A., Hall, S., Hunter, K., Jaap, A., Lowden, K., MacDougall, L., McKendrick, J.H., Mtika, P., Moscardini, L., Reid, L., Ritchie, M., Robson, D., Shanks, R., Sebastian Stettin, S. and Wilson, A. (2023). Beyond the Pandemic – Poverty and School Education in Scotland. *Scottish Educational Review*, 54(2): 238–64.

McMullen, J.D., Jones, S., Campbell, R., McLaughlin, J., McDade, B., O'Lynn, P. and Glen, C. (2020). 'Sitting on a Wobbly Chair': Mental Health and Wellbeing Among Newcomer Pupils in Northern Irish Schools. *Emotional and Behavioural Difficulties*, 25(2): 125–38.

Mersky, J.P., Janczewski, C.E. and Topitzes, J. (2017). Rethinking the Measurement of Adversity: Moving Toward Second-Generation Research on Adverse Childhood Experiences. *Child Maltreatment*, 22(1): 58–68.

Metz, A., Burke, K., Albers, B., Louison, L. and Bartley, L. (2020). *A Practice Guide to Supporting Implementation: What Competences Do We Need?* Chapel Hill, NC: University of North Carolina Publications.

Mikahere-Hall, A. (2019). Tuhono Maori: Promoting Secure Attachments for Indigenous Maori Children. *Ata: Journal of Psychotherapy Aotearoa New Zealand*, 23(1): 49–59.

Miller, C. and Saxton, J. (2011). 'To See the World as if It Were Otherwise': Brain Research Challenges the Curriculum of 'Organized Chunks'. *Drama Australia Journal*, 35(1): 118–32.

Miller, K. and Flint-Stipp, K. (2024). The Unintended Consequences of Integrating Trauma-Informed Teaching into Teacher Education. *Teaching Education*, 35(4): 424–42.

Missouri Department of Mental Health and Partners (MDMHP) (2014). *The Missouri Model: A Developmental Framework for Trauma Informed Approaches*. Jefferson City, MO: Missouri Department of Mental Health.

Mok, M.M.C. and Moore, P.J. (2019). Teachers and Self-Efficacy. *Educational Psychology*, 39(1): 1–3.

Monnat, S.M. and Chandler, R.F. (2015). Long-Term Physical Health Consequences of Adverse Childhood Experiences. *The Sociological Quarterly*, 56(4): 723–52.

Morgan, A. (2018). *Different Ways of Being an Educator: Relational Practice*. Bloomington, IN: Balboa Press.

Morgan, N. and Saxton, J. (1987). *Teaching Drama: A Mind of Many Wonders*. London: Hutchinson.

Morrison, T. (2005). *Staff Supervision in Social Care: Making a Real Difference for Staff and Service Users*. Shoreham-by-Sea: Pavilion Publishing.

Moss, P. (2016). Why Can't We Get Beyond Quality? *Contemporary Issues in Early Childhood*, 17(1): 8–15.

Moss, P. (2019). *Alternative Narratives in Early Childhood: An Introduction for Students and Practitioners*. London: Routledge.

Moss, L. and Dunkley, E. (2024). Pupil Behaviour 'Getting Worse' at Schools in England, Say Teachers. Available at: https://www.bbc.co.uk/news/education-68674568 [Last accessed 1 November 2024].

Motta, R.W. (2012). Secondary Trauma in Children and School Personnel. *Journal of Applied School Psychology*, 28(3): 256–69.

Muir, C. (2024). 'Moving Beyond Surviving to Support the Ability to Thrive: Sharing the Experiences of Young People Whose Parents Use Substances', in W. McGovern, A. Gillespie, T. Brandon and A. McInnes (eds), *Developing and Implementing Teaching in Sensitive Subject and Topic Areas: A Comprehensive Guide for Professionals in FE and HE Settings*. Leeds: Emerald Publishing Limited, pp. 143–9.

Munford, R. (2022). Children and Young People in the Care System: Relational Practice in Working with Transitions and Challenges. *Australian Social Work*, 75(1): 1–4.

Murray, J. (2023). What Is the Purpose of Education? A Context for Early Childhood Education. *International Journal of Early Years Education*, 31(3): 571–8.

NASUWT (2023). *Behaviour in Schools*. Birmingham: NASUWT.

National Child Traumatic Stress Network (NCTSN) (2017). *Creating, Supporting, and Sustaining Trauma-Informed Schools: A System Framework*. Los Angeles, CA: National Center for Child Traumatic Stress.

National Child Traumatic Stress Network (NCTSN) (n.d.). About Child Trauma. Available at: https://www.nctsn.org/what-is-child-trauma/about-child-trauma [Last accessed 1 November 2024].

National Institute for Health and Care Excellence (NICE) (2018). Post Traumatic Stress Disorder. Available at: https://www.nice.org.uk/guidance/ng116/resources/

posttraumatic-stress-disorder-pdf-66141601777861 [Last accessed 1 November 2024].

National Trauma Transformation Programme (NTTP) (2023). A Roadmap for Creating Trauma-Informed and Responsive Change: Guidance for Organisations, Systems and Workforces in Scotland. Available at: https://www.traumatransformation.scot/implementation/ [Last accessed 4 April 2025].

Neelands, J. (1992). *Learning Through Imagined Experience*. London: Hodder & Stoughton.

Neelands, J. and Goode, T. (2000). *Structuring Drama Work: A Handbook of Available Forms in Theatre and Drama*. Cambridge: Cambridge University Press.

Neimeyer, R.A. (2001). *Meaning Reconstruction and the Experience of Loss*. Washington, DC: American Psychological Association.

Nemer, S.L., Sutherland, K.S., Chow, J.C. and Kunemund, R.L. (2019). A Systematic Literature Review Identifying Dimensions of Teacher Attributions for Challenging Student Behavior. *Education and Treatment of Children*, 42(4): 557–78.

Nespor, J. (1987). The Role of Beliefs in the Practice of Teaching. *Journal of Curriculum Studies*, 19(4): 317–28.

Neufeld, G. (2012). Brussels Address: Keys to Well-Being in Children and Youth. Delivered at the European Union Parliament, November 13, 2012. Available at: https://neufeldinstitute.org/wp-content/uploads/2017/12/Neufeld_Brussels_address.pdf [Last accessed 29 November 2024].

NHS Education for Scotland (2017). *Transforming Psychological Trauma: A Knowledge and Skills Framework for the Scottish Workforce*. Edinburgh: NES.

NHS Education for Scotland (NES) (2021). *Children and Young People's Mental Health and Wellbeing: A Knowledge and Skills Framework for the Scottish Workforce*. Edinburgh: NES.

NHS Education for Scotland (NES) (2023a). *A Roadmap for Creating Trauma-Informed and Responsive Change: Guidance for Organisations, Systems and Workforces in Scotland*. Edinburgh: NES.

NHS Education for Scotland (NES) (2023b). *National Trauma Transformation Programme*. Edinburgh: NES.

NHS Education for Scotland (NES) (2024). *Post Traumatic Stress Disorder (PTSD)*. Edinburgh: NES.

NHS (Highland) (2018). Adverse Childhood Experiences, Resilience and Trauma Informed Care: A Public Health Approach to Understanding and Responding to Adversity (The Annual Report of the Director of Public Health). Inverness: Public Health Directorate.

Nicholson, J. (2022). Towards Understanding the Lives and Educational Experiences of Children and Their Drug Using Caregivers: Connecting Home and School. PhD thesis, University of Glasgow.

Nicholson, J. (2025). Young People Affected by Drug Use: Implications for Teacher Education. *Journal of Education for Teaching*, online. Available at: https://www.tandfonline.com/doi/full/10.1080/02607476.2025.2480087 [Last accessed 15 April 2025].

Nicholson, J., Perez, L., Kurtz, J., Bryant, S. and Giles, D. (2023). *Trauma-Informed Practices for Early Childhood Educators: Relationship-Based Approaches That Reduce Stress, Build Resilience and Support Healing in Young Children* (Second edition). New York: Routledge.

Nickerson, A.B., Reeves, M.A., Brock, S.E., Jimerson, S.R. (2009). *Identifying, Addressing and Assessing PTSD at School.* New York: Springer.

Nutbrown, C. (2021). Early Childhood Educators' Qualifications: A Framework for Change. *International Journal of Early Years Education*, 29(3): 236–49.

O'Brien, N. and Dadswell, A. (2020). Reflections on a Participatory Research Project Exploring Bullying and School Self-Exclusion: Power Dynamics, Practicalities and Partnership Working. *Pastoral Care in Education*, 38(3): 208–29.

Olson, K. (2009). *Wounded by School: Recapturing the Joy in Learning and Standing Up to Old School Culture.* New York: Teachers College Press.

Olszewski, D., Burkhart, G. and Bo, A. (2010). *Children's Voices: Experiences and Perceptions of European Children on Drug and Alcohol Issues.* Lisbon: European Monitoring Centre for Drugs and Drug Addiction (EMCDDA).

O'Neill, C. (2017). Seal Wife – Random Observations. *Drama Australia Journal*, 41(1): 27–9.

Organisation for Economic Co-operation and Development (OECD) (2007). *Understanding the Brain: Towards a New Learning Science.* Paris: OECD.

Organisation for Economic Cooperation and Development (OECD) (2019). *OECD Learning Compass 2030: Conceptual Learning Framework.* Paris: OECD.

Organisation for Economic Cooperation and Development (OECD) (2021). *Starting Strong VI: Supporting Meaningful Interactions in Early Childhood Education and Care.* Paris: OECD.

Organisation for Economic Cooperation and Development (OECD) (online-a). Who We Are. Available at: https://www.oecd.org/en/about.html [Last accessed 2 April 2025a].

Organisation for Economic Cooperation and Development (OECD) (online-b). Starting Strong Teaching and Learning International Survey. Available at: https://www.oecd.org/en/about/projects/starting-strong-talis.html [Last accessed 7 February 2025b].

Osgood, J. (2006). Deconstructing Professionalism in Early Childhood Education: Resisting the Regulatory Gaze. *Contemporary Issues in Early Childhood*, 7(1): 5–14.

O'Toole, C. (2022). 'Childhood Adversity and Education: Integrating Trauma-Informed Practice Within School Wellbeing and Health Promotion Frameworks', in R. McLellan, C. Faucher and V. Simovska (eds), *Wellbeing and Schooling: Cross Cultural and Cross Disciplinary Perspectives.* Cham: Springer, pp. 107–20.

O'Toole, C. and Dobutowitsch, M. (2023). The Courage to Care: Teacher Compassion Predicts More Positive Attitudes Toward Trauma-Informed Practice. *Journal of Child and Adolescent Trauma*, 16(1): 123–33.

Overstreet, S. and Chafouleas, S.M. (2016). Trauma-Informed Schools: Introduction to the Special Issue. *School Mental Health*, 8: 1–6.

Palma, C., Abdou, A.S., Danforth, S. and Griffiths, A.J. (2023). Are Deficit Perspectives Thriving in Trauma-Informed Schools? A Historical and Anti-Racist Reflection. *Equity and Excellence in Education*, 57(1): 76–92.

Papatheodorou, T. (2009). 'Exploring Relational Pedagogy', in T. Papatheodorou and J. Moyles (eds), *Learning Together in the Early Years: Exploring Relational Pedagogy*. Abingdon: Routledge, pp. 3–17.

Parameswaran, U.D., Molloy, J. and Kuttner, P. (2024). Healing Schools: A Framework for Joining Trauma-Informed Care, Restorative Justice, and Multicultural Education for Whole School Reform. *The Urban Review*, 56: 186–209.

Parker, R. (2024). *Attachment Aware Schools: A Critical Perspective*. Cham: Palgrave Macmillan.

Parkes, C.M. (2008). *Love and Loss: The Roots of Grief and Its Complications*. London: Routledge.

Payne, A.A. and Welch, K. (2018). The Effect of School Conditions on the Use of Restorative Justice in Schools. *Youth Violence and Juvenile Justice*, 16(2): 224–40.

Perry, B. (2009). Examining Child Maltreatment Through a Neurodevelopmental Lens: Clinical Applications of the Neurosequential Model of Therapeutics. *Journal of Loss and Trauma*, 14(4): 240–55.

Perry, B. and Szalavitz, M. (2017). *The Boy Who Was Raised as a Dog* (Second edition). New York: Basic Books.

Perry, B. and Winfrey, O. (2021). *What Happened to You? Conversations on Trauma, Resilience, and Healing*. London: Bluebird.

Phifer, L.W. and Hull, R. (2016). Helping Students Heal: Observations of Trauma-Informed Practices in the Schools. *School Mental Health*, 8(1): 201–5.

Pietrzak, R.H. and Southwick, S.M. (2011). Psychological Resilience in OEF-OIF Veterans: Application of a Novel Classification Approach and Examination of Demographic and Psychosocial Correlates. *Journal of Affect Disorders*, 133(3): 560–8.

Pinyu, D. (2024). The Influence of Teacher-Student Relationship on Students. *Learning. Lecture Notes in Education Psychology and Public Media*, 40(1): 240–6.

Porges, S.W. (2017). *The Pocket Guide to the Polyvagal Theory*. New York: W.W. Norton & Company.

Porges, S.W. (2022). Polyvagal Theory: A Science of Safety. *Frontiers in Integrative Neuroscience*, 16: 1–15.

Porter, L. (2006). *Behaviour in Schools Theory and Practice for Teachers* (Second edition). Maidenhead: Open University Press.

Portwood, S.G., Lawler, M.J. and Roberts, M.C. (eds) (2023). *Handbook of Adverse Childhood Experiences: A Framework for Collaborative Health Promotion*. Cham: Springer.

Poulou, M. and Norwich, B. (2002). Cognitive, Emotional and Behavioural Responses to Students with Emotional and Behavioural Difficulties: A Model of Decision-Making. *British Educational Research Journal*, 28(1): 111–38.

Price, C.L. and Steed, E.A. (2016). Culturally Responsive Strategies to Support Young Children with Challenging Behavior. *YC Young Children*, 71(5): 36–43.

PSHE Association (2022). *Programme of study for PSHE Education: Key Stages 1–5*. London: PSHE Association.

Quadara, A. and Hunter, C. (2016). *Principles of Trauma-Informed Approaches to Child Sexual Abuse: A Discussion Paper*. Sydney: Royal Commission into Institutional Responses to Child Sexual Abuse.

Raphael, B. (1984). *The Anatomy of Bereavement: A Handbook for the Caring Professions*. London: Routledge.

Record-Lemon, R.M. and Buchanan, M.J. (2017). Trauma-Informed Practices in Schools: A Narrative Literature Review. *Canadian Journal of Counselling and Psychotherapy*, 51(4): 286–305.

Reynolds, S., MacKay, T. and Kearney, M. (2009). Nurture Groups: A Large-Scale, Controlled Study of Effects on Development and Academic Attainment. *British Journal of Special Education*, 36(4): 204–12.

Richardson, H. (2022). There Is No 'I' in Identity: A Dialogic, Social and Discursive Exploration of Professional Identity Within Inter-Agency Interactions. Doctorate of Applied Educational Psychology thesis, Newcastle University.

Riley, P. (2009). An Adult Attachment Perspective on the Student–Teacher Relationship and Classroom Management Difficulties. *Teaching and Teacher Education*, 25(5): 626–35.

Riley, P. (2010). *Attachment Theory and the Teacher-student Relationship: A Practical Guide for Teachers, Teacher Educators and School Leaders*. London: Routledge.

Riley, P. (2013). Attachment Theory, Teacher Motivation & Pastoral Care: A Challenge for Teachers and Academics. *Pastoral Care in Education*, 31(2): 112–29.

Roberts-Holmes, G. and Bradbury, A. (2016). Governance, Accountability and the Datafication of Early Years Education in England. *British Educational Research Journal*, 42(4): 600–13.

Roberts-Holmes, G. and Moss, P. (2021). *Neoliberalism and Early Childhood Education: Markers, Imaginaries and Governance*. London: Routledge.

Robertson, H., Goodall, K. and Kay, D. (2021). Teachers' Attitudes Towards Trauma-Informed Practice: Associations with Attachment and Adverse Childhood Experiences (ACEs). *Psychology of Education Review*, 45(2): 62–74.

Roffey, S. (2011). *The New Teachers' Survival Guide to Behaviour* (Second edition). London: SAGE Publications.

Roffey, S. and O'Reirdan, T. (2001). *Young Children and Classroom Behaviour, Needs, Perspectives and Strategies* (Second edition). London: David Fulton Publishers.

Rogers, C.R. (1967). *On Becoming a Person: A Therapist's View of Psychotherapy*. London: Constable.

Rogers, C.R. (1983). *Freedom to Learn for the 80s*. Columbus, OH: Charles Merrill.

Rogers, C.R. (1990). 'The Interpersonal Relationship in the Facilitation of Learning', in H. Kirschenbaum and V.L. Henderson (eds), *The Carl Rogers Reader*. London: Constable, pp. 304–11.

Rose, J., McGuire-Snieckus, R., Gilbert, L. and McInnes, K. (2019). Attachment Aware Schools: The Impact of a Targeted and Collaborative Intervention. *Pastoral Care in Education*, 37(2): 162–84.

Rossen, E. and Cowan, K. (2013). The Role of Schools in Supporting Traumatized Students. *Principal's Research Review*, 8(6): 1–8.

Roy, J. (2021). Children Living with Parental Substance Misuse: A Cross-Sectional Profile of Children and Families Referred to Children's Social Care. *Child and Family Social Work*, 26(1): 122–31.

Ruch, G. (2002). From Triangle to Spiral: Reflective Practice in Social Work Education, Practice and Research. *Social Work Education*, 21(2): 199–216.

Rutter, M. (2006). 'The Promotion of Resilience in the Face of Adversity', in A. Clarke-Stewart and J. Dunn (eds), *Families Count: Effects on Child and Adolescent Development. The Jacobs Foundation Series on Adolescence*. New York: Cambridge University Press, pp. 26–52.

Rutter, M. (2013). Annual Research Review: Resilience–Clinical Implications. *Journal of Child Psychology and Psychiatry, and Allied Disciplines*, 54(4): 474–87.

Saleem, F.T., Howard, T.C. and Langley, A.K. (2022). Understanding and Addressing Racial Stress and Trauma in Schools: A Pathway Toward Resistance and Healing. *Psychology in the Schools*, 59(12): 2506–21.

Samji, H., Wu, J., Ladak, A., Vossen, C., Stewart, E., Dove, N., Long, D., and Snell, G. (2022). Review: Mental Health Impacts of the COVID-19 Pandemic on Children and Youth – A Systematic Review. *Child and Adolescent Mental Health*, 27(2): 173–89.

Sanders, M. and Thompson, G. (2022). *Polyvagal Theory and the Developing Child*. New York: W.W. Norton & Company.

Satchwell-Hirst, M. (2017). 'Neuroscience and Emotional Development', in D. Colley and P. Cooper (eds), *Attachment and Emotional Development in the Classroom*. London: Jessica Kingsley Publishers, pp. 49–63.

Savolainen, H., Malinen, O.-P. and Schwab, S. (2020). Teacher Efficacy Predicts Teachers' Attitudes Towards Inclusion – A Longitudinal Cross-Lagged Analysis. *International Journal of Inclusive Education*, 26(9): 958–72.

Schmid, M., Ludtke, J., Dolitzsch, C., Fischer, S., Eckert, A. and Fegert, J.M. (2020). Effects of Trauma Informed Care on Hair Cortisol Concentration in Youth Welfare Staff and Client Physical Aggression Towards Staff: Results of a Longitudinal Study. *BMC Public Health*, 20(21): 1–11.

Schore, A. (2022). Right Brain-to-Right Brain Psychotherapy: Recent Scientific and Clinical Advances. *Annals of General Psychiatry*, 21(46): 1–12.

Schore, A.N. (2000). Attachment and the Regulation of the Right Brain. *Attachment & Human Development*, 2(1): 23–47.

Schore, J.R. and Schore, A.N. (2008). Modern Attachment Theory: The Central Role of Affect and Regulation in Development and Treatment. *Clinical Social Work Journal*, 36: 9–20.

Scott, J.J., Vernon, L. and Metse, A.P. (2023). The International Framework for School Health Promotion: Supporting Young People Through and After the COVID-19 Pandemic. *The Journal of School Health*, 93(10): 920–9.

Scottish Association for Mental Health (SAMH) (2017). *Going to Be .... Well Trained. SAMH Survey on School Staff Training in Mental Health*. Glasgow: SAMH.

Scottish Attachment in Action (SAIA) (2022). *Mapping Attachment Informed Trauma Sensitive Practice in Scottish Education*. Cardross: SAIA.

Scottish Government (2012). *Common Core of Skills, Knowledge and Understanding and Values for the 'Children's Workforce', in Scotland: Final Common Core and Discussion Questions*. Edinburgh: Scottish Government.

Scottish Government (2013). *Better Relationships, Better Learning, Better Behaviour*. Edinburgh: Scottish Government.

Scottish Government (2017). *Developing a Positive Whole School Ethos and Culture: Relationships, Learning and Behaviour*. Edinburgh: Scottish Government.

Scottish Government (2018). *Delivering for Today, Investing for Tomorrow. The Government's Programme for Scotland 2018–19*. Edinburgh: Scottish Government.

Scottish Government (2020a). *Support for Learning: All Our Children and All Their Potential*. Edinburgh: Scottish Government.

Scottish Government (2020b). *The Independent Care Review. The Promise*. Edinburgh: Scottish Government.

Scottish Government (2020c). *Achieving Excellence and Equity: 2021 National Improvement Framework and Improvement Plan*. Edinburgh: Scottish Government.

Scottish Government (2021a). *Trauma-Informed Practice: A Toolkit for Scotland*. Edinburgh: Scottish Government.

Scottish Government (2021b). *Interim Evaluation of the National Trauma Training Programme Local Delivery Trials*. Edinburgh: Scottish Government.

Scottish Government (2022a). *Getting It Right for Every Child (GIRFEC): Policy Statement*. Edinburgh: Scottish Government.

Scottish Government (2022b). *Keeping the Promise to Our Children, Young People and Families*. Edinburgh: Scottish Government.

Scottish Government (2023a). *Behaviour in Scottish Schools 2023: Research Report*. Edinburgh: Scottish Government.

Scottish Government (2023b). *A Roadmap for Creating Trauma-Informed and Responsive Change: Guidance for Organisations, Systems and Workforces in Scotland (Executive Summary)*. Edinburgh: Scottish Government.

Scottish Government (2023c). *Access to Childcare Fund Phase 2: Evaluation Report*. Edinburgh: Scottish Government.

Scottish Government (2023d). *2023 National Improvement Framework (NIF) and Improvement Plan: Summary Document*. Edinburgh: Scottish Government.

Scottish Government (2023e). *National Guidance for Child Protection in Scotland 2021 – Updated 2023*. Edinburgh: Scottish Government.

Scottish Government (2024a). *Poverty and Income Inequality in Scotland: 2020–23*. Edinburgh: Scottish Government.

Scottish Government (2024b). Psychological Trauma and Adversity Including ACEs (Adverse Childhood Experiences). Available at: https://www.gov.scot/publications/psychological-trauma-and-adversity [Last accessed 12 May 2025].

Scottish Government (2024c). *Improving Relationships and Behaviour in Schools: Ensuring Safe and Consistent Environments for All. Joint Action Plan 2024–27*. Edinburgh: Scottish Government.

Scottish Government (2024d). *National Trauma Transformation Programme (NTTP)*. Edinburgh: Scottish Government.

Scottish Government (2024e). *Follow-up Evaluation of the National Trauma Transformation Programme Local Authority Delivery Trials*. Edinburgh: Scottish Government.

Scottish Government (online). Curriculum for Excellence: Experiences and Outcomes. Available at: https://education.gov.scot/media/wpsnskgv/all-experiencesoutcomes18.pdf [Last accessed 7 February 2025].

Scottish Parliament (2014). *The Children and Young People (Scotland) Act*. Edinburgh: Scottish Parliament. Available at: https://www.legislation.gov.uk/asp/2014/8/contents/enacted [Last accessed 1 November 2024].

Scottish Parliament (2024). *United Nations Convention on the Rights of the Child (Incorporation) (Scotland) Bill*. Edinburgh: Scottish Parliament. Available at: https://www.parliament.scot/bills-and-laws/bills/s5/united-nations-convention-on-the-rights-of-the-child-incorporation-scotland-bill [Last accessed 28 October 2024].

Scottish Social Services Council (SSSC) (2024). Introduction to CPL. Available at: https://learn.sssc.uk.com/cpl/introduction [Last accessed 7 February 2025].

Seith, E. (2019). 'Scottish Schools Get Rid of Exclusion "Reflex"', *TES Magazine*, 19 December 2019, n.p.

Seith, E. (2024a). 'Teacher Absence in Scotland Hits Highest Level in over a Decade', *TES Magazine*, 7 March 2024, n.p.

Seith, E. (2024b). 'More than 550 Probationers Opt Out of Induction Scheme', *TES Magazine*, 8 March 2024, n.p.

Senaratne, D.N.S., Thakkar, B., Smith, B.H., Hales, T.G., Marryat, L. and Colvin, L.A. (2024). The Impact of Adverse Childhood Experiences on Multimorbidity: A Systematic Review and Meta-Analysis. *BMC Medicine*, 22(315): 1–14.

Sharkey, J.D., Mullin, A., Felix, E.D., Maier, D. and Fedders, A. (2024). Supporting Educators and Students: A University–Community Partnership to Implement Trauma-Informed Practices in Schools. *School Mental Health*, 16(3): 879–93.

Shin, M. and Partyka, T. (2017). Empowering Infants Through Responsive and Intentional Play Activities. *International Journal of Early Years Education*, 25(2): 127–42.

Shonkoff, J.P. and Garner, A.S. (2012). The Lifelong Effects of Early Childhood Adversity and Toxic Stress. *Pediatrics*, 129(1): 232–46.

Shonkoff, J.P., Slopen, N. and Williams, D.R. (2021). Early Childhood Adversity, Toxic Stress, and the Impacts of Racism on the Foundations of Health. *Annual Review of Public Health*, 42: 115–34.

Short, R., Case, G., and McKenzie, K. (2018). The Long-Term Impact of a Whole School Approach of Restorative Practice: The Views of Secondary School Teachers. *Pastoral Care in Education*, 36(4): 313–24.

Siegel, D. (1999). *The Developing Mind: How Relationships and the Brain Interact to Shape Who We Are*. New York: Gulliford Press.

Siegel, D. (2020). *The Developing Mind: How Relationships and the Brain Interact to Shape Who We Are* (Third edition). New York: Guilford Press.

Siegel, D. and Payne Bryson, T. (2012). *The Whole-Brain Child*. London: Hachette UK.

Signorelli, A., Morganti, A. and Pascoletti, S. (2021). Boosting Emotional Intelligence in the Post-Covid. Flexible Approaches in Teaching Social and Emotional Skills. *Formare*, 21(3): 41–58.

Silverman, P.R. (1999). *Never Too Young to Know: Death in Children's lives.* Oxford: Oxford University Press.

Sims, M. (2017). Neoliberalism and Early Childhood. *Cogent education*, 4: 1–10.

Skinner, B.F. (1993). *About Behaviourism.* London: Penguin.

Smith, D., Fisher, D. and Frey, N. (2015). *Better than Carrots or Sticks: Restorative Practices for Positive Classroom Management.* Alexandria, VA: ASCD.

Smith, E. and Grace, L. (2011). Vocational Educators' Qualifications: A Pedagogical Poor Relation? *International Journal of Training Research*, 9(3): 204–17.

Smyth, J., Down, B., and McInerney, P. (2010). 'Hanging in with Kids' in Tough Times: Engagement in Contexts of Educational Disadvantage in the Relational School. *British Journal of Educational Studies*, 59(3): 347–8.

Smyth, J., Down, B., and McInerney, P. (2014). *The Socially Just School: Making Spaces for Youth to Speak Back.* London: Springer.

Soneson, E., Puntis, S., Chapman, N., Mansfield, K.L., Jones, P.B. and Fazel, M. (2023). Happier During Lockdown: A Descriptive Analysis of Self-Reported Wellbeing in 17,000 UK School Students During Covid-19 Lockdown. *European Child and Adolescent Psychiatry*, 32(6): 1131–46.

Sonu, S., Marvin, D. and Moore, C. (2021). The Intersection and Dynamics Between COVID-19, Health Disparities, and Adverse Childhood Experiences. *Journal of Child and Adolescent Trauma*, 14: 517–26.

South Lanarkshire Council (2023). South Lanarkshire Council Youth, Family and Community Learning Pathfinder Initiative: Implementation and Impact. *Longitudinal Research Report.* Hamilton: South Lanarkshire Council.

Spilt, J.L., Koomen, H.M.Y. and Thijs, J.T. (2011). Teacher Wellbeing: The Importance of Teacher–Student Relationships. *Educational Psychology Review*, 23(4): 457–77.

Spodek, B. and Saracho, O.N. (1999). The Relationship Between Theories of Child Development and the Early Childhood Curriculum. *Early Child Development and Care*, 152(1): 1–15.

Spurling, N., McMeekin, A., Shove, E., Southerton, D. and Welch, D. (2013). *Interventions in Practice: Re-Framing Policy Approaches to Consumer Behaviour.* Manchester: Sustainable Practices Research Group.

Srivastav, A., Strompolis, M., Moseley, A. and Daniels, K. (2020). The Empower Action Model: A Framework for Preventing Adverse Childhood Experiences by Promoting Health, Equity, and Well-Being Across the Life Span. *Health Promotion Practice*, 21(4): 525–34.

Sroufe, A. and Siegel, D. (2011). The Verdict Is In: The Case for Attachment Theory. *Psychotherapy Networker*, 35(2): 35–53.

Steiny, J. (2009). Learning Walks: Build Hearty Appetites for Professional Development. *Journal of Staff Development*, 30(2): 31–6.

Steptoe, A., Marteau, T., Fonagy, P. and Abel, K. (2019). ACEs: Evidence, Gaps, Evaluation and Future Priorities. *Social Policy and Society*, 18(3): 415–24.

Stokes, H. and Tom Brunzell, T. (2019). Professional Learning in Trauma Informed Positive Education: Moving School Communities from Trauma Aware to Trauma Affected. *School Leadership Review*, 14(2): 1–13.

Stroebe, M.S. and Schut, H. (1999). The Dual Process Model of Coping with Bereavement. *Death Studies*, 23(3): 197–224.

Stroebe, M.S. and Schut, H. (2005). To Continue or Relinquish Bonds: A Review of Consequences for the Bereaved. *Death Studies*, 29(6): 477–94.

Stroebe, M.S. and Schut, H. (2010). The Dual Process of Coping with Bereavement. A decade on. *Omega – Journal of Death and Dying*, 61(4): 237–89.

Substance Abuse and Mental Health Services Administration (SAMHSA) (2014). *Concept of Trauma and Guidance for a Trauma Informed Approach*. Rockville, MD: Office of Policy, Planning and Innovation.

Sylva, K., Siraj-Blatchford, I. and Taggart, B. (2006). *Assessing Quality in the Early Years. Early Childhood Environment Rating Scale: Extension (ECERS-E), Four Curricular Subscales*. Stoke on Trent: Trentham Books.

Szuhany, K.L., Malgaroli, M., Miron, C.D. and Simon, N.M. (2021). Prolonged Grief Disorder: Course, Diagnosis, Assessment, and Treatment. *Focus*, 19(2): 161–72.

Tanyu, M., Spier, E., Pulizzi, S., Rooney, M., Sorenson, I., Fernandez, J., American Institutes for Research (2020). Improving Education Outcomes for Students Who Have Experienced Trauma and/or Adversity. *OECD Education Working Papers*, No. 242, Paris: OECD Publishing.

Tassone, M. (2025). Literacy Assessment in the Early Years of Schooling in an Era of Neoliberalism. *Journal of Early Childhood Literacy*, 25(2): 422–462.

Taylor, L. and Barrett, W. (2022). The Importance of Trauma-Informed Approaches in Education – The Impact of Implementing a Brain-Based Approach to Supporting Learners Across a Scottish Local Authority. *International Journal of School Social Work*, 6(2): 1–30.

Taylor, P. (1998). *Redcoats and Patriots: Reflective Practice in Drama and Social Studies*. Portsmouth, NH: Heinemann Educational Books.

Taylor, P. (2000). *The Drama Classroom: Action, Reflection and Transformation*. London: Routledge.

Taylor-Robinson, D.C., Straatmann, V.S. and Whitehead, M. (2018). Adverse Childhood Experiences or Adverse Childhood Socioeconomic Conditions? *The Lancet*, 3: 262–3.

Tett, L. and Hamilton, L. (2019). 'Introduction: Resisting Neoliberalism in Education', in L. Tett and L. Hamilton (eds), *Resisting Neoliberalism in Education: Local, National and Transnational Perspectives*. Bristol: Policy Press, pp. 1–10.

The Lines Between (2025). *Evaluation of the Wee Breathers: Final Report*. Edinburgh: The Lines Between.

Thomas, M.S., Crosby, S. and Vanderhaar, J. (2019). Trauma-Informed Practices in Schools Across Two Decades: An Interdisciplinary Review of Research. *Review of Research in Education*, 43(1): 422–52.

Thorburn, M. (2014). Educating for Well-Being in Scotland: Policy and Philosophy, Pitfalls and Possibilities. *Oxford Review of Education*, 40(2): 206–22.

Tobin, M. (2016). *Childhood Trauma: Developmental Pathways and Implications for the Classroom*. Melbourne: Australian Council for Educational Research (ACER).

Trauma Informed Oregon (online). Trauma Informed Oregon. Available at: https://traumainformedoregon.org/ [Last accessed 7 February 2025].

Trawick-Smith, J.W. (2014). *Early Childhood Development: A Multicultural Perspective, Pearson New International* (Sixth edition). Harlow: Pearson Education Limited.

Treisman, K. (2017). *Working with Relational and Developmental Trauma in Children and Adolescents*. Abingdon: Routledge.

Trivedi, H. and Harrison, N. (2022). *Attachment Aware and Trauma-Informed Schools Programmes: Positive Practice Examples from Local Authorities*. Oxford: Oxford University.

Tsappis, E., Garside, M., Wright, B. and Fearon, P. (2022). Promoting Secure Attachment. *Paediatrics and Child Health*, 32(5): 191–7.

Ungar, M. (2013). Resilience, Trauma, Context, and Culture. *Trauma, Violence & Abuse*, 14(3): 255–66.

United Nations (UN) (1989). *The United Nations Convention on the Rights of the Child (UNCRC)*. New York: Office of the High Commissioner for Human Rights.

United Nations Educational, Scientific and Cultural Organization (UNESCO) (2013). *Education for All Global Monitoring Report: Teaching and Learning for Development*. Paris: UNESCO.

U.S. Department of Education (2015). *Every Student Succeeds Act (ESSA)*. Washington, DC: U.S. Department of Education.

Usher, E.L. and Pajares, F. (2008). Sources of Self-efficacy in School: Critical Review of the Literature. *Review of Educational Research*, 78(4): 751–96.

Van der Kolk, B.A. (2014). *The Body Keeps the Score: Brain, Mind, and Body in the Healing of Trauma*. New York: Viking.

Van Gulden, H. (2000). Stable and Resilient Children. Available at: https://womensaidorkney.org.uk/wp-content/uploads/2014/08/Stable-Resilient-Children.pdf [Last accessed 11 March 2025].

Van Gulden, H. and Vick, C. (2010). *Learning the Dance of Attachment: An Adoptive/Foster Parent's Guide to Nurturing Healthy Development* (Second edition). Minneapolis, MN: Van Gulden and Vick.

Velleman, R. and Templeton, L. (2016). Impact of Parents' Substance Misuse on Children: An Update. *British Journal of Psychiatric Advances*, 22(2): 108–17.

Venet, A.S. (2023). *Equity-Centered Trauma-Informed Education*. New York: Routledge.

Verschueren, K. and Koomen, H.M.Y. (2012). Teacher-Child Relationships from an Attachment Perspective. *Attachment & Human Development*, 14(3): 205–11.

Vygotsky, L (1978). *Mind in Society: The Development of Higher Psychological Processes*. Cambridge, MA: Harvard University Press.

Wagner, B.J. (1999). *Dorothy Heathcote: Drama as a Learning Medium*. Portland, ME: Calendar Islands Publishers.

Walkley, M. and Cox, T.L. (2013). Building Trauma-Informed Schools and Communities. *Children and Schools*, 35(2): 123–6.

Wallbank, S. and Wonnacott, J. (2015). The Integrated Model of Restorative Supervision for Use Within Safeguarding. *Community Practice*, 88(5): 41–5.

Walsh, W., McCartney, G., Smith, M. and Armour, G. (2019). Relationship Between Childhood Socioeconomic Position and Adverse Childhood Experiences (ACEs): A Systematic Review. *Journal of Epidemiology and Community Health*, 73(12): 1087–93.

Wang, H. and Hall, N.C. (2018). A Systematic Review of Teachers' Causal Attributions: Prevalence, Correlates, and Consequences. *Frontiers in Psychology*, 9(2305): 1–22.

Wang, H., Hall, N.C. and Taxer, J.L. (2019). Antecedents and Consequences of Teachers' Emotional Labor: A Systematic Review and Meta-analytic Investigation. *Educational Psychology Review*, 31(3): 663–98.

Wassink-de Stigter, R., Kooijmans, R., Asselman, M.W., Oferman, E.C.P., Nelen, W. and Helmond, P. (2022). Facilitators and Barriers in the Implementation of Trauma-Informed Approaches in Schools: A Scoping Review. *School Mental Health*, 14: 470–48.

Watson, K.R. and Astor, R.A. (2025). A Critical Review of Empirical Support for Trauma-informed Approaches in Schools and a Call for Conceptual, Empirical and Practice Integration. *Review of Education*, 13(1–e70025): 1–40.

Webber, L. (2017). A School's Journey in Creating a Relational Environment Which Supports Attachment and Emotional Security. *Emotional and Behavioural Difficulties*, 22(4): 317–31.

Webster, E.M., Hodges, H.R. and Corcoran, F. (2025). The Impact of Family Resilience in Promoting School Readiness for Children with Adverse Childhood Experiences. *Early Childhood Education Journal*, 53(3): 821–33.

Weinberg, M. and Tronick, E. (1996). Infant Affective Reactions to the Resumption of Maternal Interaction After the Still-Face. *Child Development*, 67(3): 905–14.

Weiner, B. (1985). An Attributional Theory of Motivation and Emotion. *Psychological Review*, 92(4): 548–73.

White, S., Edwards, R., Gillies, V. and Wastell, D. (2019). All the ACEs: A Chaotic Concept for Family Policy and Decision-Making? *Social Policy and Society*, 18(3): 457–66.

Wilkin, A., Moor, H., Murfield, J., Kinder, K. and Johnson, F. (2006). *Behaviour in Scottish Schools*. Edinburgh: Scottish Executive.

Wingrave, M. (2011). 'Nurture Groups and Inclusion', in M. McMahon, C. Forde and M. Martin (eds), *Contemporary Issues in Learning and Teaching*. London: SAGE Publications, pp. 90–101.

Woodcock, S. and L.M. Woolfson (2019). Are Leaders Leading the Way with Inclusion? Teachers' Perceptions of Systemic Support and Barriers Towards Inclusion. *International Journal of Educational Research*, 93(1): 232–42.

Worden, J.W. (1996). *Children and Grief: When a Parent Dies*. New York: Guilford Press.

Worden, J.W. (2010). *Grief Counselling and Grief Therapy: A Handbook for the Mental Health Practitioner* (Fourth edition). London: Routledge.

World Bank (2011). *World Development Report 2011: Conflict, Security and Development – Overview*. Washington, DC: The World Bank Publications.

World Health Organisation (2024). *Covid-19 Epidemiological Update.* Geneva: World Health Organisation.

Wu, M.-H., Chiao, C. and Lin, W.-H. (2024). Adverse Childhood Experience and Persistent Insomnia During Emerging Adulthood: Do Positive Childhood Experiences Matter? *BMC Public Health*, 24(287): 1–9.

Wu, Y., Hartman, D.T., Brown, L., Wang, Y., Vidales, D., Grandchamp, J., Enriquez, R., Moriarty, N., Goldfarb, D. and Goodman, G.S. (2024). Collective Trauma: Childhood Abuse, Perceived Discrimination, and COVID-19. *Psychological Trauma*, 16(S1): S115–24.

Ximenes, R. de B.B., Ximenes, J.C.M., Nascimento, S.L., Roddy, S.M. and Leite, A.J.M. (2019). Relationship Between Maternal Adverse Childhood Experiences and Infant Development: A Systematic Review (Protocol). *Medicine*, 98(10): 1–4.

YouTube (2022). Tronick's Still Face Experiment. Available at: https://youtu.be/f1Jw0-LExyc [Last accessed 11 November 2024].

Zakszeski, B.N., Ventresco, N.E. and Jafe, A.R. (2017). Promoting Resilience Through Trauma-Focused Practices: A Critical Review of School-Based Implementation. *School Mental Health*, 9(4): 310–21.

Zee, M. and Koomen, H.M.Y. (2016). Teacher Self-Efficacy and Its Effects on Classroom Processes, Student Academic Adjustment, and Teacher Well-Being: A Synthesis of 40 Years of Research. *Review of Educational Research*, 86(4): 981–1015.

Zuckerman, B. and Tronick, E. (2023). The Still-Face Paradigm: Training Model for Relational Health. *Journal of Developmental and Behavioral Pediatrics*, 44(2): e135–36.

Index